MW00855658

# The Online Classroom

## Resources for Effective Middle Level Virtual Education

A Volume in Research in
The Handbook of Resources in Middle Level Education

Series Editors

Micki M. Caskey
*Portland State University*
Steven B. Mertens
*Illinois State University*

# The Handbook of Resources in Middle Level Education

Vincent A. Anfara, Jr. (founding editor),
Micki M. Caskey, and Steven B. Mertens, Editors

*The Legacy of Middle School Leaders: In Their Own Words* (2011)
edited by L. Tracy W. Smith and C. Kenneth McEwin

*Clinical Preparation at the Middle Level: Practices and Possibilities* (2015)
edited by Penny B. Howell, Jan Carpenter, and Jeanneine Jones

*Encyclopedia of Middle Grades Education (2nd ed.)* (2016)
edited by Steven B. Mertens, Micki M. Caskey, and Nancy Flowers

*Imagine a Place: Stores from Middle Grades Educators* (2017)
edited by Jan Carpenter, Amy Lutz, Linda Samek, Micki M. Caskey,
William L. Greene, Younghee M. Kim, Jay Casbon, and Maureen Musser

*Literature Reviews in Support of the
Middle Level Education Research Agenda* (2018)
edited by Steven B. Mertens & Micki M. Caskey

*The Online Classroom: Resources for
Effective Middle Level Virtual Education* (2018)
edited by Brooke B. Eisenbach and Paula Greathouse

# The Online Classroom

## Resources for Effective Middle Level Virtual Education

**Edited by**

**Brooke B. Eisenbach**
*Lesley University*

**Paula Greathouse**
*Tennessee Tech University*

**Middle Level Education Research
Special Interest Group**

**INFORMATION AGE PUBLISHING, INC.**
Charlotte, NC • www.infoagepub.com

**Library of Congress Cataloging-in-Publication Data**

CIP record for this book is available from the Library of Congress
http://www.loc.gov


ISBNs:   978-1-64113-459-0 (Paperback)

978-1-64113-460-6 (Hardcover)

978-1-64113-461-3 (ebook)

Copyright © 2018 Information Age Publishing Inc.

All rights reserved. No part of this publication may be reproduced, stored
in a retrieval system, or transmitted, in any form or by any means, electronic,
mechanical, photocopying, microfilming, recording or otherwise, without written
permission from the publisher.

Printed in the United States of America

MIDDLE LEVEL EDUCATION RESEARCH
SPECIAL INTEREST GROUP

The Handbook of Research in Middle Level Educationis endorsed by the Middle Level Education Research Special Interest Group, an affiliate of the American Educational Research Association.

As stated in the organization's Constitution, the purpose of **MLER** is to improve, promote, and disseminate educational research reflecting early adolescence and middle-level education.

# CONTENTS

## SECTION III: COMMUNITY

## SECTION IV: STRATEGIES

## SECTION V: DIVERSE POPULATIONS

# ACKNOWLEDGMENTS

We would like to dedicate this volume to all of the middle level students who participate in virtual education, and to all of the teachers, administrators, teacher educators, and researchers who seek to ensure virtual education is accessible and purposeful in meeting the unique needs of middle level learners.

We would like to thank all of the chapter contributors for their research, focus, and attention to virtual middle level education. As this form of education continues to grow, we appreciate the continued focus on ensuring virtual learners receive a quality education that addresses their social, emotional and academic needs.

We would like to give a special thanks to Micki Caskey and Steve Mertens for their valued mentorship and support throughout the compilation, editing, and review of this handbook, and to the AERA Middle Level Education Research Special Interest Group for their research and support of middle level learners and educators.

*The Online Classroom:*
*Resources for Effective Middle Level Virtual Education,* pp. ix–ix
Copyright © 2018 by Information Age Publishing
All rights of reproduction in any form reserved.

# INTRODUCTION

**Brooke B. Eisenbach**
*Lesley University*

**Paula Greathouse**
*Tennessee Tech University*

It is not difficult to recall the countless hours that we (Brooke and Paula) spent as children, spreading our stuffed animals around our living room or bedroom floor, reciting the day's "lesson," and doing our best to replicate what we experienced as children in the classroom within our imaginative play. However, had anyone mentioned all those years ago that our future classrooms would one day replace paper and pencil with laptops and tablets, or that our future students would someday attend our class sessions by virtual means, we would have scratched our heads and considered their suggestions nothing more than the work of science fiction. Yet, here we are today, bracing ourselves for the fast-paced, ever-changing world of modern public education.

As I (Brooke) transitioned from a position as a traditional middle level teacher to an instructional role within a public virtual school, I felt shocked by the way that this change caused me to reevaluate every aspect of my approach to teaching. Despite my background and training in middle level education, and the expertise I acquired due to my years of middle

*The Online Classroom:*
*Resources for Effective Middle Level Virtual Education,* pp. xi–xvi
Copyright © 2018 by Information Age Publishing
All rights of reproduction in any form reserved.

school teaching, I was ill prepared to transfer my knowledge to the virtual context. I was not sure how to adapt my pedagogy in a way that met the developmental needs of my students within this new technological space. I was at a loss for developing the close-knit community and teacher-student relationships, which I once valued within the brick-and-mortar environment. In addition, I struggled to find effective ways of meeting the needs of the diverse learners that I encountered on the other end of the phone, text message, or online instructional session. Regardless of the books I read, the virtual workshops I attended, and the assistance of my new virtual colleagues, I struggled as an online educator. It simply did not translate as I expected that it would.

We were veteran, award-winning, public school teachers, who transitioned from our role as secondary classroom educators to university education faculty members. Yet, before making the move to higher education, we took time to learn more about the experience of online K–12 learning in an effort to prepare our future teacher candidates to teach in this new landscape. Drawing on my (Brooke's) experiences within the middle level virtual classroom, we began to collaborate to reevaluate the curriculum within our respective teacher education courses. We asked ourselves, would our curriculum prepare our teacher candidates for virtual middle level classrooms? The answer was no. In our attempt to rectify this gap in our curriculum, we discovered a shortage of research and resources for virtual middle level teachers. It seemed virtual education appeared in the dead of night, and the resources necessary for middle level virtual educators to address the needs of middle level learners was slow to catch up.

Researchers estimated that more than 2 million K–12 students were enrolled in some form of online school, district, or state virtual course during the 2015–2016 school year (Evergreen Education Group, 2015). As of 2015, middle level students represented 14% of learners taking virtual courses to supplement their current coursework and 28% of full-time virtual school students (Evergreen Education Group, 2015). Today's middle level students have been signing into virtual education courses at a rapidly growing rate.

Research in virtual education reveals a gap in knowledge about effective instruction of online students. As more teachers leave the traditional classroom for a position in virtual education, they bring with them experience, education, and training related to traditional pedagogical techniques, but limited knowledge of effective means of teaching and reaching virtual learners (Baran, Correia & Thompson, 2011; Eisenbach, 2015; Kreber & Kanuka, 2006). They often find that the techniques and instructional strategies that they relied upon within the brick-and-mortar setting to teach and connect with students are simply not translating effectively within the online classroom setting (Powell, Rabbitt, & Kennedy, 2014). This gap in knowledge and resources may prove detrimental to meeting the needs of the academic, social, and emotional needs of today's virtual learner.

Given the unique nature of the developmental needs of middle level learners, virtual teachers and instructional designers face the challenge of engaging, motivating, and meeting the academic, social, and emotional needs of this demographic with limited resources. To date, texts on this topic have centered on understanding the development of virtual education (Chubb et al., 2012), forming and maintaining an effective virtual classroom (Christopher, 2014; Clark & Kwinn, 2007), and K–12 virtual students (Cavanaugh & Blomeyer, 2010; Ebert, 2014). However, given the ever-changing nature of the virtual classroom, many of these texts are already outdated, and others focus more on understanding and working with elementary or secondary students, rather than giving specific attention to middle level learners and their unique needs.

We contend that it is essential that teachers find ways to address these developmental needs within this digital context. This volume of the *Handbook of Resources on Middle Level Education* provides necessary resources for today's virtual middle level teachers, administrators, and teacher educators as they move from teaching within the traditional school toward curriculum design and effective pedagogy within the virtual context. Primarily, this text focuses on offering virtual teachers and teacher educators the tools and information necessary to address the specific needs of middle level learners within the blended or virtual classroom environment in ways that draw on the framework set forth in *This We Believe: Keys to Educating Young Adolescents* (National Middle School Association [NMSA], 2010).

We developed this volume based on three assumptions: (a) middle level learners will continue to enroll in virtual classrooms at an ever-increasing rate; (b) virtual educators need to design curriculum and engage pedagogy that addresses the unique developmental needs of the middle level learners; and (c) virtual teacher preparation and resources are unique to the pedagogy and resources necessary and available to the traditional middle level teacher. Given these assumptions, we invited researchers and virtual teachers to share their research, resources, tips, strategies, words of guidance, and stories in working with middle level students within the online classroom setting.

We organized this Handbook according to five key tenets of *This We Believe* (NMSA, 2010). Section I draws on the need for middle level virtual teachers to understand the developmental uniqueness of middle level virtual learners and use this knowledge in ways that will make them effective in the virtual classroom. In Chapter 1, Suzanne Wolfinger introduces readers to the virtual middle level student and discusses ways in which virtual stakeholders can support their success. Kerry Rice and Shannon

Skelcher continue this discussion in Chapter 2, providing readers with insights into what makes an effective virtual middle level teacher.

Section II spotlights the importance of quality middle level virtual teachers, as they are key in making the middle school experience meaningful and successful (NMSA, 2010). In Chapter 3, Shelly Furuness provides resources that teacher education programs can use in preparing teacher candidates for the virtual middle level classroom. Barbara Smith offers resources for building professional learning communities and providing leadership opportunities for virtual teachers in Chapter 4. Mark Stevens and Mary Rice end this section in Chapter 5 by offering virtual teachers resources and strategies for collaborating as they build the virtual middle level curriculum.

Section III spotlights community. The authors of *This We Believe* posited, "A successful school for young adolescents is an inviting, supportive, and safe place—a joyful community that promotes in-depth learning and enhances students' physical and emotional well-being. In such a school, human relationships are paramount" (NMSA, 2010, p. 53). Drawing on this belief, Jillian Wendt, Amanda Rockinson-Szapkiw, and Kyleigh Harrell offer resources and strategies for building and sustaining community in the middle level virtual classroom in Chapter 6. In Chapter 7, Brooke Eisenbach, Paula Greathouse, and Mary Kirk advance resources and strategies that virtual educators can employ in creating a community of care. Natalie Duvall and Matthew Duvall close this section in Chapter 8 with a discussion on the importance of relationships at the middle level and suggest resources and strategies that support virtual student mentoring.

Section IV addresses the call for effective curriculum, instruction, and assessment for middle level learners. In *This We Believe,* NMSA (2010) maintained, "Teaching and learning strategies employed in middle grades classrooms should be as diverse, varied, and lively as the students themselves (p. 69). In Chapter 9, Jeremy Wendt and Jason Beach recommend resources and strategies for curriculum design and instruction as teachers transition from brick-and-mortar to the virtual classroom. Eve Bernstein and Andrea Mosenson propose resources and strategies for motivating and engaging the middle level virtual learner in Chapter 10. In Chapter 11, Ebony Terrell Shockley, Arquimen Chicas, Cachanda Orellana, and Meri Robinson draw attention to the need for virtual teachers to employ culturally relevant pedagogy and suggest resources and strategies to accomplish this goal. This section ends with Nancy Gallavan and Shannon Maiden discussing resources and strategies for developing and facilitating assessments in the virtual classroom in Chapter 12.

Section V builds on the need for middle school teachers to make "sound pedagogical, research-based decisions reflecting the needs, interests, and special abilities of students" (NMSA, 2010, p. 28). In Chapter 13, Sucari

Epps offers insights into the developmental needs of students with disabilities and provides resources and strategies in meeting these needs instructionally within the virtual classroom. In Chapter 14, Jennifer Gallup and Cory Bennett continue this discussion by proposing resources and strategies for virtual teachers in meeting the needs of students with disabilities within virtual STEM courses.

Each chapter, grounded in research and rich with strategies and resources, provides information necessary to assist educators as they transition from the traditional classroom, or their teacher preparation program, to the world of middle level virtual teaching. The Handbook concludes with an appendix of online resources and applications as noted by authors throughout each chapter. We understand technology is ever changing, and for this reason, many of the suggested online applications, websites, or platforms offered within this text will give-way to new technological tools. However, we believe these approaches, strategies, and suggested resources can serve as a starting point for the reader's own development as a virtual educator. It is our hope that virtual teachers, teacher educators, and those responsible for the crafting and implementation of virtual education will use this resource handbook as a necessary support in designing curriculum and providing effective instruction, classroom support, and a sense of community for today and tomorrow's growing population of virtual middle level learners.

## REFERENCES

Baran, E., Correia, A., & Thompson, A. (2011). Transforming online teaching practice: Critical analysis of the literature on the roles and competencies of online teachers. *Distance Education, 32*(3), 421–439.

Cavanaugh, C., & Blomeyer, R. (2010). *What works in K–12 online learning.* Eugene, OR: International Society for Technology in Education.

Christopher, D. (2014). *The successful virtual classroom: How to design and facilitate interactive and engaging live online learning.* New York, NY: AMACOM.

Chubb, J. E., Hill, P. T., Laurans, E., Halderman, M., Battaglino, T. B., Hess, F. M., & Finn, C. E., Jr. (2012). *Education reform for the digital era.* Washington DC: Thomas B. Fordham Institute.

Clark, R. C., & Kwinn, A. (2007). *The new virtual classroom: Evidence-based guidelines for synchronous e-learning.* San Francisco, CA: Pfieffer.

Ebert, H. (2014). *So, you want to teach in your pajamas: An inside guide to K–12 virtual education* [Kindle version]. Retrieved from https://www.amazon.com/You-Want-Teach-Your-Pajamas-ebook/dp/B00KQIJ0XO

Eisenbach, B. B. (2015). *Stories of care in the virtual classroom: An autoethnographic narrative inquiry* (Doctoral Dissertation). Retrieved from Scholar Commons at http://scholarcommons.usf.edu/etd/5477

Evergreen Education Group. (2015). *Keeping pace with K–12 digital learning: An annual review of policy and practice* (12th ed.). Retrieved from https://www.inacol.org/resource/keeping-pace-with-k-12-digital-learning-12th-edition/

Kreber, C., & Kanuka, H. (2006). The scholarship of teaching and learning and the online classroom. *Canadian Journal of University Continuing Education, 32*(2), 109–131.

National Middle School Association. (2010). *This we believe: Keys to educating young adolescents*. Westerville, OH: Author.

Powell, A., Rabbitt, B., & Kennedy, K. (2014). *iNACOL blended learning teacher competency framework*. Retrieved from https://www.inacol.org/resource/inacol-blended-learning-teacher-competency-framework/

# SECTION I

## OVERVIEW

CHAPTER 1

# CHARACTERISTICS OF VIRTUAL MIDDLE SCHOOL STUDENTS

## Who They Are and How We Support Their Success

**Suzanne Wolfinger**
*Drexel University*

Personalization is a term referred to often in K–12 schools where educators strive daily to differentiate curriculum materials to suit each individual student's learning needs. Learning needs are addressed through personalized learner-centered activities that replace the older, industrial-age classroom model in which educators lecture and students listen. The trend of individualization in the 21st century classroom continues to gain momentum in public education, but educators and administrators must be cautious to avoid a hasty implementation of this approach to learning and consider the inherent complexity of effective personalization.

Implementing meaningful personalization is a complicated process for any educator who tries to assess the balance between a learner's disposition

*The Online Classroom:*
*Resources for Effective Middle Level Virtual Education,* pp. 3–22
Copyright © 2018 by Information Age Publishing
All rights of reproduction in any form reserved.

and academic performance to create a personalized learning plan. K–12 fully online virtual school educators face unique challenges. For example, online educators may never actually meet their learners in person to observe their learning, and they may need to rely mostly on the available online curriculum design to individualize instruction, with fewer options for personalization than their peers have in brick-and-mortar schools (Lowes, 2007). Truly understanding a virtual student's learning needs and disposition can be difficult in an online environment, and this challenge has been compounded by the gap in education research regarding who adolescent online learners are and what may help them succeed in a fully online virtual school.

Since virtual schools first emerged in the southeastern United States in 1997 (Barbour & Reeves, 2009), they have become a popular school choice for many families. Although statistics show many virtual school students perform below grade level on standardized exams (Molnar et al., 2015), the perceived benefits (i.e., personalization, flexibility, advanced learning opportunities) of online learning continue to attract learners and families to this type of school model. To support academic achievement, virtual educators and learning coaches (often parents/guardians) need to understand the attributes of young adolescent online learners and the academic support they need to succeed. Additionally, the new role of parents in the virtual school model must also be studied closely (Molnar et al., 2014). "At present, virtual education lacks a firm understanding of what high performance looks like" (Dillon & Tucker, 2011, p. 52), and current online educator professional development tends to focus more on learning new technologies than guidance on quality instruction (Lowes, 2007).

## ACHIEVEMENT CONTRIBUTORS IN THE VIRTUAL CLASSROOM

In an effort to facilitate middle school virtual learner success in the online context, we need to identify what contributes to academic achievement. Recent exploratory research indicates that successful middle school virtual students may possess the same personal characteristics that foster academic achievement in the virtual school setting (Wolfinger, 2016). In her research, Wolfinger (2016) identified the following personal characteristics: driven, autonomous, diligent, aware, confident, communicative, engaged, cooperative, and computer literate. Her research also revealed components of virtual educator and learning coach support that may promote academic success for these same learners: synchronous instruction, responsive teacher communication, a household routine, learning coach attentiveness, learning coach direction, learning coach assistance, and the supportive structure and design of a virtual school program itself. This chapter discusses virtual learner characteristics and offers virtual educators and learning coaches a set of strategies and effective practices intended to support the development of these characteristics in virtual middle school students enrolled in fully online virtual school programs.

## Characteristic: Driven

A person who is driven is motivated, and a learner who is driven is determined to succeed and accomplish goals, using sustained effort to do so (Wolfinger, 2016). Motivation, or drive, is a characteristic that has previously been associated with the description of an "ideal" virtual school student, mostly evidenced among high school students who participated in early studies regarding virtual schools (Barbour & Reeves, 2009). Drive has also been connected to the characteristics of autonomy and engagement in adults (Pink, 2009), and notably, these are common characteristics possessed by successful virtual middle school students (Wolfinger, 2016). Because it can be difficult to discern whether a virtual middle school student is driven to learn in the online environment, the following questions were developed for virtual educators to use to help determine the level of virtual learner motivation affecting academic achievement. The intent of these questions is to prompt a conversation between the virtual educator, virtual learner, and learning coach in the home to determine whether the virtual student would benefit from further development of this characteristic:

- Does the learner use opportunities to improve course grades?
- Does the learner have goals to achieve passing/exceptional grades in courses?
- Does the learner often work ahead in lesson completion when there is extra time to do so?
- Does the learner and/or learning coach recognize the benefit of education toward the learner's future?
- Can the learner identify motivators that stimulate personal academic achievement in school?

**Virtual educator strategy.** All virtual learners may benefit from the use of a daily or weekly journal intended for reflection of what motivates them from their perspective, or in some cases, what keeps them from feeling motivated. For virtual learners who prefer digital journals, virtual educators can suggest they use Google Slides or other types of documents located on Google Drive to record their reflections. Each virtual learner can securely share journal entries with virtual educators, and virtual educators can build relationships by engaging virtual learners through comments directly placed in the online journal. Virtual educators can begin with these suggested virtual learner journal prompts, asking virtual learners to respond to each prompt by explaining whether or not the prompt describes them and why. Journal prompts include:

- I want to succeed
- I am a hard worker
- I have goals that I want to reach in school
- Doing well in school is important to me
- I strive to do well in school every day

Some virtual learners may be motivated by daily responses in their journals, while other virtual learners may prefer weekly comments. This frequency of interaction will be more evident as virtual educators learn more about each virtual learner. Virtual educators need to consider how virtual learners' interests revealed in the journal entries could be incorporated into online assignments to increase motivation. Those virtual learners who are motivated through interaction may benefit from online programs intended to motivate various types of learners. Turning work into play can increase motivation (Pink, 2009), and a website like Kahoot. com is a game-based program that encourages interaction with learners both locally and globally. This type of website may provide a new experience for those virtual learners who are motivated by new challenges and enjoyment. Interactive assessments, like those created using Quizizz.com, may help sustain motivation for virtual learners who are motivated by the challenge of taking assessments and scoring well.

**Learning coach effective practice.** Setting academic goals, creating a daily routine, and providing overall direction during the day can promote academic achievement of adolescent virtual learners and help them remain motivated (Wolfinger, 2016). The aforementioned learning coach practices are supported by research conducted in brick-and-mortar settings that suggest parental expectations, such as goals and routines, may have a significant impact on learner achievement relative to constant parental supervision (Fan & Chen, 2001; Jeynes, 2005). It is possible that regardless of the school setting, virtual or brick-and-mortar, the tone set by the learning coach and the presence of parental expectations may affect standards or goals students set for themselves, thereby influencing motivation. Learning coaches could use a whiteboard to outline household daily routines, or Google Calendars for an online alternative, and add assignment deadlines or daily goals developed by the learner and learning coach. Learning coaches need to avoid short-term rewards or incentives to increase motivation, and instead encourage learners to focus on accomplishing their goals and doing their best. Short-term rewards may actually decrease intrinsic motivation in the long term, even though they may seem to motivate the learner at first (Pink, 2009).

## Characteristic: Autonomous

Autonomous is an adjective used to describe a person who is independent, and the ability to be mostly self-directed during the school day is what defines a virtual learner as an independent learner (Wolfinger, 2016). Virtual educators must determine whether a virtual learner is relying heavily on learning coach or virtual educator support to achieve academically, or whether a struggling learner may be new to online learning and needs additional scaffolding to succeed. Research suggests that there may be a correlation between a virtual learner's autonomy and the number of years enrolled in a virtual program (Wolfinger, 2016). The literature explains how people struggle to succeed in an autonomous environment when all they have known is a controlled or structured environment (Pink, 2009). In the virtual school setting, it is possible that middle level virtual learners who have been enrolled in a virtual school for several years have developed autonomy with each successive year, whereas middle level learners who have recently transferred to a virtual school from a brick-and-mortar environment may not have developed the characteristic to the same degree. Virtual educators can use the following reflection questions to determine whether a virtual learner may need support to foster autonomy:

- Does the learner blame others for poor performance in school?
- Can the learner communicate to you the reasoning for completing lessons and assignments in a particular chronological order?
- Does the learner attempt to resolve questions or issues independently before asking a virtual educator or learning coach for help?
- Does the learner take initiative to contact the virtual educator rather than depending on the learning coach to communicate for the learner?
- Does the learner take the initiative to use additional resources when there is a question or need for additional information regarding an assignment?

**Virtual educator strategy.** If a virtual learner relies significantly on learning coach or virtual educator support to complete online lessons efficiently and successfully, virtual educators need to work together with the learning coach and learner to create a structured plan that provides the virtual learner with planning support to help prioritize lessons and assignments. As the virtual learner begins to thrive with the plan, the coach or educator can add more daily activities to the list of schoolwork to be completed independently. For those virtual learners who are unable to achieve academically without considerable scaffolding from the learning coach or virtual educator, consider creating a roster for those virtual learners at Mobymax.com. This website has an online program that provides differentiated instruction for most subjects. Closing the gap in skills for struggling virtual learners may ultimately increase their level of independence through supportive instructional level activities.

Virtual learners new to online learning may benefit from a transition plan to bolster their autonomy in the virtual setting. Virtual educators can provide intensive support to new families during the first several months: daily telephone check-in calls, home visits, or weekly one-on-one virtual meetings. Consider connecting new families with seasoned families who have been with the virtual school for several years to serve as mentors. The autonomy of new learning coaches and new learners may develop more quickly with a mentorship rather than by struggling on their own during their first several months in the program. This intensive support can be provided to new families until the virtual educator agrees with the learning coach that the household routine is supportive of academic achievement and the virtual learner is progressing toward becoming a successful independent learner as evidenced through gradebook scores.

**Learning coach effective practice.** Learning coaches need to set the expectations for autonomy the first day of school by navigating through the online program with the virtual learner to familiarize the student with the online lessons and to establish a plan for the types of tasks the virtual learner can complete successfully and independently. The learning coach needs to remain involved with the virtual learner's daily plan and be available to discuss any concerns the virtual learner may have about the lessons assigned each day. The smartphone application, Rememberthemilk.com, is a calendar tool designed for students 13 years and older that may be helpful to use to establish a household routine. Another online tool, Toodledo.com, enables learning coaches and virtual learners to create a daily to do list and then prioritize the tasks. Learning coaches need to involve the virtual learner in the development of any plan to establish shared ownership of the plan, shared expectations, and a timeline for building an appropriate level of autonomy.

## Characteristics: Diligent

A diligent person makes a steady, consistent effort, and a diligent virtual learner makes a steady, consistent effort to complete course work, taking time to do so without rushing to completion (Wolfinger, 2016). Research indicates that diligence is a characteristic supportive of academic achievement among older adolescent students enrolled in virtual school programs, showing that the more time learners spend in a learning management system, the better they achieve academically compared to learners who spend less time in the learning management system (Liu & Cavanaugh, 2011). Successful virtual middle school learners who were deemed diligent learners exhibited similar behavior, with sustained time on task (Wolfinger, 2016), suggesting diligence may be an indicator of success for middle school learners in virtual school. "Compared to traditional classroom instructors, online instructors lack the regular set of cues about students' confusion or frustration during the learning process" (Liu & Cavanaugh, 2011, p. 396), so it is difficult for a virtual educator to determine if time spent in a learning management system is due to diligence or inefficiency. Virtual educators must rely on other available information to determine whether a virtual learner is putting forth consistent effort to achieve in the virtual setting, including evidence such as the quality of written work, actual time spent on assessments, and the frequency of poorly completed assignments. Virtual educators may use the following reflection questions to guide the data to collect and questions to ask during conversations with the virtual learner and learning coach to gauge a virtual learner's level of diligence:

- Does the learner spend the time necessary to fully comprehend concepts rather than skip over parts of a lesson to finish the lesson quickly?
- Does the learner consistently read e-mail communications to remain informed regarding course information?
- Does the learner spend adequate time on tests, quizzes, or other assignments to strive for the best result?
- Does the learner search for additional resources when needed for successful completion of an assignment?
- Does the learner attempt to understand errors or mistakes made?

**Virtual educator strategy.** Virtual educators need to consider using peer modeling as an effective way to introduce virtual learners to practices that will help them become more diligent with their schoolwork. Research suggests that using peer models to promote the learning of skills may be more effective than teacher modeling (Schunk & Hanson, 1985), and although virtual students are not physically in the same building together, peer modeling can occur in the virtual classroom. Using student work as an example, virtual educators can ask virtual learners to demonstrate how they proofread for accuracy or revise to add ideas, and these sessions could be mini-lessons lasting 10 minutes. Virtual educators can also ask diligent students to contribute their effective practices to a list of suggestions to share with the class via e-mail or message board postings. Ideas could address how diligent learners proofread their writing, monitor their comprehension, and check their assessments before submitting them for feedback and a grade. Virtual educators need to also consider allowing learners to revise assignments more than once to receive the highest score possible, showing virtual learners that a consistent effort is worthwhile, and providing online resources that virtual learners can use to help guide their efforts. In addition, virtual educators can recommend a site such as Grammarly.com that virtual learners can use to locate grammar errors in their writing.

**Learning coach effective practice.** Learning coaches can help learners self-monitor their behavior to reinforce diligent practices. The learning coach and virtual learner together can create a checklist of behaviors that the virtual learner need to practice regularly. For example, prior to completing a reading comprehension assignment, the virtual learner can use a checklist that may include some of the following tasks: sit in a quiet space, have your notebook with you, get post-it notes to write down questions, skim the reading passage once and find words that are unfamiliar, and so on. Self-monitoring behavior checklists can be created and personalized using the Interventioncentral.org website. The self-monitoring checklists can be printed and posted in the virtual learner's work area as a visual aid. If virtual learners are not motivated to make a consistent and steady effort to do their best with their schoolwork, learning coaches need to consider discussing with learners the importance of always trying your best. Pink (2009) suggested that some people may be motivated to complete more routine tasks if they understand the big picture and why the task is important in the long term, in addition to being given flexibility with how the task is completed. Learning coaches need to encourage virtual learners to revise and improve their work when an academic goal is not achieved in a course and establish an expectation that the virtual learner will be thorough and strive for understanding of skills rather than rushing to completion. When a virtual learner has a question, ask the learner to discuss which resources can be used to research the answer to the question independently. The virtual learner needs to ask the learning coach for assistance only after exhausting available resources; the virtual learner can create a checklist to outline the steps to take until the virtual learner internalizes these behaviors.

## Characteristic: Aware

Awareness refers to having a realization or perception, and a virtual learner's realization is a "knowing" of what is needed to achieve academically in virtual school (Wolfinger, 2016). Learners who are aware of their own learning process can regularly gauge whether or not their efforts are effective toward achieving academic goals, positively affecting motivation (Schunk, 1991). Research suggests that successful middle level virtual learners and their learning coaches possess an awareness of student learning styles that may enable them to regulate learning activities to fit their needs in the virtual setting (Wolfinger, 2016). Awareness is inclusive of, but not limited to, understanding learning styles, when to take a break and regroup, and which resources are most helpful to a virtual learner (Wolfinger, 2016). The following list of reflection questions for virtual educators may reveal whether or not a lack of awareness is impacting a learner's academic achievement:

- Can the virtual learner and learning coach identify a learning style that fits the learner best (e.g., visual, kinesthetic, aural)?
- Is the virtual learner or learning coach aware of academic strengths and needs for improvement?
- Is the virtual learner aware of when to slow down the pacing of a lesson if it seems difficult?
- Can the virtual learner explain strategies used to remain focused during lesson completion or assessment preparation?
- Does the virtual learner know how to prioritize lessons and assignments effectively each day?
- Does the virtual learner know when to take a break from schoolwork to refocus and reenergize?

**Virtual educator strategy.** Virtual educators need to consider asking learners and learning coaches to complete the free questionnaire located on the Vark-Learn.com website. In addition to identifying learning styles for students, this website provides strategies to use that are supportive of each learning style, which can easily be translated to the virtual setting. The website Thrively.com is another tool that helps educators understand learners' interests to tailor activities effectively. Virtual educators can adjust their pedagogy once they are aware of each virtual learner's learning style in an effort to provide more personalized instruction and appropriate resources for learner use. For virtual learners who may struggle with pacing, virtual educators can provide a general guideline regarding time that could be spent working on each lesson. For example, perhaps a virtual learner needs to spend generally one hour on a science lesson; this provides the learning coach with a timeframe to help monitor the virtual learner's progress in that lesson to ensure the learner is not spending too little or too much time on it. Several online timers are available as a resource for keeping track of time spent on lessons, such as those located on the Online-stopwatch.com website. Virtual educators can recommend these timers, or other household and smartphone timers, to ensure virtual learners are aware of when to take breaks and that breaks are an appropriate length of time.

**Learning coach effective practice.** Learning coaches need to check in with virtual learners periodically during school hours to monitor student progress, whether it is having a conversation with the learner or logging into the learning management system to remain aware of learner status. It is important that the learning coach is available to provide the student guidance or assistance that could take the form of coaching rather than constant supervision (Wolfinger, 2016). It is critical that learning coaches designate an appropriate place in the home as a daily learning area that is supportive of each virtual learner's individual needs. For example, if the virtual learner is easily distracted, ensure the learning environment is free of distractions, such as televisions, cell phones, and video games. To remain aware of a virtual learner's online engagement, consider installing a free parental control application such as the one located at Kidlogger.net. Learning coach awareness is an important component of parental involvement in virtual education, and research indicates that learner engagement may be influenced by whether an adult provides appropriate support, highlighting the need for learning coaches to remain vigilant (Frid, 2001).

## Characteristic: Confident

A confident person is certain; confident virtual learners are certain they will do well and succeed in school (Wolfinger, 2016). A clear connection is present between learner confidence and academic achievement (Bandura, 1993; Zimmerman, Bandura, & Martinez-Pons, 1992). Bandura (1993) explained that a high level of self-efficacy, or confidence, in one's abilities could influence a learner's personal goals, motivation, and academic achievement, thereby connecting the attributes of confidence and drive. If learners have low self-efficacy, they expect failure; however, learners with high self-efficacy expect success (Bandura, 1993). Research also suggests that self-confidence can influence autonomy, and it is connected to self- awareness and technological skills (Rice, 2006; Roblyer, Davis, Mills, Marshall, & Pape, 2008). Confidence is key in perseverance and engagement in activities (Bandura, 1993), making confidence a critical characteristic to foster in an online environment where virtual learners may be expected to be autonomous and self-motivated. Virtual educators can use the following questions to discern whether a virtual learner needs additional support to foster self-confidence:

- Does the virtual learner have a positive attitude toward learning?
- Has the virtual learner earned passing grades in previous school years?
- Is the virtual learner able to confront a challenge without becoming frustrated, upset, or disengaged?
- Does the virtual learner have previous experience with virtual school?
- Does the virtual learner visualize succeeding or failing each day?

**Virtual educator strategy.** Confidence is linked to success, and if a virtual learner is struggling, it is possible the virtual learner lacks confidence (Wolfinger, 2016). To build a virtual learner's confidence, virtual educators may want to address any gap in skills causing a lack in confidence. Virtual educators can use a website such as Activelylearn.com that supports learners by addressing barriers to reading, or the website Prodigygame.com—an interactive math program that supports learners at many different math instructional levels. In addition to supplemental programs, virtual educators can help build virtual learner confidence through synchronous instruction in either small group or one-on-one tutoring sessions that build upon skills and reinforces confidence. Then, they can expand synchronous instruction to include more challenging tasks as learners develop confidence. Research suggests that both virtual learners and learning coaches in middle school value teacher responsiveness as an academic support in the virtual setting (Wolfinger, 2016), and this notion is supported by Schunk (1991) who indicated that student self-efficacy may be measured by teacher feedback, connecting confidence with teacher interaction. Virtual educators need to consider forming a peer-tutoring group to cultivate more confidence in virtual learners already deemed confident, and help those who are less secure begin to feel more confident in their skills. Self-efficacy is improved when learners observe their peers completing work successfully (Schunk & Hanson, 1985), and research indicates students may persist longer at difficult tasks when interacting with their peers (Frid, 2001). Virtual educators can arrange peer tutoring sessions in their virtual classrooms or organize structured peer-tutoring sessions through platforms such as Google Hangouts.

**Learning coach effective practice.** Learning coaches need to be generally present in the household during the school day to provide educational support and bolster learner confidence. Active parental involvement is a potential indicator of student success in K–12 virtual schools (Lee & Figueroa, 2012). It is central to student success that a learning coach is able to recognize when a student is struggling and may need coaching support. Learning coaches need to provide appropriate, constructive feedback and encouragement, rather than focusing solely on areas of potential weakness. Pickhardt (2017) suggested that to foster self-confidence in adolescents, parents need to be generally encouraging of learners in the following ways: (a) support their goals, (b) help them learn from their mistakes, (c) promote persistence in a challenging situation, (d) give them space to solve problems independently, and (e) avoid connecting praise with how it makes the parent feel. The focus needs to be on how success makes the adolescent feel.

## Characteristic: Communicative

A communicative person is willing to talk to people, and communicative virtual learners are comfortable speaking with virtual educators, learning coaches, and classmates (Wolfinger, 2016). Communication is key to academic success (Wolfinger, 2016), and virtual learners must be able, and willing, to ask a learning coach or virtual educator for help when they have concerns regarding online lessons, assignments, or the mastery of concepts. Adolescent learners' self-efficacy may be affected negatively if they are unwilling to communicate concerns (Kim, Park, & Cozart, 2014), ultimately affecting academic achievement (Bandura, 1993). The characteristic of communication may be also related to a virtual learner's level of self-awareness and their understanding of which resources to use to achieve academically—resources including virtual educators and learning coaches. To determine if a virtual learner needs additional guidance or support to become more communicative, virtual educators can use the following reflection questions associated with learner communication skills:

- Does the virtual learner contact the virtual educator with questions or when additional support is needed?
- Does the virtual learner speak to virtual educators with ease while on the telephone?
- Does the virtual learner communicate issues or questions to the learning coach without prompting from the learning coach?
- Can the virtual learner clearly explain struggles with schoolwork in addition to what is going well?
- Does the virtual learner interact with classmates in a synchronous virtual class or through asynchronous message board discussions?

**Virtual educator strategy.** Research indicates that virtual learners and learning coaches value teacher responsiveness, whether the communication is via the telephone or through e-mail (Wolfinger, 2016). Virtual educators may need to initiate and foster regular communication with virtual learners who struggle to communicate, perhaps scheduling weekly telephone calls or meetings in the virtual classroom to discuss course progress. Virtual educators need to consider trying various methods of communication, such as using Skype or text messaging through the website Remind.com, to help determine which method is most effective for each virtual learner.

Building relationships and building trust with virtual learners can be a challenge in the virtual setting. Making interactions more personal using web cameras may help foster a stronger connection between virtual educators and virtual learners. Virtual educators could use a website such as Padlet.com or an application similar to ChatterPix Kids to help virtual learners build relationships amongst themselves through the sharing of photographs and encouraging informal communication. Virtual educators need to also consider developing a way for virtual learners to carry out informal conversations in programs such as Google Hangouts or through the virtual school learning management system itself, as research indicates that adolescent learners may benefit from informal peer communication, aside from interaction via structured instructional sessions (Barbour & Plough, 2012).

**Learning coach effective practice.** Learning coaches need to model how to communicate effectively and comfortably with virtual educators by initiating contact with virtual educators via the telephone and using speakerphone to converse together in a telephone conference. It may be beneficial for learning coaches to create a telephone call agenda with the virtual learner before the telephone call is made, outlining what will be discussed, to help allay any anxiety. Learning coaches can also encourage virtual learners to contact virtual educators through whatever means is at first most comfortable for the virtual learner, using e-mail if preferred, with an expectation that the virtual learner will ultimately initiate telephone conversations. Learning coaches need to model communication practices such as reading e-mails sent by virtual educators, and set the expectation that virtual learners read e-mails daily to remain informed and understand the purpose of written communication. For those virtual learners who struggle with communication with their learning coaches, learning coaches can create a plan together with the learner to discuss online lesson progress at agreed upon specific intervals during the day. For example, the learning coach and virtual learner can agree to review lesson objectives together at the beginning of a lesson and discuss any learner concerns at that point. The learning coach can then check in with virtual learner approximately 20 minutes later to discuss progress and monitor comprehension of the information in the lesson. An expectation can then be set to discuss what the virtual learner recalls from the online lesson when the lesson is completed. A communication plan may help to remove the onus from the virtual learner, who may opt to remain silent rather than ask for help.

### Characteristic: Engaged

When people are engaged, they are interested in what they are doing, and engaged learners are interested in what they are doing, whether it is the virtual class they are attending, an online video they are watching, online lesson activities they are completing, or online passages they are reading (Wolfinger, 2016). Research involving older adolescent students showed that learners who were engaged within their learning management system for extended periods of time performed better academically than learners who did not show sustained time in their online assignments (Liu & Cavanaugh, 2011), indicating that it is important to engage learners so they remain active in a learning management system. The level of awareness that a virtual learner and learning coach have about a learner's strengths, needs for improvement, and interests may influence engagement. Disengagement could possibly be a symptom caused by a lack of one of the other common characteristics discussed in this chapter (Wolfinger, 2016). The following reflection questions may help virtual educators identify whether or not disengagement in virtual learning is an issue:

- Does the virtual learner state that he or she enjoys learning in general?
- Does the virtual learner ask questions to gain additional information about lesson content?
- Can the virtual learner have a conversation about lesson content using higher order skills?
- Does the virtual learner actively participate in synchronous virtual classes?
- Does the virtual learner participate in activities that are not required, but available for enrichment or socialization?
- Does the virtual learner seem disinterested learning specific content (e.g., math, science)?

**Virtual educator strategy.** Virtual educators need to strive to provide learners with multiple opportunities to engage in learning each day, whether it is providing educational videos, independent projects, or opportunities for synchronous student-led virtual classes where learners create the information and present it using a website such as Educreations.com. It is important for virtual educators to understand the learning style of virtual learners to engage them in the virtual setting and personalize their learning experience. Virtual educators need to try to determine the reason for any student disengagement by using the reflections questions associated with each characteristic within this chapter. Many key characteristics influence engagement and ultimately academic achievement, so diagnosing the cause of disengagement is critical in effectively addressing it.

**Learning coach effective practice.** Learning coaches need to be curious about what virtual learners are working on each day and frequently interact with them, connecting lesson content with real world situations and outside interests to help virtual learners understand the relevance of their education to future goals. Coaches need to provide consistent support during the day while enabling virtual learners to work toward independence. However, learning coaches need to be cautious about using rewards to help engage learners. Pink (2009) explained that research studies involving children have shown that "if-then" rewards can actually have a negative effect on motivation and engagement in the long term because the approach takes away some of the child's autonomy. Instead, learning coaches need to add variety into daily tasks that may seem routine and attempt to incorporate a fun factor into the learning plan. The learning coach and virtual educator need to work together to create a plan that helps the virtual learner remain engaged actively.

## Characteristic: Cooperative

A cooperative person is able to work with others, and a cooperative virtual learner is able to work effectively with the learning coach, virtual educator, and peers (Wolfinger, 2016). A cooperative learner-learning coach relationship in a virtual school program may be the most important relationship within the virtual school context (Borup, West, Graham, & Davies, 2014). It is reasonable to assume that young adolescent online learners may need to interact more often with their learning coaches than older learners, because generally they are home together daily. The following list of reflection questions may help virtual educators evaluate the level of cooperation between a virtual learner and learning coach, as well as evaluate a learner's ability to accept feedback and work cooperatively with a virtual educator and peers to accomplish academic goals:

- Does the virtual learner work well with the virtual educator and the learning coach?

- Is the virtual learner able to accept constructive feedback from the virtual educator or learning coach without resistance?
- Does the virtual learner tend to help others when help is needed?
- Does the virtual learner do well in a teamwork setting?
- Is the virtual learner generally compliant without being disengaged?

**Virtual educator strategy.** Virtual educators need to set reasonable expectations for assignments and provide clear directions to alleviate any confusion or misinterpretation of information that could lead to a disagreement between the virtual learner, learning coach, and virtual educator regarding expected outcomes. It is important to have a shared goal for cooperation to thrive in the virtual setting. Rubrics are effective tools for conveying requirements for tasks and in sharing how points are assigned and websites such as Rubistar.4teachers.org enable educators to customize rubrics for course assignments. To encourage cooperation in a team setting, use the virtual classroom as a cooperative learning opportunity by organizing virtual learners into small groups and assigning tasks to be completed together. Cooperative learning may be most effective if the virtual educator is familiar with students' learning characteristics to ensure appropriate grouping and suitable tasks for the group to maximize the learning experience. For example, if a virtual learner is struggling with diligence, the virtual learner may not be best suited to be the note taker of the group. Virtual educators can also ask virtual learners to create virtual classroom guidelines to foster cooperation while learners are working together during learner-led activities in the virtual classroom throughout the school year. Virtual educators can also coach virtual learners through conflict resolution by role-playing, providing learners with strategies they can use to achieve a win-win outcome where no one really loses in the end. Virtual educators need to communicate regularly with learning coaches to reinforce cooperation strategies both in the online classroom and at home.

**Learning coach effective practice.** Learning coaches need to model cooperation in the household and guide virtual learners through discussions about how different perspectives can be informative and how understanding various points of view add to the learning process. Coaches can encourage virtual learners to be autonomous, but explain that they should not expect that everything would be done only their way. They can also create a positive learning environment in the household where everyone in the household contributes to certain decisions about school, and ensure the environment is relatively stress-free. If there is more than one learner engaged in online learning in the home, the learning coach could encourage the virtual learners in the household to help one another with activities and assignments. Having expectations and shared academic goals using a daily routine developed along with the virtual learner may help avoid frustration, which in turn, may lead to increased levels of cooperation.

## Characteristic: Computer Literate

Literate refers to having knowledge about a topic, and a virtual learner who is computer literate has a general knowledge about computers and use of the Internet (Wolfinger, 2016). Computer literacy is significant in the virtual setting. Research suggests that older adolescent online learners who have had experience with computers are content and motivated in a virtual program (Kim, Kim, & Karimi, 2012). Research also indicates that successful middle school virtual students are, at a minimum, proficient with computers (Wolfinger, 2016). Learning coach computer literacy connects to virtual learner success because research shows that a parent's level of self-efficacy with a task influences their expectations of learners regarding that same task (Brody, Flor, & Gibson, 1999). For example, if learning coaches are not computer proficient, they may not expect their virtual learners to navigate computer programs proficiently, which may affect virtual learners' expectations for themselves. Because online learners work with computers daily and must navigate the Internet and a learning management system, it is critical that virtual educators determine whether a lack of computer skills in the learner's household may affect academic achievement. The following questions may help virtual educators determine if a virtual learner and learning coach are capable of effectively using a computer in a virtual school setting:

- Can the virtual learner demonstrate knowledge of how to use the Internet?
- Does the virtual learner know any keyboard shortcuts?
- Does the virtual learner have any prior experience using a computer?
- Is the learning coach uncomfortable using a computer?

**Virtual educator strategy.** Virtual educators need to consider creating a simple class survey to gauge the level of computer proficiency of each virtual learner and learning coach at the beginning of the school year. Google Forms is an efficient survey tool as well as the questioning option on Tricider.com. Virtual educators can also ask about the virtual learner and learning coach's level of comfort working with computers during the initial conversation with family. If the virtual school does not provide an online orientation, virtual educators need to consider scheduling orientation sessions in the virtual classroom that provide an overview of the learning management system. Websites such as Typing.com and Typingclub.com can help learners and learning coaches improve typing skills, which could help improve efficiency while working on the computer. Administrators need to consider offering a computer technology course for each virtual learner to support basic skills, information about Internet safety, and opportunities to learn advanced computer skills.

**Learning coach effective practice.** Learning coaches need to be proficient in and comfortable with navigating an online learning management system to support virtual learners effectively in a virtual school. Learning coaches need to spend time each day on the computer to become familiar with the learning management system and its features. They can also watch how their virtual student navigates a particular course as a means to understand the learning management system.

## CONCLUSION

Education is more complex in the 21st century than ever before, with many learners considered digital natives who have never known life without a computer or smartphone. Virtual education is a popular school choice for many of these students, but in spite of their familiarity with technology, many virtual learners continue to perform below grade level on standardized exams and struggle in the virtual school model (Molnar et al., 2014). Shifting the focus away from standardized curriculum and toward individualization and personalization is the only way to begin to understand how to support each virtual learner's success—but it is a challenge.

Virtual schools have amazing potential to be groundbreaking, learner-centered, and a true educational fit for virtual middle level learners, but virtual educators and administrators must develop a deep understanding of the virtual learners they are serving for academic achievement to be truly attainable for each and every online learner. The insights, resources, and strategies in this chapter are intended to be useful for virtual educators as they work together with families toward creating and implementing an effective, personalized, and engaging learning experience for virtual learners.

## REFERENCES

Bandura, A. (1993). Perceived self-efficacy in cognitive development and functioning. *Educational Psychologist, 28*(2), 117–148.

Barbour, M. K., & Plough, C. (2012). Odyssey of the mind: Social networking in cyberschool. *The International Review of Research in Open and Distance Learning, 13*(3), 1–18.

Barbour, M. K., & Reeves, T. C. (2009). The reality of virtual schools: A review of the literature. *Computers & Education, 52*(2), 402–416.

Borup, J., West, R. E., Graham, C. R., & Davies, R. S. (2014). The adolescent community of engagement: A framework for research on adolescent online learning. *Journal of Technology & Teacher Education, 22*(1), 107–129.

Brody, G. H., Flor, D. L., & Gibson, N. M. (1999). Linking maternal efficacy beliefs, developmental goals, parenting practices, and child competence in rural single-parent African American families. *Child Development, 70*(5), 1197–1208.

Dillon, E., & Tucker, B. (2011). Lessons for online learning. *Education Next, 11*(2). Retrieved from http://educationnext.org/lessons-for-online-learning/

Fan, X., & Chen, M. (2001). Parental involvement and students' academic achievement: A meta-analysis. *Educational Psychology Review, 13*(1), 1–22.

Frid, S. (2001). Supporting primary students' on-line learning in a virtual enrichment program. *Research in Education, 66*(1), 9–27.

Jeynes, W. H. (2005). A meta-analysis of the relation of parental involvement to urban elementary school student academic achievement. *Urban Education, 40*(3), 237–269.

Kim, P., Kim, F. H., & Karimi, A. (2012). Public online charter school students: Choices, perceptions, and traits. *American Educational Research Journal, 49*(3), 521–545.

Kim, C., Park, S. W., & Cozart, J. (2014). Affective and motivational factors of learning in online mathematics courses. *British Journal of Educational Technology, 45*(1), 171–185.

Lee, M., & Figueroa, R. (2012). Internal and external indicators of virtual school learning success: A guide to success in K–12 virtual learning. *Distance Learning, 9*(1), 21–28.

Liu, F., & Cavanaugh, C. (2011). High enrollment course success factors in virtual school: Factors influencing student academic achievement. *International Journal on E-Learning. 10*(4), 393–418.

Lowes, S. (2007). Professional development for online teachers. In C. Cavanaugh & R. L. Blomeyer (Eds.), *What works in K–12 online learning* (pp. 161–178). Eugene, OR: International Society for Technology in Education.

Molnar, A., Huerta, L., Shafer, S. R., Barbour, M. K., Miron, G., & Gulosino, C. (2015). *Virtual schools in the U.S. 2015: Politics, performance, policy, and research evidence.* Boulder, CO: National Education Policy Center.

Molnar, A., Rice, J. K., Huerta, L., Shafer, S. R., Barbour, M. K., Miron, G., Gulosino, C., & Horvitz, B. (2014). *Virtual schools in the U.S. 2014: Politics, performance, policy, and research evidence.* Boulder, CO: National Education Policy Center.

Pickhardt, C. (2017, March 6). *Raising a self-confident adolescent* [Web log post]. Retrieved from https://www.psychologytoday.com/blog/surviving-your-childs-adolescence/201703/raising-self-confident-adolescent

Pink, D. H. (2009). *Drive: The surprising truth about what motivates us.* New York, NY: Riverhead Books.

Rice, K. L. (2006). A comprehensive look at distance education in the K–12 context. *Journal of Research on Technology in Education, 38*(4), 425–447.

Roblyer, M. D., Davis, L., Mills, S. C., Marshall, J., & Pape, L. (2008). Toward practical procedures for predicting and promoting success in virtual school students. *American Journal of Distance Education, 22*(2), 90–109.

Schunk, D. H. (1991). Self-efficacy and academic motivation. *Educational Psychologist, 26*(3 & 4), 207–231.

Schunk, D. H., & Hanson, A. R. (1985). Peer models: Influence on children's self-efficacy and achievement. *Journal of Educational Psychology, 77*(3), 313–322.

Wolfinger, S. (2016). *An exploratory case study of middle school student academic achievement in a fully online virtual school.* (Unpublished doctoral dissertation). Drexel University, Philadelphia, PA.

Zimmerman, B. J., Bandura, A., & Martinez-Pons, M. (1992). Self-motivation for academic attainment: The role of self-efficacy beliefs and personal goal setting. *American Educational Research Journal, 29*(3), 663–676.

# CHAPTER 2

# THE EFFECTIVE MIDDLE LEVEL VIRTUAL TEACHER

**Kerry Rice and Shannon Skelcher**
***Boise State University***

The rapid pace of technological advancements, along with decreasing budgets and a focus on preparing learners for a 21st century workforce are a few of the drivers for the proliferation of online and blended learning in K–12 education contexts. Other notable reasons for online learning enrollment include access to highly qualified teachers, flexible scheduling, credit recovery, and dual credit options. Growth in online learning remains steady, with estimated enrollments in the millions, and projected enrollment growth in North America of 13% by 2021 (Chang, 2017). When looking at grade distribution of fully online schools, we see an interesting pattern emerge with fewer enrollments in the elementary years, compared to the national distribution by grade level. High school enrollment sees a greater distribution and the middle school years are mixed, with a smaller enrollment distribution in sixth grade, and greater enrollment distribution in grades seven and eight (Rice et al., 2014).Supplemental program enrollments are harder to pin down, partly because there is no single tracking system in place and partly because of the varied approaches to offering part

*The Online Classroom:*
*Resources for Effective Middle Level Virtual Education*, pp. 23–37
Copyright © 2018 by Information Age Publishing
All rights of reproduction in any form reserved.

time online courses, be they state-led, district-led, or some other provider-led program such as dual credit.

Although the exact enrollment numbers may not be known, what we do suspect is that online learning is fully entrenched across all grade levels, particularly high school, and notably middle school. This growth in online learning brings with it a new set of challenges with respect to teacher preparation and measures of effectiveness. Currently, there is no federal requirement that differentiates between online teacher preparation and mainstream teacher preparation. The onus for ensuring the criteria for judging the quality of teacher preparation programs has traditionally been the purview of states and managed through accreditation processes and resource allocation (Rice, 2014).With guidance from standards such as those established by the International Association for K–12 Online Learning (2011) for quality online teaching and blended learning competencies (Powell, Rabbitt, & Kennedy, 2014), a few states have adopted teaching standards specifically addressing the competencies and skills online or blended teachers should possess. Georgia and Idaho are two states that have legislated online teaching endorsements. Michigan, Louisiana, South Carolina, South Dakota, Utah, Vermont, and Minnesota are examples of states that have specific standards, suggested guidelines, or recommendations (Archambault, DeBruler, & Freidhoff, 2014).

What this means is that our knowledge of best practice in online teaching has come not only from guidance provided by standards, but also from the on the ground, emerging experiences and practices of virtual school teachers and their programs. One challenge in identifying best practice and effectiveness measures for online teaching identified in literature is the "difficulty of conceiving the role of the teacher in online courses within the long established conceptual framework that we have built in the context of conventional, face-to-face teaching" (Anderson, Rourke, Garrison, & Archer, 2001, p. 14). No longer can our conception of classroom teaching be limited by physical location, time, pace, and path. Teaching online requires working knowledge of pedagogy, but with the additional understanding of how to leverage and use technology in a context and delivery modality that was unheard of in the past. In the case of middle level education, this entails applying that knowledge to the unique developmental needs of pre- and postadolescent youth.

## THE MIDDLE SCHOOL YEARS

A critical shift in the K–12 educational experience occurs in the transition between elementary and middle school. In addition to the challenges expected in association with changes in educational environments, adolescent learners are developing a sense of social self that can affect their achievement, motivation, and engagement in these crucial years (Eccles et al., 1993; Harter, Whitesell, & Kowalski, 1992; Midgley, Anderman, & Hicks, 1995; Roeser & Eccles, 1998). With a disposition toward self-doubt and uncertainty, adolescent students can be severely limited in their engagement and motivation, which in turn can result in poor academic achievement (Ryan & Patrick, 2001). For example, an internal change that follows the transition to middle school is a distinct, negative shift in students' overall intrinsic motivation (Eccles, Midgley, & Adler, 1984; Eccles et al., 1993; Harter et al., 1992; Midgley et al., 1995). In what Anderman and Maehr (1994) defined as "the problem of adolescence," students can find themselves lacking motivation for school and instead shift their focus to extraneous activities opposite to academic content (p. 298). Further, the adolescent student may respond to scholastic changes by reconsidering attitudes toward coursework (Rudolph, Lambert, Clark, & Kurlakowsky, 2001) such as using avoidance to shift any blame for potential academic failure from themselves (Anderman & Maehr, 1994). This allows the student to place responsibility for low performance on lack of study, instead of accepting ownership for inability and therefore preserving their self-image and esteem.

With a decrease in intrinsic motivation, it should be no surprise that students may face adversity in areas of self-esteem, anger control, and in their overall emotional stability as they enter middle school (Kazdin, 1993; Roeser & Eccles, 1998). In fact, research has demonstrated a dramatic increase in discipline issues in middle school compared to elementary school (Theriot & Dupper, 2009). Additionally, self-esteem initially decreases as adolescents face a growing sense of self-awareness as well as increasing pressure to achieve as they become more aware of nearing adulthood (Anderman & Maehr, 1994; Eccles et al., 1984). Studies also revealed that peer relationships could take priority over academic achievement as middle schoolers are developing deeper relationships with their friends (LaFontana & Cillessen, 2010). Conversely, a student struggling to develop these relationships could experience poorer academic performance (Wentzel & Caldwell, 1997).

Applying what we know about the struggle to both transition and succeed in middle school, teachers need to be aware of their position as both a practicing, professional educator as well as an example of a successful adult. While we often perceive teachers as role models and mentors to their students, the effect of these interactions is especially present in the research of teacher influence on student social development, motivation, confidence, and engagement (Midgley et al., 1995; Roeser & Eccles, 1998). Teacher relationships and perceived levels of caring are also correlated with student academic and prosocial goals (Wentzel, 1997). A goal of the middle school teacher should be to support and encourage student's current achievements and learning toward future successes and application, as opposed to a narrowing in on current failures (Anderman & Maehr, 1994). Negative interactions with a teacher can dramatically influence a student's motivation, and may deteriorate an ability for many students to proceed through the course (Ryan & Patrick, 2001). In looking at the emotional and motivational needs of middle school students, it becomes apparent that the middle school teacher requires not only knowledge of content and pedagogy, but also must take on the role of mentor and counselor (Theriot & Dupper, 2009).

## BEST PRACTICE IN ONLINE TEACHING

The primary purpose of education is to promote intellectual development. However, middle school in particular, is a time of discovery, and growth that requires a focus on both educational needs and developmental needs (Jackson & Davis, 2000). It is this nuanced approach, taking into consideration academic needs while at the same time attending to the emotional and motivational needs of middle schoolers, that perhaps best defines the qualities of successful middle school teachers. When we look at the literature surrounding best practice in online teaching, we find striking similarities. For example, DiPietro, Ferdig, Black, and Presto (2010) identified 37 distinct characteristics of best practice reported by online teachers themselves. They categorized these characteristics into a framework consisting of general characteristics associated with personal and instructional characteristics, classroom management strategies, and pedagogical strategies. While these best practice characteristics may appear typical for any delivery modality, digging deeper one sees an extensive focus on the need to (a) meet learners developmental and emotional needs, (b) connect with learners on a deeper level than perhaps one would in a traditional classroom, and (c) find ways to engage learners through more personalized instructional approaches.

In exploring the intersection of pedagogy, technology, and content, DiPietro (2010) eloquently writes about the degree to which online teachers' pedagogic beliefs translate into practice and inform the instructional practices they use. Making and maintaining strong academic and emotional connections with students while engaging in "fluid practice" were key beliefs of online teachers and supported practices intended to engage learners in ways beyond those in place- and time-based classroom settings. These studies are a good starting place at providing important insight into effective online teacher practice. Our exploration of the literature provided additional insight into potential effectiveness measures for virtual middle school teachers. We have chosen to categorize our results from a review of the literature into four areas of need based on our understanding of the very specific developmental needs of this unique age group: building community, promoting engagement, fostering relationships, and supporting learner agency.

## Building Community

Adolescents at the middle level place greater importance and pressure on developing peer relationships, with these friendships often taking priority over academic pursuits (LaFontana & Cillessen, 2010). It is important, however, that we encourage the building of this community, as research has shown that those who fail to establish these relationships can find themselves struggling both emotionally and academically (Wentzel & Caldwell, 1997). The online environment creates a barrier for students to engage in this relational contact due to a physical separation, paired with an electronic communication medium requiring nuanced and increased responsiveness to accommodate the missing face-to-face interactions (Aragon, 2003; Rovai, 2001). Students are not alone in their struggle to connect. In the virtual environment, teachers often experience feelings of disconnect from the teaching profession, their peers, and from their students. Hawkins, Barbour, and Graham (2012) described a low sense of community among teachers in the virtual environment, highlighting that some felt working online hindered their ability to work with their colleagues throughout the day.

The struggle for both teachers and students to connect online helps us understand the necessity for the development of an online learning community within the classroom. An online learning community is defined as when "a group of people who communicate with each other across the Internet to share information, learn more about a topic, or work on a project of mutual interest" (Porter, 2004, p. 193).The virtual educator, as the leader of this community, is ultimately responsible for building a meaningful relationship with the students, leading and encouraging peer interactions, and developing a structure and communication practices for the community within their classroom (Beck & Normann, 2009; Heuer & King, 2004). This is especially true for students new to the online setting, who will have less time to prioritize community-building and interpersonal connections as they navigate their new learning environment (Brown, 2001). In developing an online learning community, Beck and Normann (2009) emphasized that frequent and consistent interaction is essential—leading to a community of open communication, collaboration, and the exchange of information. To develop this interaction virtually, teachers should consider the regular use of discussion boards, blogs, wikis, and e-mail. Teachers may also consider social opportunities in a face-to-face setting, including field trips, community project collaborations, peer mentoring, involvement with the local newspapers, and other collaborative meet-ups (Bryans-Bongey, 2016).

Some families choose the online environment to avoid the (at times, negative) socialization that may have occurred at a brick-and-mortar school (Bryans-Bongey, 2016). Additionally, geographic barriers can result in students being unable to attend socialization opportunities or events, despite a desire to connect. Fortunately, teachers can take measures for students who can only meet in the virtual space, but would still like the opportunity to socialize "outside" of school. Barbour and Plough (2009) encouraged virtual schools to consider implementing private social networks for both the teachers and students to interact more freely. Such a network can act as a virtual staff room for instructors to meet and interact outside the learning management system, allowing teachers to plan with one another, share best practices, and discuss student issues (Hawkins, Barbour, & Graham, 2012). Through the establishment of social networks online schools have demonstrated an increase in student motivation and a sense of connectedness, as well as an increase in overall school community (Barbour & Plough, 2009). While research has not addressed the positive outcomes such a community could have on parents or caretakers involved in the educational process, we must imagine that by creating a separate space for work, and a separate space for community, a school can alleviate feelings of isolation for all involved stakeholders.

For many students, the middle school environment presents one of the first opportunities in which they have different teachers in each subject. A significant part of this transition is that the typical, individual classroom educator at the middle school level may not have the opportunity to interact with students beyond a limited class session, nor consider the students as holistically as the elementary educator is able to do. Without the common-day bonding that is available at earlier grade levels, the middle school educator needs to have a system of communication with colleagues, parents, and students to consider a student in all of their strengths and weaknesses (Treagust, Jacobowitz, Gallagher, & Parker, 2001). The need for building community is even more evident in online environments with the physical separation in time and place.

## Promoting Engagement

Adolescence is a developmental stage in which students begin seeking both autonomy and independence, and a time in which their intellectual abilities can be underestimated (Lounsbury, 2000). The online teacher should act as a facilitator within the class, and should engage the student while also respecting student capabilities. In a study by An, Shin, and Lim (2009), they found that college level students enrolled in an online course preferred the course instructor to be hands-off when facilitating discussions. The more involved an instructor became in classroom discussions, the less the students interacted with their peers. This study provides good insight into the importance of instructor facilitation with tempered involvement to encourage peer interaction, and ultimately, classroom community, in the online environment. Of course, teachers cannot expect the middle school student to work completely independently, which highlights the struggle for the middle school teacher—finding balance between virtual presence and engagement, with proper pedagogical challenges that encourage student growth and independence.

Teacher and student relationships and interactions may influence the engagement of the middle school student, positively (or negatively), affecting their motivation and academic achievement (Midgley et al., 1995; Roeser & Eccles, 1998). In looking at the virtual environment, middle school teachers face a geographic barrier that requires a different approach to reaching their students. In a study about middle school student's online engagement, Louwrens and Hartnett (2015) addressed three types of engagement—behavioral, cognitive, and emotional—and provided practical advice on how to utilize each one. First, teachers can improve students' behavioral engagement through the development of activities utilizing Web 2.0 resources, ultimately increasing the student buy-in. Second, teachers can improve students' cognitive engagement by including activities in which peers offer feedback to one another, again emphasizing a need for a classroom community. Third, Louwrens and Hartnett (2015) suggested improving students' emotional engagement by developing a learning community that allows students to feel safe and cared for in the virtual space. In this study, the students appreciated the opportunity to engage and learn more about their peers, noting that this added engagement increased their likelihood to work together and problem solve as a class, rather than constantly relying on the teacher.

## Fostering Relationships

Parents and guardians may have an outsized role in online middle school education. For example, a parent may have primary responsibility for the facilitation of lesson content, while the teacher serves as the provider of materials and expert on strategies. While no longer entirely responsible for direct instruction, the online teacher now has an additional responsibility to maintain consistent contact with the caretaker, guiding them in how to facilitate learning and maintain student motivation. This essential shift in roles allows the teacher the freedom to individualize and foster a student's approach to their own learning (Litke, 1998). It is good practice to keep constant, timely, and positive communication with parents and caretakers (Gill, 2007), including them in communications with students, and requesting that at-home supervisors also keep the teacher apprised of observations and concerns (Murphy & Rodríguez-Manzanares, 2009). Providing and maintaining expectations for these communications is crucial—best approaches include regular contact and deliberate use of multiple forms of communication, such as e-mail and/or text messaging (Belair, 2012; Rice & Carter, 2015). Consistent communication benefits the parent and is reassuring for the student (Borup, Stevens, & Waters, 2015). One essential initiative is the development of individual plans for communication that best fit the needs of facilitators and students, particularly in problem solving student issues and cooperating on scheduling and conferencing (Borup, West, Graham, & Davies, 2014).

Parents and caretakers must negate the lack of a direct presence from the teacher: supplementing roles of encouragement, modeling, and reinforcement (Liu, Black, Algina, Cavanaugh, & Dawson, 2010). Motivation is among the most important facilitator roles that needs attention shared strategies among teachers and caregivers are instrumental (Hasler-Waters, 2012). Facilitators at home with the students also need to demonstrate self-efficacy, and middle school can be particularly challenging for them, as adolescent students often begin seeking independence from their parents (Hoffman, 1984). The parent or guardian, now taking on the role as both supervisor and caretaker, must have support from the teacher to negotiate abstraction or ambiguities about adult participation in the facilitated lessons (Borup, Graham, & Davies, 2013). As students mature, the parent or caregiver will need to take on a more professional or organizational ethos or attitude, and the online middle school educator may be the facilitator of this development (Harvey, Greer, Basham, & Hu, 2014).

## Supporting Learner Agency

If supports are not evident and considering the increased disadvantages that adolescents face in maintaining motivation, the online setting could be a potential impediment to students' feelings of self-efficacy and self-regulation. Instructors must recognize that teaching practices in the face-to-face environment do not automatically transfer into the online setting; nor do students perceive learning in these environments to be alike (Mullen & Tallent-Runnels, 2006). In distance education, teachers ask students to work more independently and in a more ambiguous learning setting—one requiring a greater commitment to time-management, self-regulation, and self-efficacy (Sankaran & Bui, 2001). The delivery of instruction must result from careful planning and the promotion, encouragement, and maintenance of student self-confidence and motivation. A well-developed course would establish clear learning objectives, step-by-step assignment instructions, review exercises to reinforce material learned, and sample questions that offer students opportunities to practice their skills in a low-stakes environment (Sankaran & Bui, 2001).

In addition to the course design, instructors must consider the individual student needs in terms of encouragement, technical assistance, and academic proficiency. Teachers could consider adapting a variety of presentation methods within their content. In the online environment, teachers may notice a shift from their role as a leader of the classroom to becoming a partner to each student's individual learning process (McCombs & Vakili, 2005). The use of a needs assessment may assist a teacher in better understanding their students' learning style, academic standing, prior school experiences, and personality—allowing the teacher to adapt to individual needs (Egan & Gibb, 1997; Wagner, 1993). DiPietro (2010) observed that one element of the face-to-face classroom is still vital online—the feeling of connection created between instructor and student. A stronger relationship and corresponding trust and access will provide students the foundation to build their independence on.

The research also speaks to the importance of teacher self-efficacy—a teacher who demonstrates self-efficacy can have a positive influence on a students' own self-efficacy (Goddard, Hoy, & Hoy, 2000). Teachers demonstrating high levels of self-efficacy are more capable in creating classroom environments of organization and growth, as well as maintaining interpersonal connections that relieve pressures and stress (Caprara, Barbaranelli, Steca, & Malone, 2006). Overall, collective efficacy, a systematic sense of support through a system of peers, can ensure the success of students in need of models of appropriate, mature learners interacting in a professional environment (Cantrell & Hughes, 2008). The cohesion of teachers, administrators and other staff members in monitoring students' progress and potential issues before they are installed more permanently is crucial to supporting the efficacy of teachers and students alike (Cauley & Jovanovich, 2006).

## CONCLUSION

Middle school learners present a unique set of needs in virtual environments. Middle school is a time when academic development is highly dependent on socioemotional development, all of which occur in an interface that lacks immediacy and physical presence. In addition to the obvious technological skills that online teachers must possess, more nuanced capabilities are critical to meet the needs of these learners. An overview of the literature provides some evidence that four areas of investigation show promise for providing insight into potential effectiveness measures for virtual middle school teachers: community building, promoting engagement, fostering relationships, and supporting learner agency. We address each of these areas in the following list including recommendations of measures of effectiveness that gleaned from the research. While we address each area separately, we recognize that there is significant overlap; for example, engagement may be highly dependent on community building.

To build community, the virtual middle school teacher:

- Supports both academic and emotional needs of learners through well-developed communication and feedback loops;
- Designs tasks and establishes environments that mix student-status;
- Engages in activities that promote frequent and consistent interaction (i.e., student-student, student-teacher, teacher-parent, teacher-teacher);
- Uses a variety of communication tools (i.e., discussion boards, blogs, wikis, and e-mail);
- Provides social networking opportunities for both the teachers and students to interact more freely; and
- Engages in face-to-face social opportunities (i.e. field trips, community project collaborations, peer mentoring, and involvement with the local newspapers).

To promote learner engagement, the virtual middle school teacher:

- Uses peer-to-peer supports, interactions, and collaboration;
- Understands the available tools, what they do, and the pedagogy behind their use;
- Provides purpose for educational content;
- Develops real world or interest-based tasks; and
- Conducts live, synchronous lessons for learners who lack self-directness.

To build and foster enduring relationships the virtual middle school teacher:

- Consistently/purposefully interacts with students and families;
- Advocates mutual respect with students;
- Appreciates students' psychological well-being; and
- Develops student comfort and feelings of belonging in the school.

To build a classroom culture that supports learner agency the virtual middle school teacher:

- Emphasizes task goals, not performance goals;
- Avoids overemphasizing grades and competition;
- Engages learners to serve as partners with peers to improve collective success;
- Creates opportunities for student self-determination and rule making;
- Demonstrates self-efficacy as a model to students; and
- Communicates with peers and administrators to improve efficacy and self-regulation.

## REFERENCES

An, H., Shin, S., & Lim, K. (2009). The effects of different instructor facilitation approaches on students' interactions during asynchronous online discussions. *Computers & Education, 53*(3), 749–760.

Anderman, E. M., & Maehr, M. L. (1994). Motivation and schooling in the middle grades. *Review of Educational Research, 64*(2), 287–309.

Anderson, T., Rourke, L., Garrison, D. R., & Archer, W. (2001). Assessing teaching presence in a computer conference context. *Journal of Asynchronous Learning Networks, 5*(2), 1–17.

Aragon, S. R. (2003). Creating social presence in online environments. *New Directions for Adult and Continuing Education, 2003*(100), 57–68.

Archambault, L., DeBruler, K., & Freidhoff, J. (2014). K–12 online and blended teacher licensure: Striking a balance between policy and preparedness. *Journal of Technology and Teacher Education, 22*(1), 83–106.

Barbour, M., & Plough, C. (2009). Helping to make online learning less isolating. *TechTrends, 53*(4), 56–60.

Beck, D. E., & Normann, S. A. (2009). Implementing successful online learning communities. In P. L. Rogers, G. A. Berg, J. V. Boettcher, C. Howard, L. Justice, & K. D. Schenk (Eds.), *Encyclopedia of distance learning* (2nd ed.) (pp. 1134–1141). Hershey, PA: IGI Global.

Belair, M. (2012). The investigation of virtual school communications. *TechTrends, 56*(4), 26–33.

Borup, J., Graham, C. R., & Davies, R. S. (2013). The nature of parental interactions in an online charter school. *American Journal of Distance Education, 27*(1), 40–55.

Borup, J., Stevens, M. A., & Waters, L. H. (2015). Parent and student perceptions of parent engagement at a cyber charter high school. *Online Learning, 19*(5), 69–91.

Borup, J., West, R. E., Graham, C. R., & Davies, R. S. (2014). The adolescent community of engagement: A framework for research on adolescent online learning. *Journal of Technology and Teacher Education, 22*(1), 107–129.

Brown, R. (2001). The process of community building in distance learning classes. *Journal of Asynchronous Learning Networks, 5*(2), 18–35.

Bryans-Bongey, S. (2016). Meeting the holistic needs of K–12 online learners: Designing schools for the future. *Internet Learning, 4*(2), 7–24.

Cantrell, S. C., & Hughes, H. K. (2008). Teacher efficacy and content literacy implementation: An exploration of the effects of extended professional development with coaching. *Journal of Literacy Research, 40*(1), 95–127.

Caprara, G. V., Barbaranelli, C., Steca, P., & Malone, P. S. (2006). Teachers' self-efficacy beliefs as determinants of job satisfaction and students' academic achievement. A study at the school level. *Journal of School Psychology, 44*(6), 473–490.

Cauley, K., & Jovanovich, D. (2006). Developing an effective transition program for students entering middle school or high school. *The Clearing House: A Journal of Educational Strategies, Issues and Ideas, 80*(1), 15–25.

Chang, R. (2017, March 17). Virtual schools market in North America expected to grow 13% by 2021. *The Journal.* Retrieved from https://thejournal.com/articles/2017/03/07/virtual-schools-market-in-north-america-expected-to-grow-13-percent-by-2021.aspx

DiPietro, M. (2010). Virtual school pedagogy: The instructional practices of K–12 virtual school teachers. *Journal of Educational Computing Research, 42*(3), 327–354.

DiPietro, M., Ferdig, R. E., Black, E. W., & Presto, M. (2010). Best practices in teaching K–12 online: Lessons learned from Michigan virtual school teachers. *Journal of Interactive Online Learning, 9*(3), 10–35.

Eccles, J. S., Midgley, C., & Adler, T. F. (1984). Grade-related changes in the school environment: Effects on achievement motivation. In J. G. Nicholls (Ed.), *The development of achievement motivation* (pp. 283–331). Greenwich, CT: JAI Press.

Eccles, J. S., Midgley, C., Wigfield, A., Buchanan, C. M., Reuman, D., Flanagan, C., & MacIver, D. (1993). Development during adolescence: The impact of stage-environment fit on young adolescents' experiences in schools and in families. *American Psychologist, 48*(2), 90–101.

Egan, M. W., & Gibb, G. S. (1997). Student-centered instruction for the design of telecourses. *New Directions for Teaching and Learning, 1997*(71), 33–39.

Gill, L. (2007). *Connected students: A study of the viability of online learning for middle school.* (Doctoral dissertation). Retrieved from ProQuest Dissertations and Theses database. (AAT 304699026)

Goddard, R. D., Hoy, W. K., & Hoy, A. W. (2000). Collective teacher efficacy: Its meaning, measure and impact on student achievement. *American Educational Research Journal, 37*(2), 479–507.

Harter, S., Whitesell, N. R., & Kowalski, P. (1992). Individual differences in the effects of educational transitions on young adolescent's perceptions of competence and motivational orientation. *American Educational Research Journal, 29*(4), 777–807.

Harvey, D., Greer, D., Basham, J., & Hu, B. (2014). Student perspective: Experiences of middle and high school students in online learning. *American Journal of Distance Education, 28*(1), 14–26.

Hasler-Waters, L. (2012). *Exploring the experiences of learning coaches in a cyber charter school: A qualitative case study.* (Doctoral dissertation). Retrieved from ProQuest Dissertations and Theses database. (AAT 3569079)

Hawkins, A., Barbour, M. K., & Graham, C. R. (2012). "Everybody is their own island": Teacher disconnection in a virtual school. *International Review of Research in Open and Distance Learning, 13*(2), 123–144.

Hoffman, J. (1984). Psychological separation of late adolescents from their parents. *Journal of Counseling Psychology, 31*(2), 77–91.

Heuer, B. P., & King, K. P. (2004). Leading the band: The role of the instructor in online learning for educators. *The Journal of Interactive Online Learning, 3*(1), 1–11.

International Association for K–12 Online Learning. (2011). *National standards for quality online teaching, Version 2.* Vienna VA: Author. Retrieved from https://www.inacol.org/wp-content/uploads/2015/02/national-standards-for-quality-online-teaching-v2.pdf

Jackson, A., & Davis, G. (2000). *Turning points 2000: Educating adolescents in the 21st century.* New York, NY: Teachers College Press.

Kazdin, A. E. (1993). Adolescent mental health: Prevention and treatment programs. *American Psychologist, 48*(2), 127–141.

LaFontana, K. M., & Cillessen, A. H. (2010). Developmental changes in the priority of perceived status in childhood and adolescence. *Social Development, 19*(1), 130–147.

Litke, C. D. (1998). Virtual schooling at the middle grades: A case study. *Journal of Distance Education, 13*(2), 33–50.

Liu, F., Black, E., Algina, J., Cavanaugh, C., & Dawson, K. (2010). The validation of one parental involvement measurement in virtual schooling. *Journal of Interactive Online Learning, 9*(2), 105–132.

Lounsbury, J. H. (2000). *Understanding and appreciating the wonder years.* Westerville, OH: National Middle School Association. Retrieved from https://www.amle.org/portals/0/pdf/mlem/wonder_years.pdf

Louwrens, N., & Hartnett, M. (2015). Student and teacher perceptions of online student engagement in an online middle school. *Journal of Open, Flexible and Distance Learning, 19*(1), 27–44.

McCombs, B. L., & Vakili, D. (2005). A learner-centered framework for e-learning. *Teachers College Record, 107*(8), 1582–1600.

Midgley, C., Anderman, E., & Hicks (1995). Differences between elementary and middle school teachers and students: A goal theory approach. *The Journal of Early Adolescence, 15*(1), 90–113.

Mullen, G. E., & Tallent-Runnels, M. K. (2006). Student outcomes and perceptions of instructors' demands and support in online and traditional classrooms. *Internet & Higher Education, 9*(4), 257–266.

Murphy, E., & Rodríguez-Manzanares, M. A. (2009). Teachers' perspectives on motivation in high-school distance education. *International Journal of E-Learning & Distance Education, 23*(3), 1–24.

Porter, L. R. (2004). *Developing an online curriculum: Technologies and techniques.* Hershey, PA: Idea Group.

Powell, A., Rabbitt, B., & Kennedy, K. (2014). *iNACOL blended learning teacher competency framework.* Vienna, VA: International Association for K–12 Online Learning. Retrieved from https://www.inacol.org/wp-content/uploads/2015/02/iNACOL-Blended-Learning-Teacher-Competency-Framework.pdf

Rice, K. (2014). Research and history of policies in K–12 online and blended learning. In R. E. Ferdig & K. Kennedy (Eds.), *Handbook of research on K–12 online and blended learning* (pp. 51–81). Pittsburgh, PA: ETC Press.

Rice, J. K., Huerta, L., Shafer, S. R., Barbour, M. K., Miron, G., Gulosino, C., & Horvitz, B. (2014). *Virtual schools in the U.S. 2014: Politics, performance, policy, and research.* Boulder, CO: National Educational Policy Center.

Rice, M., & Carter, R. A., Jr. (2015). With new eyes: Online teachers' sacred stories of students with disabilities. In M. Rice (Ed.), *Exploring pedagogies for diverse learners online* (pp. 205–226). Bingley, England: Emerald Group.

Roeser, R. W., & Eccles, J. S. (1998). Adolescents' perceptions of middle school: Relation to longitudinal changes in academic and psychological adjustment. *Journal of Research on Adolescence, 8*(1), 123–158.

Rovai, A. P. (2001). Building classroom community at a distance: A case study. *Educational Technology Research and Development, 49*(4), 33–48.

Rudolph, K. D., Lambert, S. F., Clark, A. G., & Kurlakowsky, K. D. (2001). Negotiating the transition to middle school: The role of self-regulatory processes. *Child Development, 72*(3), 929–946.

Ryan, A. M., & Patrick, H. (2001). The classroom social environment and changes in adolescents' motivation and engagement during middle school. *American Educational Research Journal, 38*(2), 437–460.

Sankaran, S. R., & Bui, T. (2001). Impact of learning strategies and motivation on performance: A study in web-based instruction. *Journal of Instructional Psychology, 28*(3), 191–198.

Theriot, M. T., & Dupper, D. R. (2009). Student discipline problems and the transition from elementary to middle school. *Education and Urban Society, 42*(2), 205–222.

Treagust, D. F., Jacobowitz, R., Gallagher, J. L., & Parker, J. (2001). Using assessment as a guide in teaching for understanding: A case study of a middle school science class learning about sound. *Science Education, 85*(2), 137–57.

Wagner, T. (1993). Systemic change: Rethinking the purpose of school. *Educational Leadership, 51*(1), 24–28.

Wentzel, K. R. (1997). Student motivation in middle school: The role of perceived pedagogical caring. *Journal of Educational Psychology, 89*(3), 411–419.

Wentzel, K. R., & Caldwell, K. (1997). Friendships, peer acceptance, and group membership: Relations to academic achievement in middle school. *Child Development, 68*(6), 1198–1209.

# SECTION II

## PREPARATION

CHAPTER 3

# PREPARING TEACHERS FOR THE VIRTUAL MIDDLE LEVEL CLASSROOM

**Shelly Furuness**
*Butler University*

Regardless of the type of environment in which one teaches, successful middle level teachers create results-driven curriculum to meet the specific developmental needs of the 21st century middle level student. Creating a safe learning environment, whether it be face-to-face or virtual, is no easy undertaking. Duncan and Barnett (2009) contended that "many K–12 teachers currently teaching in online environments lack both the theoretical and practical understandings of teaching and learning online" (p. 358) and have advocated for the inclusion of 21st century skills competencies in teacher education because "few preservice teachers bring the skills and experiences that are needed to transform today's classrooms" (p. 360).

Despite the expansion of online learning and virtual classrooms, most teacher preparation programs have not had a consistent or dedicated focus on learning to teach in the virtual environment. When preservice teachers do not experience sustained, intentional opportunities for learning how to teach in virtual spaces, attempts to do so will remain pedagogically

*The Online Classroom:*
*Resources for Effective Middle Level Virtual Education*, pp. 41–60
Copyright © 2018 by Information Age Publishing
All rights of reproduction in any form reserved.

unsophisticated and limited. To counter this challenge, teacher preparation programs can prepare preservice teachers to transition to the virtual classroom, a task that is "not straightforward and may require rethinking teacher education" (Koehler & Mishra, 2009, p. 61). Teacher education programs can begin by creating opportunities with explicit, metacognitive modeling of an instructor's synthesized technological, pedagogical, and content knowledge as well as opportunities for preservice teachers to practice this synthesis.

Beginning in the summer of 2013, a collaborative partnership between an exurban school district—meaning it is typical of those prosperous communities that lie just beyond the ring of suburban neighborhoods—and a middle-secondary teacher preparation program sought to investigate practices for preparing preservice and in-service teachers for 21st century learning environments. Over the course of 3 years, we experimented with the creation of online teaching and learning opportunities for a variety of purposes and with varying degrees of student choice. Such opportunities included both voluntary and compulsory summer enrichment and remediation programs for incoming fifth through ninth grade students, as well as compulsory remediation aimed at improving Lexile scores and overall performance on academic tasks requiring specific content literacy skills. We discovered that being a good online teacher requires all the same skills as being a good face-to-face teacher, just more so. In this chapter, we offer resources and strategies for teacher education programs as they prepare future teachers to root their planning and instruction in the virtual middle level environment.

## TECHNOLOGICAL, PEDAGOGICAL, AND CONTENT KNOWLEDGE–TPACK FRAMEWORK

For decades, Lee Shulman (1987) has helped educators to understand that the most purposeful and intentional teaching exists at the deepest intersection of a teacher's pedagogical and content knowledge. The overlapping space in knowledge bases regarding how one teaches (pedagogy) and what one teaches (content) is pedagogical content knowledge. The virtual classroom adds a third domain—technological knowledge. This domain requires the recognition that to be effective in virtual contexts, a teacher must have some knowledge and understanding about the function and use of technologies in learning and in the content area. The key is the recognition that a teacher must possess or gain *some* knowledge and understanding about the function and use of technology.

Being an effective online teacher does not require technological expertise. Further, having expertise in technology will not make for an effective online teacher if the pedagogical knowledge base and skills are lacking. The goal of the technological, pedagogical, and content knowledge (TPACK) framework is for teachers to combine their knowledge about methods of teaching and learning, the content, and the function and uses of technologies in ways that result in complex virtual learning environments (Koehler & Mishra, 2009). To be clear, online teaching is not as simple as moving a class into the virtual space wholesale. Instead, successful technology-rich, online teaching results from thoughtful planning across multiple domains of teacher knowledge. Trainor (2014) pointed out that "what makes the TPACK framework successful for technology integration is the explicit and metacognitive 'how' and 'why' behind the technology use, not simply the 'what' " (p. 7). It is this location, the intersection of the "how," "what," and "why," that preservice teachers must see modeled in practice, alongside other opportunities for development and application, to address the technological demands of the 21st century virtual classroom. Therefore, as one begins to teach online, it is necessary to remember what one already knows about good teaching practices, therefore, it is a matter of adding the technological knowledge (not expertise) to that framework. While that demand may seem overwhelming at first, remembering that one's depth and breadth of knowledge in the areas of pedagogy and content is always growing may provide the novice online educator with some perspective regarding one's knowledge base in technology.

## PREPARING PRESERVICE TEACHERS FOR DEVELOPMENTALLY APPROPRIATE PRACTICES IN VIRTUAL MIDDLE SCHOOL CLASSROOMS

Regardless of whether a middle school class is fully online or blended (a combination of online and face-to-face), teacher educators must begin to prepare preservice teachers with what is already known about teaching to the needs of the middle level learner. Since the early 1990s, the unique needs and characteristics of this age cohort have been well documented (Scales, 1991) and middle school practices aligned to those unique needs have been defined (WNET Education: Concept to Classroom, n.d.). The Association for Middle Level Education (2012) continued to delineate the most essential, primary attribute for successful middle level teaching as being "developmentally responsive—using the nature of young adolescents as the foundation on which all decisions are made" (p. xii). It is important that teacher do not forget or abandon the foundational theories in the ever-changing learning environments of the 21st century. With these foundational theories and philosophies in mind, educators begin to build their virtual classroom practice. Table 3.1 provides an overview of the seven developmental needs specific to 11–15-year olds in their schooling experience (Caskey & Anfara, 2014; National Middle School Association, 1999; Scales, 1991; Van Hoose, Strahan, & L'Esperance, 2001), as well as considerations for the virtual classroom. These developmental attributes provide the necessary framework for understanding the middle schooler on the other side of the screen.

Teaching young adolescents requires a deep understanding of the unique characteristics of this age group, as well as a deep understanding of learning theory that is most compatible with these characteristics. In this chapter, we explore these seven developmental needs of young adolescents and we situate these needs squarely in the virtual classroom as we discuss ways to prepare preservice teachers in meeting these needs in virtual contexts.

**Table 3.1.**
**Summary of the Seven Developmental Needs**

**Physical Activity**
The adolescent body and brain undergo more changes than at any other time except from birth to age two. "Typical" weight gain can be 40–50 pounds and 0–20 inches. Growth is disproportionate, strength and flexibility are limited, and a minimum of 10 hours of sleep a night is recommended.

**Physical Development Domain**
The usual physical discomforts and anxiety that lead to fidgeting, mirror-checking, and frequent requests for passes out of the room are not present in the virtual space.

**Competence and Achievement.** In the midst of such rapid physical and uncontrollable transformation, young adolescents need many opportunities to demonstrate mastery and control over some aspects in their lives to resolve the industry vs. inferiority conflict.

**Cognitive and Identity Development Domains**
Results-driven instruction
Synchronicity
SAMR Model

**Self-Definition.** Making progress toward resolving the identity vs. role confusion conflict requires that adolescents have many opportunities to explore a wide variety of roles as they begin to look at what the future might hold.

**Identity Development Domain**
Social and Cognitive Online Presence

*(Table continues on next page)*

**Table 3.1.
(Continued)**

| | |
|---|---|
| **Creative Expression.** Opportunities that honor the varied and multiple talents people can possess go a long way toward helping adolescents both identify and develop their own talents. Opportunities that move beyond the typically narrow ways of demonstrating what one knows can be helpful during this time as adolescents grow in their ability to express themselves through speaking, writing, singing, dancing, drama, and visual arts. | **Cognitive & Identity Development Domains**<br>SAMR Model<br>Results-driven instruction |
| **Positive Social Interaction.** Though the family remains of primary importance for many, the circle of influence is increasingly wider. Positive relationships with both peers and adults outside the family provide secure, yet dynamic models for how to incorporate new ideas, views, values, and feelings into the identity that adolescents are working to create. | **Social and Emotional Development Domain**<br>Social and Cognitive Online Presence |
| **Structure and Clear Limits.** As adolescents grow, so does their need for independence, risk-taking, and freedom. The adolescent need to push boundaries must be balanced against our responsibility to ensure safety and security. Establishing clear, consistent structures and limits help adolescents develop skills and qualities associated with independence and freedom such as integrity, responsibility, and self-reliance. | **Moral Development Domain**<br>Synchronicity<br>Results-driven instruction |
| **Meaningful Participation.** All learners need their experiences to be meaningful and relevant. Considering the lack of control and uncertainty adolescents are experiencing at this given stage, providing opportunities for adolescents to give real input and experience personally relevant curriculum is vital to keeping them engaged. | **Results-Driven Instruction**<br>SAMR Model |

*Source:* WNET Education: Concept to Classroom. (n.d.).

## Preparing Preservice Teacher for Results-Driven Instructional Planning

The online environment does not change the rules of good teaching, nor does it change the needs of the young adolescents it serves. Regardless of the instructional format or platform of the class, middle school instruction should be relationally oriented, student-centered, and needs-based to promote an environment of academic success (Vatterott, 2007). The teacher as instructional planner must know even before the first day of class what it is students should know, should value, and should be able to do with the material by the end of the course. Wiggins and McTighe (2005) referred to this process as *understanding by design*. Cathy Vatterott (2007) labeled it *results-driven instruction* or backward mapping. This approach begins with the end of the experience in mind. It imagines what successful student outcomes would look like in action and then looks backward toward the first day of class to trace the path students would need to take to reach the desired results. When a teacher has imagined what a successful student would know, do, and value as a result of participating in the instructional experiences, then every class meeting, every assigned reading, every activity, and every assessment can be in direct alignment to the objectives determined at the beginning of a course. This does not mean there is not room for exploration and discovery of something unexpected, but it does mean that teachers intentionally selected instructional experiences or modified the course program based upon both the goals of instruction and the technological knowledge and skill set of the students and the teacher.

While this may sound reasonable, results-driven instructional planning is an uncommon approach in course design. For novice teachers, especially, it may be difficult to imagine what successful outcomes might look like thereby making it difficult to design instructional experiences toward those aims. More often, teachers use the known content as a *content driven* approach (Vatterott, 2007) to designing a course. In content driven planning, a teacher starts with the topic or standards to be covered and the amount of time available in the schedule. The teacher organizes the materials into chunks and determines how much time to dedicate to a topic. The content is separated into chunks and sequenced to fit the allotted time frame. Because the teacher may often have extensive experience or knowledge about the topic before teaching it, the connections between and among the readings and materials may seem strong and obvious, but students do not necessarily have the schema to make those connections. In content driven instruction, the goal becomes simply "to learn" or "to know" as much as possible about a content topic.

The bottom line is that a results-driven instructional planning process provides the teacher with the most control and direction over student learning outcomes because it requires the teacher to direct all readings, learning activities, and assignments toward specific, measurable objectives. Using this process in planning is valuable in every context, but in planning and creating an online class, it is essential to the success and sustained engagement of students. All teachers need to be skilled in this process, thus making this approach important to include within teacher education curriculums when preparing preservice teachers for the middle level virtual classroom.

**Planning process for results-driven instruction**. The framework for a results-driven instruction planning process is simple, but not simplistic. It should be the process every teacher uses to plan effectively in the online environment before making the course available to students. One conceptual mapping tool that teacher educators can offer preservice teachers is a bull's-eye target graphic. The center of the target, also known as the bull's-eye, is where teachers list the results at which they are aiming. To determine what is placed in that center spot, teachers must ask themselves, "At the end of this course, what is it that every student should understand, should know, and should be able to do as a result of the content and activities they had during the course?" Clarifying answers to this question is the most important step to creating a powerful learning experience because everything the teacher does once that is determined must be in service to ensuring that students get to that result.

The next question teachers must ask themselves is, "If students were successful in showing me the result I am aiming at, what would that success look like and how would the students be using their new knowledge, skills and understandings?" In other words, teachers must identify how they will define and assess success before they begin presenting any content to students or asking students to engage in activities. This process is a departure from more traditional planning practices where teachers present content and then create the test or project for students after most of the instruction has taken place. When teachers devise assessments *after* instruction instead of *before* instruction, the assessment tends to measure what was covered (or worse, what should have been covered, but was not). Assessments that measure the amount of content covered, as opposed to measuring what students can do with the content, remain disconnected from meaningful learning. Teachers, who are teaching in the online environment where curated content can be stored and retrieved indefinitely, and where the online environment documents content coverage, must plan assessments that allow students to show how they have reached the desired result.

Once teachers have determined the desired results, as well as successful evidence of those results, it is at that point teachers should consider the content, instructional activities, and technological tools that would best help students reach those goals. It is at this point a teacher can carefully select digital tools aligned to both student and teacher levels of technological knowledge and proficiency that would facilitate the learning. Every instructional choice needs to connect directly to one of the desired outcomes. Utilizing this framework in planning online instruction is crucial given the overwhelming, nearly infinite number of tools and activities virtual teachers could use. Teachers need to weigh innovative tools against some criteria or face the dilemma of having their action paralyzed by the endless possibility. As teachers learn about new digital tools, they can ask themselves a series of important questions:

- In what ways does the tool help students reach the desired result at which we are aiming?
- Would using this tool require specific training to use it effectively?
- Is the tool free?
- Will it work on multiple platforms?

If there are clear answers to these questions, then online teachers have a clearer rationale for using or discarding tools.

## PREPARING PRESERVICE TEACHERS FOR SUBSTITUTION, AUGMENTATION, MODIFICATION AND REDEFINITION (SAMR)

With adolescent developmental needs and learning theories guiding us and a planning framework that keeps us focused on the results our instruction is aiming at achieving, we can return to the TPACK framework to explore the substitution, augmentation, modification, and redefinition (SAMR) model made popular by Puentedura (2013). The SAMR model explored ways in which classroom tasks (virtual or face-to-face) and student activities, and thereby teaching and learning, can be enhanced or transformed through technology integration. Ultimately, the SAMR model can support preservice teachers learning to teach in technology-rich ways, transitioning into effective virtual classroom teachers.

Within the SAMR model, technology integration tools aimed at substitution and augmentation levels enhance the learning experience while allowing the teacher to develop technological knowledge and skills of the "what" and "how" variety. In other words, exploration of Substitution and Augmentation tools allow teachers to see "what" kinds of digital tools, strategies, or resources exist that are similar to what is already being used in a face-to-face context, and "how" those tools work which expands a teacher's technological knowledge. Substitution tools are those that simply replace the mediums used in face-to-face settings with digital mediums.

For example, a teacher may substitute a classroom set of textbooks for e-books. There are ample open-source sites teachers can investigate to gain access to textbook materials. Websites like Open Culture and Openstax are a good place for teachers to begin looking for free textbook and e-book options. This simple replacement potentially enhances learner access to the textbook outside the classroom. Augmentation tools add a new twist to already utilized activities and often are simply flashier, digital ways of doing something teachers or students are familiar with doing. Take, for instance, the commonly used document camera or overhead projector teachers may use to display a shared text the class might work together to annotate or correct. An example of augmentation in the SAMR model would be the use of a web tool used for PDF (portable document format) annotation in which students can all log in and collaboratively and simultaneously annotate a text while also being able to comment on annotations of others. Notability is an example of a downloadable app while Annotate is a free, easy to use web-based annotation tool. This is an augmentation because it is a new, digital twist on a common task. Augmentation enhances the learner experience through novelty and increased engagement, at least in the short-term. Teachers learning to teach in virtual classrooms can think about substitution and augmentation tools as a way of doing what they have done in a face-to-face setting in a new environment.

As teacher educators prepare preservice teachers for this new reality, it is important to embed such substitution and augmentation tools into the education coursework and field experience. After all, today's teacher educators might approach their virtual instructional training with limited knowledge of the technology and platforms necessary to meet the needs of virtual learners. Allowing preservice teachers with opportunities to research a variety of tools, and providing first-hand practice with such tools will assist them in identifying the right tool for the job once they encounter their future online learners in the virtual space. It is important that teacher preparation programs help preservice teachers recognize the dynamic nature and the adaptability of digital tools and not to become too focused on training preservice teachers in the use of a few specific ones. Doing so will help to create a flexible teacher mindset that embraces the continual exploration of new tools and new possibilities empowering teachers to see themselves as capable and competent in the providing a technologically rich learning environment. Further, inviting preservice teachers to evaluate digital tools used for their own learning process against that set of planning questions (e.g., "In what ways does this tool help students reach the desired result at which we are aiming? Would using this tool require specific training to use it effectively? Is the tool free? Will it work on multiple platforms?") becomes a powerful demonstration of how technological knowledge and skill proficiency is dynamic and easily expanded.

For instance, in many of today's teacher education courses, instructors ask preservice teachers to reflect on their observations and experiences within their associated fieldwork. Traditionally, preservice teachers typed and handed in or uploaded those reflections to a learning management system. What if instead of asking students to submit reflections via pen-and-paper or a Word document, instructors model flexible tool implementation by substituting and augmenting the reflection assignments. Preservice teachers could use a series of Voice Memos or Smart Voice Recorder to articulate their reflection response giving them practice using available tools ubiquitously while simultaneously demonstrating an easy way to support future learners who may struggle to organize thoughts on paper. Alternatively, preservice teachers could capture a series images using another ubiquitous tool—the camera available on their phones. For each image captured from their field experience, the preservice teacher could provide reflective captions. Using very familiar tools with a new purpose—expressly teaching and learning—could help preservice teachers recognize that they do have a lot of knowledge and skills they can bring to the virtual learning environment, especially if they can begin to recognize how tools can help blur the boundaries between learning in a classroom and learning in life.

Modification and redefinition tools can transform learning by not only changing what and how learners experience the content, but also revealing (redefining) why it matters. Creating experiences that make it possible for learners to try something that would otherwise be impossible without technology is transformative. Modification might include opportunities to connect students with people, places, or resources that would not otherwise be available if not for technology. For example, students being able to speak with real, live astronauts on the International Space Station would not be possible without technology. Taking a virtual museum tour or field trip is another example. In a virtual classroom, technology has the power to *modify* and *redefine* learning in simple but powerful ways by making the impossible, improbable or unfeasible a reality. For example, free video conferencing tools like Zoom, make it possible to have a real-time conversation with a person (or people) anywhere in the world on a phone or laptop. Further, learners and teachers can record and view repeatedly their video conversations. Therefore, if a teacher education program wants to show preservice teachers what it is like to teach on a different continent, or to bring together a panel of educators from around the world to discuss a topic, time, location, and money are no longer obstacles. Modifying how students access learning opportunities redefines what is possible, and preservice teachers who have experience with technology that redefines what is possible are more likely to utilize similar tools.

For those preparing preservice teachers for the online classroom, the SAMR model is a good place to start with getting them acquainted with technology because it honors what already exists and provides a growth oriented, higher-order thinking continuum shift from enhancement to transformation. Using the SAMR model is a good first, initial step in increasing technological knowledge and integration can enhance the learner experience.

The inclusion of the SAMR model in teacher education programs can help teacher educators expand preservice teachers' technology knowledge base because Web 2.0 tools are often created for a singular purpose, but can be used in multiple ways. In addition, often many tools exist to serve those singular functions. As preservice teachers become more comfortable with planning for online learning tasks, they can plan a task with the result or purpose in mind, not the web tool. In other words, this means planning with the result in mind, determining what the successful outcome would look like, and then, selecting an activity or tool that will help students reach that goal.

## PREPARING PRESERVICE TEACHERS TO NAVIGATE TIME AND SPACE IN THE VIRTUAL CLASSROOM

Teaching online can provide tremendous flexibility in when and how students choose to engage with content. This flexibility can be a benefit, but it can also become a burden to the teacher if there is not clarity regarding the structure and time commitment of the class. Online teachers can quickly find themselves teaching 24 hours a day, 7 days a week and responding to individual students as if the online class were suddenly a series of infinite individualized classes. Having a results-driven instructional plan is a good step toward combating this potential pitfall, but it is also necessary for teachers to understand from the outset exactly how to structure time in the virtual environment. Therefore, it is important to consider the design of the class—whether this will be a synchronous, asynchronous, or a combination experience. Online teachers must understand that not all virtual classrooms are set up the same way. Just as physical school environments run a multitude of different scheduling patterns ranging from tightly scheduled discrete class periods to block schedules to independent, exploratory, or enrichment projects, a variety of schedules exist in the virtual classroom space making it imperative to prepare preservice teachers for this dynamic.

A synchronous course is usually defined as one with a designated time for the teacher and students to be logged into the class and participating simultaneously. One benefit of the synchronous experience is that the teacher can easily "take attendance" and follow-up with students who are absent at a designated time. The teacher is present while students are interacting with the content to answer questions and support students in real time just as they might in a physical classroom. Additionally, the teacher in a synchronous course can manage the pace of the content materials made available to students. If the teacher does not have all the materials ready to go from the outset, the synchronous class allows the teacher to control when they make materials available to students.

One drawback of the synchronous class is it severely limits the flexibility that can come with the e-learning environment. In addition, the teacher in a synchronous class becomes the sole support for all students simultaneously working on materials, which may make it difficult to answer students' questions in a timely manner or may impede others who do not have questions. Utilizing strong differentiation strategies within the virtual environment is key and this is where the vast content that is just a click or hyperlink away can be very helpful. Again, having strong and clear results in mind from the outset will allow a teacher to gear materials and activities toward those results. Having additional support and enrichment options like related videos, infographics, games, or websites ready and embedded in the course design will help the teacher manage the virtual classroom space.

The synchronous setting is most like the traditional face-to-face set-up when it comes to management and pacing of the classroom instruction. Often, teachers making the transition to the virtual environment begin with a synchronous experience because it feels most familiar to the face-to-face classroom. In making this transition, teachers can look for digital variations for face-to-face strategies. As previously discussed, the SAMR model is a good place to begin. Digital strategies that are substitutes for common brick-and-mortar practices can help a novice virtual educator build confidence and effective practice. Teacher educators can help preservice virtual teachers in their understanding of the synchronous online experience by choosing to hold synchronous class session online or allowing students to experience *flipped* lessons. Nearly all schools utilize learning management systems (LMS). Some commonly used LMS include Blackboard, Moodle, Schoology, and Canvas. Blackboard Collaborate is a virtual platform that provides a private, virtual space for instructors and students to meet, converse, and engage in collaborative activities. Adobe Connect is another virtual conferencing or meeting space tool. Tools such as Blackboard Collaborate or Adobe Connect are important for establishing a clear teacher presence in the virtual space. These tools allow you to hold office hours or tutoring sessions with students who are seeking more support or connection to the online class community.

Any strategy teachers might use for face-to-face management or engagement likely has a digital substitute. For example, teachers who use small group discussion or literature circles can implement virtual forums with assigned roles that make sense to the task. Ensuring that each member of a group has an assigned role and responsibility supports cooperative learning and limits confusion about what teachers expect from each student. In the virtual environment, forum discussions and role assignments become a highly visible way to track participation. Teachers who frequently use Word walls to teach vocabulary can have students contribute to the creation of a glossary that serves as a tool embedded directly in most LMS platforms. Teachers can create unit specific glossaries or general course vocabulary glossaries. The glossaries allow images to be included which could be an excellent support resource for students struggling with vocabulary. Many virtual classroom environments also have a live chat feature for students to be able to ask questions while the class is in session. The digital tools or strategies teachers select will be most effective when they have a clear purpose and that purpose is transparent to students. Providing preservice teachers with opportunities to research such tools throughout their coursework, and then engage in class sessions and activities utilizing these same tools to further their own knowledge of the technology available to them as virtual teachers and to help them prepare to meet the needs of their future middle level virtual students.

Synchronous courses entail everyone being online at the same time, in real time and seeing the course material revealed little by little; an asynchronous class is one in which the students proceed through the materials individually at their own pace. Asynchronous courses are primarily content coverage driven and static in their content. Because the course is asynchronous and students determine their own pace toward completion, generally, all materials must be ready for students on day one. Students may log on at any time. They may work a little at a time or in longer binges. The benefit of the asynchronous class is that it is a very individualized for students. This allows the teacher to guide each student as the needs arise. This individualized pace may also be a drawback if the teacher is essentially teaching the class as an independent study with each student needing one-on-one attention each time they choose to engage with the course materials. For this reason, it is important to prepare preservice virtual teachers with strategies and tools to ensure their students are engaged in the asynchronous classroom, while also preparing them to address the realities such a course will pose for their own lives.

Teachers can take actions within an asynchronous course to promote deeper engagement with the material. After all, asynchronous learning has the capability of becoming an isolated event—one that does little to address the middle level learner's developmental need for relationships and connection. Given the structure of this online format, and the likelihood that many preservice teachers have limited experience with such platforms, it is important to prepare future online teachers to meet the needs of virtual middle level learners within this context.

First, given what we know about developmental attributes of young adolescents, an asynchronous course should have very clear structures and limits. Virtual teachers must be clear and consistent about their availability to students, both in terms of modes for communication and frequency. Use of video conferencing tools or live chat features (e.g., Blackboard Collaborate or Adobe Connect) can help students know with some sense of certainty when support will be available and that a real person is there to help. In addition, virtual teachers in asynchronous settings can communicate regularly and predictable regarding overall student completion progress. For example, many learning management systems, such as Moodle, Canvas, and Blackboard provide teachers space to post messages, announcements, and maintain up-to-date grades for student access. Using feedback that comes in the form of voice memos of video conferencing can also make it clear to students that a real, live teacher is on the other side of the screen reviewing the work.

Again, modeling the use of such applications is important to further supporting preservice virtual teacher development. In addition, implementing coursework that provides preservice teachers the opportunity to create and post their own announcements and example tutorial videos not only offers first-hand experience, but also provides preservice teachers with the chance to create exemplars they can later apply to their own asynchronous middle level classrooms.

## PREPARING PRESERVICE TEACHERS TO
## CREATE A SENSE OF PROXIMITY IN
## THE VIRTUAL MIDDLE LEVEL CLASSROOM

Once teachers have made a decision regarding synchronicity, they must address decisions regarding course format and layout. In virtual learning spaces, results-driven instructional planning is especially important because time has a way of getting away from us when we are online. Because there is so much content available with just a click, it is essential that teacher educators prepare preservice teachers to keep in mind the perimeters of learning objectives as well as a middle schooler's need for structure and clear limits within the virtual middle level classrooms.

Teaching in an online context is like teaching in a physical space in that one must give careful consideration for setting up the virtual classroom and its norms. Just as teacher educators prepare preservice teachers to take time to determine the physical layout and appearance of the classroom and to establish clear procedures for operating within a physical classroom space, virtual teachers need to be prepared to do the same. Working with middle level learners requires that special consideration of their needs in determining the best way to layout the virtual space. Yet, unlike lessons focused on classroom organization and student seating, virtual preservice teachers require instruction on LMS and knowledge of research that speaks to engaging and capturing the attention of the virtual learner. After all, preservice teachers who have engaged in online coursework have done so in the role of the student—not the teacher. For this reason, their knowledge of online course structure, and the steps necessary in formulating and navigating the steps to develop such a course are often limited to none. Teacher educators who model best practices in virtual settings can support preservice teachers even more by making their own processes for course design as transparent as possible. Modeling a "think aloud" about the intentional ways the course is set up within the specific LMS or showing preservice educators a virtual course design planning template are just a couple of ways that teacher educators could support preservice teachers in expanding their understanding of teaching in the virtual environment. Being explicit and transparent with preservice educators will not only demystify the planning process, but it will also model excellent reflective practices that can be utilized regardless of the LMS, the content of the courses, or the developmental level of the learner being taught.

Understanding the expected timing and synchronicity of the virtual course is the beginning point for laying out the expectations. The type of structures and protocols virtual middle level teachers will use should be in service to students reaching the pre-determined result. Teachers need to spend time teaching procedures and protocols to students to orient them to the learning environment. Efficient e-learning environment classrooms have clearly marked consistent layouts for each learning module. Modules in the virtual environment represent a unit of instruction, perhaps a single lesson or series of lessons on the same topic depending on how instructor laid out the course. The locations and protocols for students to find directions, turn in their work, and locate materials and resources should be easy to find. The formatting on the module needs to be consistent. Instructors also need to outline clearly the agenda and objectives. The location for submission of work or posts needs to be highly visible. Whatever will be a regular part of their virtual experience should be practiced avoid letting the virtual classroom become a barrier to learning. Once learners are familiar with the context and the boundaries, they will be able to focus cognitive energy and effort on the content of the course, not navigating the virtual classroom landscape.

Teacher educators can provide preservice virtual teachers with opportunities to research and learn more about effective teaching procedures and protocols for their own virtual space, as well as opportunities to create and practice strategies they can later use in acquainting their virtual learners with the virtual context. The more opportunities preservice educators have for participating in well designed, dynamic virtual learning spaces, the more effective they will be at creating those spaces for middle level students.

One suggested strategy for teaching preservice educators how to create this type of efficient e-learning environment is to model that layout using screen casting tools like Screencast-O-Matic or Camtasia. These tools allow users to capture and record screenshots while providing audio commentary. It is an excellent way for a teacher to navigate and demonstrate from the same vantage point that a student would see the material while explicitly showing and telling a student what they are seeing on the screen. Again, preservice teachers need models of effective virtual environments as learners if they are to be successful in imagining and implementing strategies on their own.

## PREPARING PRESERVICE TEACHERS IN CREATING PRESENCE

Middle school philosophy is rooted in an understanding that young adolescents are at a unique period of development where they straddle the line between childhood and adulthood. There is a recognition that the community of those influencing a middle schooler is expanding. There is push and pull between fitting in and wanting to fade into the background. Young adolescents are trying to discover who they are and whom they are like and this can lead to debilitating bouts of self-consciousness and awkward displays of silliness. While the middle school students are struggling to modulate their presence in the world, it is vital that they feel seen and noticed on their own terms.

The virtual classroom community is robust when students know the teacher is present and engaged and when there is a sense of community interaction that extends beyond the content of the course—social presence. While we know that middle school learners need consistent teacher presence and proximity (Marzano & Pickering, 2011) to remain engaged, most would agree the same is true of adult learners, too. When preparing preservice teachers for teaching in the virtual setting we must work in intentional ways to develop a sense of proximity to our learners so they can feel seen and known. Once students know the teacher is present and watching and that the other online learners are "real" people too, then students are more likely to present their thinking and take academic risks with class material. We refer to this phenomenon as cognitive presence. The virtual classroom will function best when all three types of presence—teacher presence, social presence, and cognitive presence—exist (Duncan & Barnett, 2009). So, how does one prepare preservice teachers to establish a teacher presence in an online environment?

Online learning can be very isolating; it adds a layer of challenge in connecting and learning about the lives, experiences, and cultures of students. A few simple strategies can provide teachers insight into how learners perceive themselves, and how they choose to identify themselves in the virtual space. For example, begin the course by requiring preservice teachers upload a self-selected picture or visual representation, such as an avatar of their identity so that anytime they engage in online course interactions, there is an image associated with the individual person. In addition, online learning requires them to post an introductory video upload where each preservice teacher posts a 1 to 2-minute video introduction of himself or herself to a forum and each classmate is required to respond in some way. It provides them with a variety of resources for identifying and uploading such avatars and video tools so they can, in turn, practice the process and share this resource with their own students. This also increases the sense of being in a real community while also allowing students to determine an image that best represents their own identity and building technological skills all at the same time in purposeful, contextualized ways.

Showing preservice teachers how to establish teacher presence early and how to maintain this presence throughout the duration of the course is a challenge worth undertaking. As discussed in the previous section, it begins with the development and implementation of clear structures and well-designed course format. When learners, be they middle level or preservice teachers of middle level learners, are clear about where things are located in the e-learning module, when assignments are due, and where to submit them, and when and how they are to be engaged with the material, the teacher is clearly present for them.

In addition, teachers can use many other strategies to make it clear that a teacher present in the virtual space and that the course is not on auto-pilot. For example, teachers can establish presence by predictably posting a teacher created video to open each new module, or unit of instruction. Having a real, live teacher face appear to students is certainly one way to show them a teacher presence, but there are also web tools that use speech-to-text avatars to create cartoon-like videos like Voki and GoAnimate. The video allows students to visually see and/or hear the teacher. The consistent, reliable format of providing a visual and auditory overview could accompany a demonstration of different tools used with similar functions. Further, a teacher's ability to work in references to student work or forum posts in the video goes a long way toward making a learner feel seen and noticed in the virtual space.

## Student Presence

In addition to establishing and maintaining their own presence, the online teacher must actively promote and create opportunities for students to establish individual social presence.

Another part of establishing virtual classroom climate and norms that will allow student social presence involves explicit instruction of *netiquette*. One of the greatest benefits of online teaching is that there is time to gather thoughts and time to revise those thoughts before pushing "enter." The drawback is anonymity. As evidenced by trolls on social media, when there is vast cyberspace between people and one does not have to look another person in the eye before posting, it can be easy to say the first thing that comes to mind. Teachers must teach the reflective process explicitly. The teacher must establish with students answers to questions such as (a) How should people post in forums?, (b) How should people give peer-feedback?, and (c) How should we raise questions if we do not understand the point someone is trying to make in a discussion forum? Giving purposeful attention to the creation and maintenance of social presence is a good way to close the cyberspace between e-learning classmates. Teacher educators can help preservice teachers develop these practices by using clear discussion forum rubrics for participation and criteria for asking preservice teachers to help develop these as part of their own course work. Teacher educators can also provide preservice teachers with opportunities to be discussion forum moderators and provide guided reflection protocols that help the preservice teacher recognize characteristics of both effective and ineffective discussion on line.

As is generally the case, expecting teachers to model best practice for their students requires that they see these best practices modeled. Making sure that preservice preparation provides plenty of opportunities for guided, positive practicum experiences in the good virtual settings is best practice.

## CONCLUSION

To prepare preservice educators to teach in the online environment, teacher preparation programs have to engage them in the research and practice of developing technological skills alongside knowledge of content and adolescent development. Further, teacher preparation programs can model good technology rich instruction by providing preservice teachers with an introduction to resources they will use with their own students while developing within the preservice educator a mindset open to the dynamic nature of technology evolution. All of this is necessary if educators are going to be able to bring to bear all their knowledge about the processes of teaching and learning (pedagogy), about the content and its possible relevant intersections within the lives of middle level students, and about the use and function technology as a means of crossing that vast cyberspace. Therefore, it is imperative that teacher educators address each of these elements if they are to be successful in preparing effective middle level virtual teachers. Teacher preparers must help preservice teachers learn to plan for their virtual classroom spaces carefully and intentionally. They must begin their planning with the desired results in mind from the outset. As they determine what students should know, do, and understand, they must also consider the developmental needs of the young people they are serving. Teacher preparation programs must model what good virtual educators do, so that our newly prepared colleagues can and will meet the needs of middle level learners in a variety of ways, utilizing substituting, augmenting, modifying, and redefining strategies as needed. Teacher educators must help novice teacher consider not only how they structure the time and space in the virtual environment, but also how a skillful teacher's presence and proximity to students is paramount in any effective learning environment.

## REFERENCES

Association for Middle Level Education. (2012). *This we believe in action: Implementing successful middle level schools* (2nd ed.). Westerville, OH: Author.

Caskey, M. M., & Anfara, V. A., Jr. (2014). *Research summary: Developmental characteristics of young adolescents*. Retrieved from http://www.amle.org/BrowsebyTopic/WhatsNew/WNDet.aspx?ArtMID=888&ArticleID=455

Duncan, H., & Barnett, J. (2009). Learning to teach online: What works for preservice teachers. *Journal of Educational Computing Research, 40*(3) 357–376.

Koehler, M. J., & Mishra, P. (2009). What is technological pedagogical content knowledge? *Contemporary Issues in Technology and Teacher Education, 9*(1), 60–70.

Marzano, R., & Pickering, D. (2011). *The highly engaged classroom*. Bloomington, IN: Marzano Research Laboratory.

National Middle School Association. (1999). *Research summary #5: Young adolescents' developmental needs*. Retrieved from http://www.ncmle.org/research%20summaries/ressum5.html

Puentedura, R. R. (2013, May 29). *SAMR: Moving from enhancement to transformation* [Web log comment]. Retrieved from http://www.hippasus.com/rrpweblog/archives/000095.html

Scales, P. C. (1991). *A portrait of young adolescents in the 1990s: Implications for promoting healthy growth and development*. Carrboro, NC: Center for Early Adolescence. Retrieved from https://files.eric.ed.gov/fulltext/ED346990.pdf

Shulman, L. S. (1987). Knowledge and teaching: Foundations of the new reform. *Harvard Educational Review, 57*(1), 1–22.

Trainor, M. (2014). *Teaching to the technological demands of the 21st century classroom.* (Unpublished undergraduate honors thesis). Retrieved from https://digitalcommons.butler.edu/ugtheses/194

Van Hoose, J., Strahan, D., & L'Esperance, M. (2001). *Promoting harmony: Young adolescent development and school practices.* Westerville, OH: National Middle School Association.

Vatterott, C. (2007). *Becoming a middle level teacher: Student-focused teaching of early adolescents.* New York, NY: McGraw-Hill.

Wiggins, G., & McTighe, J. (2005). *Understanding by design* (2nd ed.). Alexandria, VA: Association for Supervision and Curriculum Development.

WNET Education: Concept to Classroom. (n.d.). *Summary of the seven developmental needs.* Retrieved from http://www.thirteen.org/edonline/concept2class/afterschool/seven_dev_needs.html

CHAPTER 4

# PROFESSIONAL LEARNING AND LEADING FOR VIRTUAL MIDDLE LEVEL EDUCATORS

**Barbara Smith**
*Literacy Design Collaborative*

The 21st century has seen dramatic changes in the ways groups, organizations, institutions, and corporations function (Mullen, 2010; Wise & Rothman, 2010). Some attributed these changes to a variety of factors such as the increase in knowledge-based economies and globalization via technology (Wise & Rothman, 2010). Middle schools are not immune to these changing dynamics. Although middle school proponents have defined and disseminated broadly the middle school philosophy for decades has been, schools have struggled with how to implement effective practices for teaching young adolescents systemically and with measurable impact. In many instances, changes to middle schools have occurred at a surface level without addressing underlying issues (Anfara & Mertens, 2012). Within their organization, school leaders need fresh ideas and structures to enact change collaboratively and rapidly.

Middle schools face unique challenges that make it difficult for them to manage change and develop leaders capable of driving it. Current middle

*The Online Classroom:*
*Resources for Effective Middle Level Virtual Education,* pp. 61–82
Copyright © 2018 by Information Age Publishing
All rights of reproduction in any form reserved.

school reform efforts struggle to balance the enhancement of curriculum rigor with the social and emotional needs of adolescents (Raphael & Burke, 2012). The influx of virtual middle schools on the education landscape compounds this challenge. Virtualizing education, though a worthy goal, places additional demands on an already stressed system. The ability to use technology in pedagogically sound ways, to develop strong interpersonal relationships with students and other educators, and to balance independence with virtual teaming are necessary skills for today's virtual instructors.

Leadership throughout the virtual system is critical to its survival. Leaders must be resilient in the face of ongoing change. Unfortunately, there is a shortage of leaders. As a profession, teaching has a flat career ladder. Some teachers leave the classroom and move into administrative roles so they can continue to develop their career, gain expertise, and increase their influence. Skilled teachers may also leave the classroom environment at a time in their career when they could most affect their peers (Collay, 2013; Danielson, 2007). The isolation prevalent in today's virtual middle level classrooms and schools mean that virtual teachers experience the mentorship of other teacher leaders less frequently and have limited opportunities to develop as leaders themselves. Principals in virtual settings are less likely to notice and cultivate teacher leaders than in brick-and-mortar environments where leadership is more naturally apparent. Some districts offer teacher leadership roles, such as instructional coach, department chair, or interdisciplinary team leader; however, there are not enough of these roles for every senior teacher (Collay, 2013). To encourage experienced teachers to remain within the profession, it would be prudent for virtual schools to create more leadership opportunities for teachers and to cultivate leaders (Danielson, 2007).

Today's online platforms provide collaborative spaces for virtual teachers to network, share, and learn. This approach is innovative as it separates teacher leadership and professional learning from the constraints of the physical workplace and traditional teacher roles (Wise & Rothman, 2010). Without removing teachers from the classroom or assigning official roles, it is an opportunity for collective teacher leadership that capitalizes on the more democratic structures inherent in virtual middle school teams (Collay, 2013).

Teacher development for virtual educators in online platforms should not simply transplant traditional methods of professional learning. The traditional models are restricted by a variety of factors such as a shortage of teachers, shrinking budgets, and the recognition that pulling expert teachers out of the classroom for additional training reduces their time with the students who need their help the most (Wise & Rothman, 2010).

Therefore, an even swap of traditional to online professional learning cannot be the answer. Creating high impact opportunities for virtual educators will require fully rethinking and re-envisioning teaching leadership and professional learning.

To steer this re-envisioning, Every Student Succeeds Act (ESSA) (2015–2016) offered detailed guidance on what constitutes effective professional development for teachers. Professional learning should be collaborative, continuous, rigorous, integrated, data-driven, and classroom-focused (ESSA, 2015–2016). This definition can serve as an ad hoc mission statement for virtual middle schools seeking to create online learning communities for teachers. It exemplifies the best practices of a professional learning community (PLC). Indeed, there is alignment between ESSA, the tenets espoused by experts in the field of middle level education, and the Association for Middle Level Education with regard to "collaboration as an effective professional development process" (Bickmore, 2014, para. 13). Traditional middle level structures such as interdisciplinary teaming and common planning translate well to virtual schooling as they promote shared decision making and ongoing work-embedded learning (Bickmore, 2014). Therefore, any solution for creating effective middle level virtual teacher development through an online PLC needs to consider the ESSA standards, the National Middle School Association (NMSA) (2010) guidance, and emerging research and examples from the field.

This chapter discusses the need for innovation in professional learning for middle level virtual educators. It calls for a shift to a postmodern orientation to leadership and teacher learning within virtual schools. Too often online professional learning efforts begin with high hopes and enthusiasm that fade with time. Numerous factors, such as technological issues, flagging participation, lack of clarity over the PLC purpose, and confusion over member roles contribute to this decline (Blitz, 2013). To that end, this chapter offers six strategies for launching an effective online PLC that embodies best practices including:

Strategy 1: Message leadership as a virtual community-wide practice.

Strategy 2: Create enabling conditions but do not take over.

Strategy 3: Invest in individual, network, and cross network relationships.

Strategy 4: Know your driving purpose.

Strategy 5: Explore models of successful PLCs.

Strategy 6: Take an agnostic stance toward technology.

These strategies fall into two larger thematic sets. Strategies one through three address the changing roles for leaders and teachers. They emphasize the need to foster collaboration and shared leadership between middle level virtual teachers and virtual school administrators. These strategies align with the best practices for middle school education outlined in *This We Believe: Keys to Educating Young Adolescents* (NMSA, 2010) including leadership characteristics, shared vision, and organizational structures that foster purposeful learning and relationships. Strategies four through six address the need to design PLCs with desired outcomes in mind. These strategies are also reflective of the characteristics of successful middle schools described in *This We Believe* for the areas of curriculum, assessment, instruction and professional learning (NMSA, 2010). By enacting these strategies, middle level virtual teachers and administrators will have a guide for developing and implementing collaboration and leadership within their virtual school or classroom. These strategies marry the literature on middle school best practices with the emerging research on virtual professional learning.

## VIRTUAL PROFESSIONAL LEARNING COMMUNITIES

Professional learning communities (PLCs) have garnered increased attention, research, and discussion in recent years particularly at the middle level where teachers have been allocated time to work together. However, doubts have arisen as to its effective use (Anfara & Mertens, 2012). Repurposing some of the existing time schools have allotted for PLCs might be in order. Due to physical constraints, funding cuts, evolving technologies, and new forms of schooling, the number of online PLCs is on the rise. Changing workplace conditions where technology, rather than individuals, distributes labor and leadership has made PLCs an interesting professional development strategy (Evans, 2015). In Canada, PLCs are the most frequently used approach to school improvement (Riveros, Newton, & Burgess, 2012). In the United States, their use is widespread (Bill & Melinda Gates Foundation, 2014).

Despite their proliferation, a PLC is difficult to define. DuFour (2007) stated that the term PLC has been used so broadly that "it is in danger of losing all meaning" (p. 6). The National Comprehensive Center for Teacher Quality (NCCTQ) identified PLCs as research-based, job-embedded professional development (Croft, Coggshall, Dolan, Powers, & Killion, 2010). According to the NCCTQ, PLCs "redress teacher isolation, create shared teacher responsibility for all students, and expose teachers to instructional strategies or knowledge they did not have access to previously" (Croft et al., 2010, p. 7). Stoll, Bolam, McMahon, Wallace, and Thomas (2006) noted that PLCs are comprised of "a group of people sharing and critically interrogating their practice in an ongoing, reflective, collaborative, inclusive, learning- oriented, growth-promoting way; operating as a collective enterprise" (p. 223). As evident in these definitions, PLCs represent a shift from individualistic to collaborative learning (Uhl-Bien, Marion, & McKelvey, 2007). This shift is in alignment with the middle school philosophy for student learning. It supports the growth of a shared vision, enhances relationships, and increases teacher preparation (NMSA, 2010).

Many online teachers serving adolescent student populations face the challenge of creating effective online experiences for students without having personally experienced high quality online learning. Educators need to develop their capacity as teacher leaders within an authentic social context (Lave & Wenger, 1991). A virtual PLC uses the same technologies they use with students in a digital context. Through a variety of techniques (e.g., collaborating, sharing, analyzing, and reflecting on lessons, student work, and instructional artifacts), educators can make meaningful improvements to their teaching. An online PLC provides a platform for virtual teachers to own their professional learning and development (Riveros et al., 2012). If implemented according to these standards, an online PLC promotes sustained, authentic collaboration, and leadership within the virtual school setting. Additionally, it provides online teachers with an immersive professional learning experience that translates to improved online teaching and adoption of best practices for adolescent learners (Eaton, 2016).

## CHANGING ROLES FOR LEADERS AND TEACHERS IN VIRTUAL MIDDLE LEVEL SCHOOLS

Traditionally, educators regarded the relationship between teachers and principals as unidirectional. However, new research is altering that conception. Firestone and Martinez (2007) found that teacher leaders and principals play complementary roles in regards to leadership. Nevertheless, the enabling conditions established by the district leader effect the teacher leader's success in influencing teacher practice and their sense of agency regarding leadership. Middle schools require leaders who demonstrate courage and collaboration. They must be committed to researching and learning best practices that meet the unique needs of this age group (NMSA, 2010). The first three strategies for launching an online PLC support collaboration and shared leadership between virtual teachers and online administrators. Using these strategies helps to build shared knowledge and ownership of the thorny problems of practice in middle level systems.

## Strategy 1: Message Leadership as a Virtual Community-Wide Practice

Operating from traditional modalities, teachers do not necessarily view themselves as leaders (Helterbran, 2010). Rather than teachers owning their own leadership, administrators retain control over the process. Too often, it is incumbent on the administrator to create conditions for shared leadership. In virtual settings, shared leadership creates a sense of connectedness that helps to counteract the isolation online educators may experience (Raphael & Burke, 2012). To change this dynamic, leaders need to articulate that leadership is both an opportunity and an expectation. For example, in a study on teacher's experiences in a virtual PLC, one teacher described her principal's effect on her growth as a leader:

> Our principal has told the new teachers over and over again.... "Get involved. We want you to be as involved as possible. Speak up at our meetings." He wants us, you know, not to stand in the shadows, but to become leaders in our school, to get involved as often as we can as soon as we can. (Smith, 2016, p. 94)

Through encouragement and providing multiple opportunities to function in a leadership capacity, this principal allowed teachers to be the drivers of their own leadership. Hosting Twitter chats, leading Google community groups, or curating instructional resources on Pinterest are free, informal ways a principal can encourage a teacher to begin owning teacher leadership. Providing virtual tools with the expectation that teachers will play an explicit role in leading their peers to complete a defined task (e.g., curating resources to address student needs, leading a discussion on common topics) is a starting point for principals in promoting teacher leadership in virtual settings. However, the principal remains as the facilitator of the process.

In addition to widely distributed leadership opportunities, school and network leaders need to offer support and mentorship. The common planning time and interdisciplinary teams found in traditional middle schools have created a minimal expectation of collaboration. This expectation can be through collaboration in virtual PLCs. These PLCs combine multiple forms of classroom technologies, such as curriculum design platforms, online courses, and open education resources (OER), with facilitation protocols to ensure shared decision-making. This model begins to move teachers to the forefront as facilitators of their own leadership. Table 4.1 provides examples of PLC resources where a teacher or school leader can access additional information.

**Table 4.1.**
**PLC Resources**

| Resources | Description |
| --- | --- |
| Literacy Design Collaborative: CoreTools | Offers free online courses, a library of teacher created instructional resources, and a space to build curriculum and share instructional resources. Teachers apply shared rubrics, provide online comments and feedback, and reflect on instructional practice. https://coretools.ldc.org/ |
| Literacy Design Collaborative: How LDC Works | Provides a recording of a PLC meeting to illustrate successful practices. https://ldc.org/how-does-it-work |
| Teaching Partners | Allows teachers to create or join collaborative groups of educators with the same interests to facilitate problem solving and professional growth. It provides a space for PLCs to work as well as helps virtual educators locate supportive networks. https://teachingpartners.com |
| The Center for Teaching Quality | Catalyzes teacher leaders across the U.S. to share expertise. Training in facilitating virtual teams, focused advocacy efforts, professional learning, and networking are offered. https://www.teachingquality.org/ |
| National School Reform Faculty Harmony Education Center | Hosts more than 200 protocols to develop teaming processes, analyze success, and improve efforts. Although not explicitly written for virtual PLCs, these protocols offer questions, prompts, and process descriptions that translate well to the virtual environment. https://www.nsrfharmony.org |

Finally, leaders need to guard against personal bias. Rather than viewing only a small number of teachers as ready for leadership, they must ensure the wide dispersion of leadership opportunities. Leaders need to expect that all teachers would display leadership if provided with the appropriate conditions. An online PLC that provides a safe environment for middle level teachers to practice leadership while also learning and improving their professional practice may provide those conditions.

## Strategy 2: Create Enabling Conditions but Do Not Take Over

In today's complex virtual education landscape, traditional approaches of leadership are less applicable to remotely networked leaders. Principals are embracing new leadership dynamics (MetLife Foundation, 2013). Rather than authorizing acts of leadership by a few chosen teachers, principals are increasingly expecting all teachers to assume leadership responsibilities (Barth, 2013).

If the traditional, hierarchical models no longer apply, then operating in these environments requires new leadership models. According to Mason (2008), "Educational and institutional change is less a consequence of effecting change in one particular factor or variable, and more a case of generating momentum in a new direction by attention to as many factors as possible" (p. 35). Complexity leadership theory (CLT) provides a leadership framework that could apply in complex adaptive systems (CAS) (Lichtenstein et al., 2006). A virtual middle school is an example of this type of system. Its organizational subsystems, including multiple grade levels and disciplines, function dependently and interdependently to solve co-occurring problems and to generate outcomes (e.g., improved student academic performance). The nonlinear nature of schooling, including the overlapping interactions of individuals and groups, are characteristic of a CAS.

In CLT, leadership is defined by emergent events characterized by the actions of multiple individuals in a dynamic system (Lichtenstein et al., 2006). Instead of defining leadership through the actions of a single individual, leadership is a "systems level phenomenon" (Lichtenstein et al., 2006, p. 3). In CLT, virtual middle school leaders are encouraged to be intentional about their actions as leaders to foster the leadership of others. These leaders understand that the challenges facing virtual schools at the middle level are too complex to be solved by a single leader using a top-down approach. They view change as emergent and thus prioritize quality interactions among teams working as PLCs as a mechanism for learning and leadership.

CLT encompasses three interacting forms of leadership: administrative/managerial leadership, adaptive leadership, and enabling leadership (Schreiber & Carley, 2006; Uhl-Bien et al., 2007). Administrative/managerial leadership is a traditional, hierarchical leadership style. It provides the necessary managerial processes (i.e., payroll) that keep an organization running smoothly and stably (Schreiber & Carley, 2006; Uhl-Bien et al., 2007). Adaptive leadership emerges through collective action within the many fluid networks of a complex adaptive system. Multiple people can simultaneously be adaptive leaders within the organization and are encouraged to provide innovation and adaption (Uhl-Bien et al., 2007). Enabling leadership creates the conditions to foster collective action and adaptive leadership within the system, as well as sharing with managerial leadership for organizational benefit (Schreiber & Carley, 2006; Uhl-Bien et al., 2007). Enabling leadership is comprised of two functions that allow the system to operate. One, it fosters collective action and adaptive leadership. Two, with administrative/managerial leadership, it facilitates innovation, knowledge, and emerging outcomes (Uhl-Bien et al., 2007).

Implementing the tenets of CLT is possible in a virtual middle school. For example, managerial leadership reflected in the hierarchical role of the principal who provides the management functions allows the organization to run effectively. Adaptive leadership, with its emphasis on invention and creativity, is well suited to the myriad of instructional decisions an expert teacher must make daily and to the interactive nature of online PLCs. The collaboration and distributed leadership emphasized in enabling leadership are applicable to the complexities of today's educational system (Blitz, 2013; Evans, 2015).

When faced with improving persistent low achievement in a specific area, a traditional managerial leader might analyze the achievement data, write an improvement plan, and inform the virtual middle school faculty of the tasks and timelines necessary to execute the plan. By comparison, a principal employing CLT would enlist teams of teachers in analyzing the multiple contributing factors of the issue. The teachers would take ownership for changing student outcomes. Rather than employing a single solution to a complex problem, teams might engage in proposing and testing multiple ideas and solutions with groups of students. Teacher teams would work with the principal to monitor and make necessary adjustments to ensure the teams have adequate resources and support. Working from a CLT orientation allows the principal to meet the managerial aspects of their job while putting greater focus on enabling organizational success through innovation by the faculty.

Capacity building from within is a key priority for leaders who seek to improve instructional quality and transform middle schools (Anfara & Mertens, 2012). Applying CLT builds capacity in an accelerated and generative manner through the interaction and collective action of the networked members of the virtual school. Online PLCs enacted with leadership and adequate technical resources, including individual access to technology with a working camera, microphone, and basic office software, support rapid teacher knowledge expansion and contribute to a high level of program coherence. Online PLCs need meaningful coordination and knowledge development strategy to address the unique academic, social, and emotional needs of virtual middle schoolers (Raphael & Burke, 2012).

Educators can use CLT to examine the steps necessary for formation of PLCs in online contexts. For example, a principal can exhibit the interaction of each form of leadership within this theory. From a managerial leadership perspective, the principal must first obtain the technological licenses, hardware, and software necessary to run the PLC. The principal needs to work with teachers to remove the budgetary and logistical barriers that would make participation in the PLC difficult. Leaders need to examine time constraints that may limit teacher participation. When developing master schedules, principals should identify time for teams to meet during work hours. Alternatively, principals could provide teams financial incentives to meet outside of work hours or with other desired compensation such as being able to "bank" hours and use them later.

The principal needs to support teachers in their participation in the PLC through enabling teacher leadership. Rather than monitoring participation or reviewing the content of the PLC, principals can encourage participation and provide the time needed for participation. Principal involvement and participation in online PLCs varies. In some schools, the principal enrolls as a member of the PLC. In other schools, the principal and teachers agree that the principal will not participate. Instead, teachers brief the principal on the accomplishments of the group and notify the administration if any problems emerge. A common practice of online PLCs is to record and share PLC meetings conducted on video platforms, such as Zoom or GoToMeeting, so that members not in attendance stay abreast of the information. Teachers can provide exports of the online chat or threaded conversations from a meeting to the principal as a summary. This allows teachers to own the conversations and results while making essential content available to other parties (Smith, 2016).

If a principal does decide to participate in the group, he or she may wish to refrain from serving as a facilitator. Serving in this capacity would recreate the hierarchical structure within the online environment. Principals who choose to participate in teacher led PLCs should discuss and define their role and purpose for participating with the facilitator beforehand. The teacher facilitator and principal may agree upon a code word for the facilitator to use in the case when the principal begins to step outside the participant role. It is vitally important to the process of empowering teacher leadership that the principal give space for teachers to facilitate their own teacher learning. If the principal chooses to join the PLC, he or she needs to be a co-learner who works alongside of the other educators. In addition, principals often overlook their own professional growth needs. They could benefit from online PLCs with other school leaders and leadership mentors. A recent study that included middle school principals, found that virtual professional learning with coaching improved principals' instructional leadership skills and their ownership of school improvement (Ermeling, Tatsui, & Young, 2015).

Through the skillful application of CLT, a principal can ensure that the proper conditions exist for the online PLC to be successful without taking over the process. A PLC can be a vital support system for improving instruction. Through actions such as removing fiscal barriers and ensuring a democratic leadership structure in the PLC, a leader can create supportive conditions for collaboration, preserve teacher agency, and reduce the isolation virtual teachers may experience.

## Strategy 3: Invest in Individual, Network, and Cross Network Relationships

Online PLCs have the potential to bring another dimension to teacher leadership within the virtual school. More than at other levels, middle level teachers work together within the same grade levels or subjects. This ongoing collaboration serves multiple purposes. Middle level teachers collaborate on student academic, social, and emotional needs of the adolescents in their care. This improves their professional practice. As middle level schooling shifts from face-to-face to the virtual setting, students and teachers run the risk of losing their collaborative support system and becoming isolated. Online PLCs ensure that virtual middle level educators sustain the relationships and ongoing collaboration necessary to support the academic, social, and emotional needs of middle level students (Eaton, 2016).

Principals can use the student roster and teaching assignments to form ongoing PLCs that enable teachers who teach the same group of students or the same grade, course, and/or subject to collaborate. These PLCs form the foundation for meaningful authentic work and help the school community maintain an ongoing focus on students' academic and social needs. Additionally, school can utilize online PLCs to build teacher skills or to pursue areas of professional interest. Principals or teacher leaders can use surveys and interest inventories to form short-term interest-based groupings. Platforms, such as Sevenzo and Participate, provide access to PLCs with different areas of focus, activities, and even methods of sharing knowledge with peers.

Interactions in online PLCs facilitate new professional relationships. One teacher in a recent study on virtual PLCs shared, "I've been interacting more with people that aren't on my team because I feel like their experiences are different ... it's been a real eye opener" (Smith, 2016, p. 128). Enrollment in an online PLC allowed this teacher to formulate relationships with educators that would have been unlikely to develop otherwise. Participation in online PLCs can blur the lines of traditional hierarchies. Complex tasks such as problem solving and decision making may improve with the input of new ideas, collaboration, and innovation. Ultimately, students are the beneficiaries of increased knowledge sharing by the adults in the school.

While online PLCs can have tremendous benefits, they are also prone to limitations that can undermine their success. For example, over time participation tends to decrease. Engagement declines more quickly in online settings than traditional face-to-face collaboration (Blitz, 2013). This may be due in part to the lack of context (e.g., body language, intonation) available online (Smith, 2016). Conversely, for a teacher who feels inhibited speaking out in a public setting, the online environment is liberating. For example, new teachers and teachers who self-identify as introverted may feel more comfortable online. One shared:

> I'm able to take more leadership behind a computer screen because I feel a little bit more confident because I have time to sit and really think out what I'm typing and what I want people to understand from what's going on in my classroom. (Smith, 2016, pp. 141–142)

Providing context within a PLC requires the careful cultivation of relationships and awareness of the challenges related to developing relationships online. Using a combination of mediums, such as video and blogging, can provide the visual cues and tone that adds context and connectivity for members who miss the cues present in face-to-face interactions (DuFour, 2014).

In addition to multiple mechanisms for participant response, allowing multiple opportunities for collaboration will also sustain momentum and deepen relationships. For example, one PLC found a combination of asynchronous independent work punctuated with synchronous virtual video chats to share findings, revise work products, or troubleshoot challenges to be effective (Jacobson, 2016).

The potential for overprescribing the content, agenda, and outcomes of teacher professional learning is another limitation of the virtual PLC. In these instances, participation becomes a compliance exercise. The proactive approach of the Metropolitan School District, which administers a virtual school and blended extended day program, provides insight into this issue. The district recognized that, while building content knowledge and skills were important, they needed an informal support system to address the isolation experienced by online teachers. They created a *virtual teacher workroom* that combines professional learning modules with an informal, teacher-driven, community discussion space using the learning management system (LMS). The workroom hosted courses that used discussion boards, as well as peer and online assessments. Since learners knew they would be sharing with colleagues, they were motivated to thoroughly examine the content and apply it to their own online classrooms. The district also ensured that teachers had voice and choice in setting professional learning goals and choosing activities to earn professional growth points toward those goals (Eaton, 2016).

The three aforementioned strategies illustrate the reciprocal roles of the middle level leader and teachers within the virtual school or network, the changing nature of leadership within complex systems, and the importance of fostering networks of relationships for teachers of early adolescents. The second set of strategies center on the need to design the PLC with clarity of purpose and with the desired outcomes in mind. These ideas should be at the forefront when making decisions about the PLC's form and function.

## DESIGNING VIRTUAL PLCs

Leaders and teachers enacting virtual PLCs often fall short in the critical steps of defining desired outcomes and back mapping supports. The following strategies support collaboration and shared leadership when designing an online professional learning community.

### Strategy 4: Know Your Driving Purpose

Understanding the purpose of a PLC from the outset is critical to the group's future success. For PLCs in middle level contexts, this purpose should be informed by school goals, individual participant needs, and existing research on PLCs and professional learning at the middle level. To reap the maximum benefits of virtual PLCs, teachers should link the purpose of the PLC to their actual professional practice (Bickmore, 2014). A practice-based approach that contextualizes learning within school culture, makes teacher learning relevant and immediately applicable to the classroom, and engages educators in dialogue with feedback is preferred (Bickmore, 2014). In virtual PLCs, members engage in problem solving with a network of colleagues in ways that mirror the complexity of their daily practice. This makes the learning inseparable from work. These ideals need to reflect the group's purpose.

Middle level virtual teachers can address three specific needs through a practice-based approach. First, middle school teachers are more likely to have middle level certification, but lack disciplinary certification or experience. There is a tremendous need to increase disciplinary knowledge and skill in curriculum, instruction, and assessment at the middle level (NMSA, 2010; Raphael & Burke, 2012). Second, virtual teachers often find their technology skills outpaced by those of their students. Third, middle level virtual teachers also need frequent informal time to talk with other educators about the social, emotional, and academic needs of their students (Raphael & Burke, 2012).

Virtual PLCs can address these three needs in an integrated manner. Middle level teachers can access discipline specific resources and expertise in a situated context that episodic, generalized professional development sessions cannot replicate. For example, social studies teachers working as a virtual team can access resources and professional learning webinars on democracy and civic engagement through Facing History and Ourselves online platform. Teachers can access resources and attend such webinars at a time of their own choosing rather than attending an in-person workshop. As a team, teachers can analyze instructional resources and adapt them to meet the needs of the students they teach. While formatively assessing the results of their lessons, teachers learn from each other's successes and challenges and calibrate their own approaches and expectations for students. They discuss student responses to the material and its application to the students' needs. Engaging in this type of sustained learning helps virtual teachers to become familiar with new technologies and more capable of reading, writing, and communicating digitally and collaboratively (Morgan, 2015). Teachers can embed multiple opportunities to coordinate and troubleshoot students' social and emotional concerns into the PLC's synchronous agenda, as well as asynchronous discussion boards or threaded conversations. Password protected courses with discussion spaces on popular learning management systems (LMS), such as Canvas and Schoology, as well as subscription-based services such as the Teaching Channel Teams which provide accessibility to colleagues and a secure space for these conversations.

Using a skills-based framework can aid educators' understanding the purpose of the virtual PLC. This framework forms the architecture of the PLC's work. It can yield ongoing artifacts and evidence of teacher and student skill development. Use of a framework is essential to the PLC working interdependently and gauging progress collectively. Selecting a common framework for virtual middle level educators is challenging. The framework needs to target to the unique dimensions of each discipline, yet have unifying elements that build shared practices and coherence for students (Bickmore, 2014). The Literacy Design Collaborative (LDC) has created one example of such a framework. Since its inception in 2010, the LDC has shown evidence of positive effect on teacher practice and improving student outcomes (LDC, n.d.a). Approximately 120,000 educators use the LDC across the United States, half of whom are middle level educators (Simmons, personal communication, June 1, 2017). The Australian Institute for Teaching and School Leadership (2014) recognized the LDC for its strong professional learning content and design. Schools and networks use the LDC's online professional learning system to enact lesson study cycles. Groups of teachers collaborate in and use the learning content of the PLC to plan, teach, assess, and iterate upon standards-driven instructional plans.

The LDC has created competencies that serve as a unifying thread for ongoing professional learning that are well suited as an organizing structure for PLCs at the middle level. The LDC's competencies are a set of 20 concrete teacher skills indicators organized within four broader competencies that define standards-driven instructional planning and practice. The competencies are (a) analyze assignments aligned to standards and student learning goals, (b) construct a quality assignment prompt, (c) develop a quality instructional plan, and (d) assess outcomes and iterate instruction (LDC, 2017a).

The LDC competencies can inform a protocol for a PLC group. Table 4.2 provides an example of a protocol designed for an online PLC run by the LDC.

**Table 4.2.**
**Literacy Design Collaborative Ongoing Synchronous PLC Protocol**

| Minutes | Content |
| --- | --- |
| 5 | Hello: Hack of the week |
| 5 | Connect competencies to the LDC design process and course content: Construct a Task |
| | • LDC Teacher Competencies Review + Evidence |
| | • Where do you see evidence of the competencies in this week's course blocks? |
| | • How does the competency support the steps in the design process and the course content? |
| | • What competencies are you focusing on in your practice? |
| 10 | Turn and Talk |
| | • Connections, competencies, and other takeaways |
| | • In what ways did you utilize course content to design your Task/Module? |
| 30 | Feedback to participant's performance tasks (2-3 each week) |
| | • Apply our learning to adjust a task or ladder (instructional plan supplied by a participant) |
| | • Discuss lessons learned or troubleshoot implementation issues |
| | • Model coaching connections to critical content and examples |
| 5 | Review Questions related to this week's course blocks and discussion |
| 5 | Final Word Whip (participant reflection written in chat) |

*Note.* Adapted from "Blended Foundations Course Syllabus" (Literacy Design Collaborative [LDC], 2016)

In this PLC, educators meet weekly in a one-hour synchronous session using videoconferencing. The purpose of the PLC is to improve performance tasks that the teachers have created for use in their classrooms. The session protocol begins with a "Hack of the Week," which is a brief, collaborative, problem-solving opportunity designed to address a challenge or issue that the group is experiencing currently in their practice. Built within every PLC session is the "Hack of the Week." As members have developed trusting relationships, they are more likely to seek advice and have authentic conversations about issues. This structure also affords middle level educators the opportunity to discuss students' social, emotional, and academic needs (Raphael & Burke, 2012).

Next, within the virtual PLC, teachers use the LDC competencies to articulate a transparent purpose. They help to personalize learning goals, as well as guide the resultant work and evidence analysis. The process empowers teachers to drive their own learning and promotes collaborative inquiry and reflection. It also breaks down the isolation virtual middle level educators experience (Morgan, 2015). Members of the PLC discuss competency evidence drawing on online coursework assigned within the PLC and in their own work. Participants use the chat feature within the Zoom videoconferencing platform to "Turn and Talk" about their insights and connections between the course content and their work in designing, teaching, and iterating upon performance tasks. Of the many quality videoconferencing platforms available, participants selected Zoom because it is easy to use, offers both free and premium versions, allows a Google calendar plug in, contains registration features for tracking attendance, and allows videoconferencing, chats, screen sharing, and breakout rooms.

Members dedicate the end of the PLC to the group sharing their performance tasks. During this time, members design performance tasks aligned to standards. Teachers give each other feedback to ensure the tasks are sound before implementing them with students. Eventually, teachers analyze and iterate upon instructional techniques and resultant student work. Between synchronous sessions, members work asynchronously by posting written comments online in a discussion space. Building discipline specific skills through the development and use of rigorous curricula within a collaborative virtual community parallels the characteristics of successful schools espoused by the NMSA (2010).

## Strategy 5: Explore Models of Successful Online PLCs

The emerging body of literature on online PLCs needs to inform the PLC's design and to help the planning team and prospective PLC members visualize the structure of the PLC context. For example, Luehmann and

Tinelli (2008) studied how 15 secondary science teachers found community support through social networking technologies. The group used blogging to share, reflect, and discuss problems of practice. Members experienced cognitive and affective benefits including: the ability to discuss instructional decisions, sharing emotional responses to their own professional growth and burgeoning advocacy, and development of their sense of identity as individuals and a community. Members reported that they were able to apply their learning from the group into their real-world environments (Luehmann & Tinelli, 2008).

The virtual school of Spring Independent School District in Harris County, Texas used an online PLC to allow teachers to collaborate, learn, and participate in collective inquiry (DuFour, 2014). Their PLC used Collaborate and Elluminate because the text and video features recorded PLC sessions and instructional interactions. The recordings and text became an artifact used for collective learning and inquiry. The school principal felt that these features increased the effectiveness and transparency of the group's work (DuFour, 2014).

Similarly, Rankin County School District in Jackson, Mississippi uses the Zoom videoconferencing platform as the meeting space for a virtual PLC in which middle and high school teachers design instruction and engage in student work analysis with other teachers in their discipline. This PLC uses the LDC's online professional learning content (LDC, n.d.c; LDC, 2017b). Within one PLC in Rankin County, educators designed an assignment for high school English students asking whether Romeo and Juliet were justified in pursuing their relationship. Students were required to support their position using the text (LDC, n.d.c). The assignment's authors presented it to the PLC for analysis and revision. In a series of lively discussions and online posts, the PLC members examined the alignment of the assignment to the academic standard. The standard asked students to analyze how complex characters develop over the course of a text, interact with other characters, advance the plot, or develop the theme (LDC, n.d.c).

Finding that the alignment between the assignment and the standard needed strengthening, the PLC iterated on the assignment to enhance the alignment, clarity, and rigor. Using the comment features in the platform, members annotated the assignment with comments and the authors responded with their own comments, asked for additional clarification, and thanked members for their input (LDC, n.d.c). The final assignment read, "After reading The Tragedy of Romeo and Juliet, write an essay in which you explain how Shakespeare uses internal and external conflict over the course of the play to drive the complex characters of Romeo and Juliet to their tragic end. Support your discussion with evidence from the texts" (LDC, n.d.c, para. 2). This assignment is of higher quality as it has better alignment to the standards. The collaborative analysis and interaction of the PLC provided members with experience in instructional planning and curriculum analysis. Combining professional learning with work-embedded activities prompted robust teacher acquisition of the LDC Competencies (LDC, 2017a). It enhanced the members' shared vision and culture. It resulted in more rigorous curriculum resources authored by teachers that were then publicly shared with other educators across the United States as a digital collection on the LDC CoreTools platform (LDC, n.d.b).

Before forming a new online PLC, a planning team will benefit from reviewing accounts and videos of established, successful PLCs at the middle level. Exploring models of successful PLCs will assist the team in constructing a clear picture of what a successful PLC might look like in their setting. Revisiting and sharing these concrete examples during the early stages of PLC design will aid with group coherence and establishing vision.

## Strategy 6: Take an Agnostic Stance Toward Technology

The final strategic action involves the school leader and planning-team making preliminary decisions about the technologies that will best support the virtual PLC in accomplishing its goals. Leaders seeking to implement online PLCs at the middle level have critical decisions to make regarding the appropriate platform for hosting their virtual communities. However, it is important to note that the technology selected is only a vehicle. The facilitator and the members of the community drive the online PLC. It is fueled by the content that they create. A long-standing PLC may adopt, utilize, and retire multiple vehicles as the needs of the group change and new technologies emerge. Therefore, the initial technology selection process should occur after decisions about purpose and desired outcomes are complete. Members should monitor the alignment of technology tools and PLC goals on an ongoing basis.

Decision makers should also assess the nature and types of interactions possible within potential platforms. A well-designed online platform can serve as a group member who is readily and constantly available (Evans, 2015). Platforms like Facebook are dependent on group members to crowd source ideas and post content. This creates a sense of agency and dynamism among members. Other online platforms such as the Teaching Channel marry group conversations with access to a curated library of articles, teaching resources, and videos. One middle level teacher described the benefits of having access to this additional content:

> Let's face it, we are very visual people, and our kids are extremely visually oriented. So, it really helps us to put ourselves in the situation of our students and see if this would work (teaching techniques). A lot of us would

get together and use it (the online platform) on our own (outside of group online PLC activities). (Smith, 2016, pp. 132–133)

In a successful middle level virtual PLC, participants not only work with each other in the online environment, they interact with, learn from, and contribute to the environment. They transfer this new knowledge into better teaching with their students (Morgan, 2015). While the decision about which technology to use is important, it needs to be viewed as easily changed. Informed decisions about roles, purposeful design, and clarity of purpose are more significant as they inform the technology selection process. Middle level leaders should pay careful attention to reducing teacher isolation, personalizing learning, and providing authentic informal discussion opportunities. Features such as video conferencing, threaded conversations, and chat features common to most LMS systems and popular applications (e.g., Google Communities, Facebook) create a sense of connectedness and responsiveness among members. Technologies that incorporate goal setting, progress tracking, and evidence-based badging, and recognition for achievements, such as LDC CoreTools, EduPlanet21, and Bloomboard, enhance personalization and create agency (Eaton, 2016; Morgan, 2015; Raphael & Burke, 2012).

## CONCLUSION

In virtual middle level education, a large number of teachers report that the current professional learning opportunities are not meeting their needs (Anfara & Mertens, 2012). Professional learning communities are a potential solution. By enlisting teachers as problem-solvers to improve learning, PLCs allow for collaboration between teachers who are geographically or temporally distant. They are also effective platforms for the development of teacher leaders.

While a face-to-face PLC also offers learning and content mastery for teachers, an online PLC has several advantages. It offers greater flexibility in participation and increased opportunities to access and share knowledge. Participants in online PLCs exhibit more self-reflection about their own learning and instructional practices than participants in face-to-face PLCs (Blitz, 2013). Online PLCs improve the technology skills of virtual teachers through authentic use and reduce the sense of isolation expressed by these educators (Morgan, 2015; Raphael & Burke, 2012). There is emerging evidence that the online environment might enable leadership in a more democratic fashion. This can spark innovation and help virtual middle schools build capacity from within (Anfara & Mertens, 2012; Smith, 2016). The online environment provides teachers with immediate support and access to a network of experts and resources to address disciplinary specific academic issues as well as social emotional needs of the middle level learner (Bickmore, 2014; Morgan, 2015).

Maximizing these benefits requires more than purchasing technology and inviting teachers to periodically post and chat online. Schools must give careful consideration of the purpose of the virtual PLC. Teachers and administrators must identify the specific needs of the middle school teachers and students before the technology acquisition process begins. School and network leaders play an important role in catalyzing teachers as leaders in virtual contexts. School leadership must convey that all teachers have an opportunity to be a leader within the virtual community. Administrators setting up an online PLC for the first time must focus on creating enabling conditions without inadvertently commandeering the group. They need to allow teachers to collaborate on and problem solve for the problems of practice facing the teacher, school, or network. Online educators depend on the relationships they form in these groups to offset the feelings of isolation intrinsic to virtual education. Leaders also need to be careful not to over prescribe the form and function of a PLC, as middle level teachers need flexibility to discuss student social and emotional needs (Raphael & Burke, 2012). Virtual school leaders responsible for the design and launch of an online PLC need to establish clearly the purpose of the community, explore effective models of online PLCs, and take an agnostic stance toward technology. Employing the six strategies articulated within the chapter may help to develop both human capital and systems for promoting meaningful collaboration and leadership within virtual middle schools and networks.

## REFERENCES

Anfara, V. A., Jr., & Mertens, S. B. (2012). Capacity building is a key to the radical transformation of middle grades schools. *Middle School Journal, 43*(3), 58–64.

Australian Institute for Teaching and School Leadership. (2014). *Designing professional learning*. Retrieved from https://www.aitsl.edu.au/docs/default-source/default-document-library/designing_professional_learning_report.pdf?sfvrsn=83c1ec3c_0

Barth, R. S. (2013). The time is ripe (again). *Educational Leadership, 71*(2), 10–16.

Bickmore, D. L. (2014). *Research summary: Professional learning and professional development in the middle grades*. Retrieved from http://www.amle.org/BrowsebyTopic/WhatsNew/WNDet.aspx?ArtMID=888&ArticleID=466

Bill & Melinda Gates Foundation. (2014). *Teachers know best: Teachers' views on professional development*. Retrieved from http://k12education.gatesfoundation.org/resource/teachers-know-best-teachers-views-on-professional-development/

Blitz, C. L. (2013). *Can online learning communities achieve the goals of traditional professional learning communities? What the literature says.* (REL 2013–003). Washington, DC: U.S. Department of Education, Institute of Education Sciences, National Center for Education Evaluation and Regional Assistance, Regional Educational Laboratory Mid-Atlantic. Retrieved from https://ies.ed.gov/ncee/edlabs/projects/project.asp?ProjectID=368

Collay, M. (2013). Teaching is leading. *Educational Leadership, 71*(2), 72–76.

Croft, A., Coggshall, J. G., Dolan, M., Powers, E., & Killion, J. (2010). Job-embedded professional development: What it is, who is responsible, and how to get it done well. *National Comprehensive Center for Teacher Quality.* Retrieved from https://learningforward.org/docs/pdf/jobembeddedpdbrief.pdf

Danielson, C. (2007). The many faces of leadership. *Educational Leadership, 65*(1), 14–19.

DuFour, R. (2007). Professional learning communities: A bandwagon, an idea worth considering, or our best hope for high levels of learning? *Middle School Journal, 39*(1), 4–8.

DuFour, R. (2014). Harnessing the power of PLCS. *Educational Leadership, 71*(8), 30–35.

Eaton, M. (2016). Professional development and virtual schools: Swapping ideas and practices. *THE Journal.* Retrieved from https://thejournal.com/articles/2016/09/07/professional-development-and-virtual-schools-swapping-ideas-and-practices.aspx

Ermeling, B., Tatsui, T., & Young, K. (2015). Virtual coaching for instructional leaders: A multi-method investigation of technology-enabled external assistance. *Teachers College Record, 117*(11), 1–48.

Evans, P. (2015). Open online spaces of professional learning: Context, personalisation and facilitation. *TechTrends: Linking Research & Practice to Improve Learning, 59*(1), 31–36.

Every Student Succeeds Act (ESSA) of 2015, Pub. L. No. 114-95 § 114 Stat. 1177 (2015-2016).

Firestone, W. A., & Martinez, M. C. (2007). Districts, teacher leaders, and distributed leadership: Changing instructional practice. *Leadership & Policy in Schools, 6*(1), 3–35.

Helterbran, V. R. (2010). Teacher leadership: Overcoming 'I am just a teacher' syndrome. *Education, 131*(2), 363–371.

Jacobson, L. (2016). Tailored for a perfect fit. *Journal of Staff Development, 37*(2), 18–22.

Lave, J., & Wenger, E. (1991). *Situated learning: Legitimate peripheral participation.* New York, NY: Cambridge University Press.

Lichtenstein, B. B., Uhl-Bien, M., Marion, R., Seers, A., Orton, J., & Schreiber, C. (2006). Complexity leadership theory: An interactive perspective on leading in complex adaptive systems. *Emergence: Complexity & Organization, 8*(4), 2–12.

Literacy Design Collaborative. (n.d.a). *Research.* Retrieved from https://ldc.org/results/research

Literacy Design Collaborative. (n.d.b). *LDC library.* Retrieved from https://coretools.ldc.org/curriculumLibrary

Literacy Design Collaborative. (n.d.c). *Shakespeare's use of conflict in Romeo and Juliet.* Retrieved from https://coretools.ldc.org/mods/22e54035-a928-4c37-a394-d1142976c154

Literacy Design Collaborative. (2016). *Blended foundations course syllabus.* Retrieved from https://ldc.org/sites/default/files/Blended_Foundations_Course_Syllabus%28LDC_2016%29.pdf

Literacy Design Collaborative. (2017a). *LDC competencies.* Retrieved from https://ldc.org/sites/default/files/ldc-resource-library-files/LDC%20Teacher%20Competencies%202016_2_4-21-16.pdf

Literacy Design Collaborative. (2017b). *RSCD demo day.* Retrieved from https://www.youtube.com/watch?v=QGiwy6cCJ7A&feature=youtu.be

Luehmann, A. L., & Tinelli, L. (2008). Teacher professional identity development with social networking technologies: Learning reform through blogging. *Educational Media International, 45*(4), 323–333.

Mason, M. (2008). What is complexity theory and what are its implications for educational change? *Educational Philosophy & Theory, 40*(1), 35–49.

MetLife Foundation. (2013). *The MetLife survey of the American teacher: Challenges for school leadership.* New York, NY: Metropolitan Life Insurance Company.

Morgan, H. (2015). Online instruction and virtual schools for middle and high school students: Twenty-first-century fads or progressive teaching methods for today's pupils? *The Clearing House, 88*(2), 72–76.

Mullen, C. A. (2010). 21st-century priorities for leadership education and prospective school leaders. *Scholar-Practitioner Quarterly, 4*(4), 331–333.

National Middle School Association. (2010). *This we believe: Keys to educating young adolescents.* Westerville, OH: Author.

Raphael, L. M., & Burke, M. (2012). Academic, social, and emotional needs in a middle grades reform initiative. *Research in Middle Level Education Online, 35*(6), 1–13. Retrieved from https://files.eric.ed.gov/fulltext/EJ974945.pdf

Riveros, A., Newton, P., & Burgess, D. (2012). A situated account of teacher agency and learning: Critical reflections on professional learning communities. *Canadian Journal of Education, 35*(1), 202–216.

Schreiber, C., & Carley, K. M. (2006). Leadership style as an enabler of organizational complex functioning. *Emergence: Complexity & Organization, 8*(4), 61–76.

Smith, B. A. (2016). *Teacher leadership in online professional learning communities: A phenomenological view of co-influencing relationships* (Doctoral dissertation). Retrieved from ProQuest Dissertations & Theses Global: The Humanities and Social Sciences Collection. (AAT 10239922)

Stoll, L., Bolam, R., McMahon, A., Wallace, M., & Thomas, S. (2006). Professional learning communities: A review of the literature. *Journal of Educational Change, 7*(4), 221–258.

Uhl-Bien, M., Marion, R., & McKelvey, B. (2007). Complexity leadership theory: Shifting leadership from the industrial age to the knowledge era. *Leadership Quarterly, 18*(4), 298–318.

Wise, B., & Rothman, R. (2010). The online learning imperative: A solution to three looming crises in education. *Education Digest, 76*(3), 52–58.

CHAPTER 5

# COLLABORATING TO CREATE MIDDLE LEVEL BLENDED LEARNING ENVIRONMENTS

**Mark Stevens**
*George Mason University*

**Mary F. Rice**
*University of New Mexico*

Students at the middle level report using the Internet more often and to doing more things outside classrooms than inside the classroom with online resources (Hutchison & Henry, 2010). For young people, the Internet and the devices from which they access it are not just tools but learning spaces and spaces for transgressing the norms of what is expected of them (Rice & Stevens, 2016; Stevens, 2016). The number of middle level learners using the Internet as a primary learning space has been rapidly increasing. The Digest of Educational Statistics reported that there were approximately 15,000 middle level online course enrollments in the 2004–2005 school year and more than 150,000 five years later in 2009–2010 (U.S. Department of Education, 2015).

*The Online Classroom:*
*Resources for Effective Middle Level Virtual Education,* pp. 83–96
Copyright © 2018 by Information Age Publishing
All rights of reproduction in any form reserved.

Coursework completed over the Internet can be *fully online* (entirely through the Internet) or *blended* (where teachers deliver some instruction in a physical setting). Blended learning environments (BLEs) are the fastest growing of all current K–12 online educational innovations (Barbour, Archambault, & DiPietro, 2013; Picciano, Seaman, Shea, & Swan 2012). In BLEs, students learn part of the day in a traditional setting and do part of their work away from the school building using web-based resources that rely on two things: some type of technological device and a connection to the Internet (Staker, 2011). In addition to these requirements, teachers must integrate online and face-to-face instruction thoughtfully (Garrison & Kanuka, 2004). Some referred to BLEs as a *disruptive innovation* in education, meaning that the requirements for making a blended learning model work successful do not require small changes in practice from teachers and students, but rather an overhaul of nearly every practice on the educational landscape (Christensen, Horn, & Staker, 2013). For example, one such overhaul is the need for students in BLEs to make decisions about their own learning based on data they generate as students and set a pace for their own work in consultation with teachers (Bailey, Schneider, & Vander Ark, 2013). In this frame, the struggle for program quality becomes an additional component of the definition of blended learning itself. Essentially, "pedagogical quality" becomes synonymous with successful blended learning (Graham, 2013, p. 338).

As blended programs continue to grow at the middle level, the importance of high-quality teaching cannot be overstated. The exponential growth in online learning opportunities has necessitated teacher education programs to prepare future educators to teach in online and blended learning environments (Archambault, 2011; Dawley, Rice, & Hinck, 2010; Ferdig, Cavanaugh, DiPietro, Black, & Dawson, 2009; Kennedy & Archambault, 2012; Repetto, Cavanaugh, Wayer, & Liu, 2010). However, what about those teachers who are already in the classroom? Current practicing teachers also need support in their shift from face-to-face educators to blended learning teachers.

As blended learning continues its ascension in the pantheon of educational innovations of the 21st century, teachers and administrators need support in their efforts to implement blended learning pedagogies. Because educators often find it best to implement innovations within the frame of familiar or somewhat familiar practices, in this chapter, we highlight the need for collaboration among all stakeholders when designing and transitioning to blended learning environments at the middle level before providing examples of collaboration within these environments to meet the needs of diverse middle level learners.

## IDENTIFYING KEY COMPONENTS OF COLLABORATION FOR HIGH QUALITY BLENDED LEARNING CURRICULUM

Curriculum for young adolescents needs to be intellectually engaging (Brinegar & Bishop, 2011; Reidel & Draper, 2011). However, curriculum must also be culturally relevant and responsive to students' needs as unique beings (Garcia & Chun, 2016), and needs to consider the intellectual, emotional, physical, and social growth of adolescents (Farkas, 2011). Whenever possible, curriculum needs to support young adolescents' autonomy and agency as people who can make choices and who have individual preferences for *what* and *how* they want to learn (National Middle School Association, 2010). But, how does this curriculum translate to the blended learning environment? Three activities are necessary for success in developing curriculum that promotes engagement and addresses the unique needs of middle level learners (Stevens & Rice, 2016a, 2016b):

- Working in a middle level professional learning community (PLC) to design BLEs;
- Using understandings of middle level learners in BLEs; and
- Activating administrative support in a middle level site.

### Working in Middle Level Professional Learning Communities to Design BLEs

Research has demonstrated the importance of middle level educators' shared commitment to developing curriculum that supports student learning because the middle level is usually the first time that students change teachers and subjects all day long (DuFour, 2007). Professional learning communities (PLCs) offer teachers opportunities to collaborate with colleagues to develop curriculum and encourages shared reflection on teaching and learning (Clark, Moore, & Carlson, 2008; Owen, 2014). While most teacher reflection for improved practice occurs privately or with an administrator, mentor, or supervisor, reflection in a PLC is more public. Reflection within a PLC is highly collaborative and enables iterative processes of creation, sharing, organizing, and revising that lead to continued learning (Rahman, 2011; Sims & Penny, 2014). Within PLCS devoted to curriculum building, the public reflection on that curriculum's success or failure can assist educators with navigating the complexities of technology integration and developing pedagogical approaches that meet the needs of diverse middle level learners as they develop BLEs (Dallas, 2006).

### Using Understandings About Middle Level Learners in BLEs

The combination of learning through technology and face-to-face interaction in a BLE holds so much possibility for exciting, energetic, and engagement (Grover, Pea, & Cooper, 2015). However, while middle level learners are capable of sustained engagement, often teachers do not expose learners to curriculum that fits their background and interest and over which they have some control (Kim & Chang, 2010). This control can be over the content itself, the process of learning the content, or the product they use to demonstrate content knowledge. For example, in the past, computers were mostly used in classrooms to do rote exercises like practice math facts, today students must learn to use computers as they grow to think logically about problems that rely on mathematical principles (Horn & Staker, 2014). For teachers who are looking for examples of high blended learning in action, Edutopia (2017) hosts a site where educators can watch videos of students doing blended learning and learn about personalized learning in blended environments with diverse learners. Teachers can visit these resources during PLCs to facilitate conversations about the unique needs of the middle level learner and engage teachers in researching and discussing potential routes for reaching and teaching the blended learning student.

An additional benefit of BLEs for middle level students is that they enable differentiation (Baecher, Artigliere, Patterson, & Spatzer, 2012). Differentiation in the context of blended learning is more than just assigning a student harder or easier tasks, it is about helping students identify their strengths and leverage those to build an opportunity structure within a class, a school setting, and community at large. For example, a student might become interested in the human body and use Internet resources to learn how the body works. Then, the student might learn how to make and upload resources so that others can learn about the body. At this point, the student had two lines of opportunity: one for pursuing anatomy and physiology and the other for building modules and resources that teach others about these or other similar topics.

In collaborating to design a differentiated BLE curriculum, teachers can explore numerous resources within a PLC to support curriculum and content development. We highlight several of these resources in Table 5.1.

### Activating District and School-Based Support for BLEs at the Middle Level

It is not enough for teachers to *want* to design BLEs to serve their middle level populations better; they need support from multiple entities to accomplish these designs. School districts often design BLEs primarily

**Table 5.1.**
**Web Resources for Personalized Support**

| Website | Address |
| --- | --- |
| Supporting Student Success through Time and Technology | www.Timeandlearning.org |
| Personalized Learning | www.Fueleducation.com |
| Dos and Don'ts of Middle Level Blended Learning | http://blog.istation.com/the-dos-and-donts-of-middle-school-blended-learning |
| A Roadmap for Implementing Blended Learning at the School Level | https://www.inacol.org/wp-content/uploads/2015/02/a-roadmap-for-implementation.pdf |

for that district's students (Watson & Murin, 2014). In fact, growth within single district programs—run by a single district for that district's students—is outpacing all other segments of blended learning that includes charter schools, private schools, and vendor-based companies (LaFrance & Beck, 2014). Because districts play such an important role in the success of BLEs, it is vital to consider building-level administrators' responses to official directives from district leadership regarding BLEs while still informally attending to the nuances of their own school contexts.

## What Middle Level Administrators Can Do

Even with strong teachers, middle level building administrators can do much to support collaboration in the design of curriculum for blended learning. Specifically, school leaders can dedicate planning time for teachers as they design and monitor BLEs. They can also promote sharing of these successes with all school stakeholders, advocate for additional technological access, and share the effect of BLEs with the community. In this way, administrators are accessing those points of contact that are within their control, to not only maintain open dialogue and communication with stakeholders, but also serve as ongoing assessment and reflection of the blended learning process. Accountability can be key to ensuring that schools and classrooms are meeting the needs of the students.

**Provide dedicated PLC planning time**. Teachers indicate that they need time built into the daily schedule to participate in PLCs, and not an assigned time after school (DuFour, 2007). All too often, administrators expect teachers to devote personal time to classroom planning, grading, and preparation. It is important that teachers be provided dedicated time during the school day to attend to PLC engagement to ensure they have the time and attention necessary to engage fully one another in the research, discussion, and planning necessary for blended learning implementation.

**Sharing successes with school staff.** Administrators can allow PLCs involved in BLE curricular design and implementation to give presentations of their work. When possible, they need to encourage students to share their work with all school personnel as well. Teachers hearing about BLEs and the effect they have on meeting the needs of diverse middle level learners from their colleagues may urge others be more receptive to changing the way they approach learning in their own middle level classrooms. Applications that teachers can use to share the BLE experience can include Padlet, where users can publicly post and respond to each other, and even evolving collaborative discussions through sites like Twitter.

**Advocate for ever-increasing technological access.** In a chapter about BLEs, this is an obvious idea, but one that usually receives little attention. One thing to keep in mind is that technologies, such as computers, will need to be replaced about every 4 years or so. Computers wear out. Their software systems need constant updating and increasing bandwidth is necessary to run the latest software.

Costs and maintenance concerns come with the inclusion of blended learning environments in school contexts. For example, Positive Learning (2016) hosts a blog that offers seven ways to get funding for technology in classrooms. In addition, the federal government offers money for classroom technologies. Finally, if not having technology is a matter of not knowing what to choose, select teacher leaders and parents and have them request and review devices and applications and make recommendations.

**Provide occasions for teachers to share outside of the school faculty.** When teachers present the effect of BLEs to help diverse learners to the community, it allows parents and community members to see the benefits of this approach to learning. It also clears up any misconceptions that community members may have surrounding this learning approach. You do not want to the community to think that BLEs mean that students are going to be working on the computers while teachers do nothing. Further, through the sharing of what transpires in a BLE, teachers can inform community members of the cognitively sophisticated word their middle level learners achieve. Administrators can utilize several resources to get the word out. For example, administrators can post the work that both students and teachers in BLEs do on school websites, blogs, and twitter feeds. They can also display work in the gym during athletic contests or during other community events.

## What District Level Administrators Can Do

While building-level administrators carry much of the responsibility to support teachers' collaboration in designing and implementing BLEs, district level administrators need to work to ensure these efforts are successful. Specifically, they can provide training for teachers to help them develop the technological skills they will need to be effective within a BLE. They can also encourage schools with the greatest diversity or challenges to include BLEs in core classes. However, most importantly, they can guarantee (to the greatest extent possible) the technological infrastructure necessary for BLEs to be effective.

**BLEs in schools with the greatest diversity and challenges.** Often it is easier to begin BLE initiatives in schools that are already well-resourced (Sandoval & Harven, 2001). In most cases, new schools situated in higher socioeconomic communities already have technological infrastructure to support BLEs, parent/guardians that understand technology enhanced learning to a greater degree, and highly effective teachers. What districts might want to consider is looking to middle schools who house a more diverse population, for example schools with high numbers of English language learners or students with special needs. Bringing these more diverse middle schools on board with BLEs can be effective in promoting academic success, as the structure of BLEs lends itself to meeting the many needs of diverse students.

Principals in diverse middle schools can make decisions to fund both computer acquisition, and BLE professional development, for teachers using computers to serve diverse middle level learners. For example, principals can provide teacher development efficiently and cost-effectively by looking for guidance from both ongoing district BLE professional development and scholars working to develop approaches that benefit diverse learners. Administrators at the district level can encourage BLE development by actively seeking to establish PLCs devoted solely to BLEs, ones made up of teachers from across their districts, regardless of content area. It would also benefit these PLCS if district administrators collaborate with peers from other districts around the country. Logically speaking the more support, the stronger the blended learning environment.

**Guarantee the technological infrastructure to make BLEs work.** District personnel usually have a desire to be innovative and as part of that, some take up large-scale projects and buy expensive equipment and program access without a long-term vision for how to implement these projects in schools. Districts can alleviate some of the problems that result from this rush to find the latest and greatest tool by finding out *exactly* what the district and schools will need to make BLEs successful (Cuban, 2009; Parks, Oliver, & Carlson, 2016). Districts that are serious about implementing new tools and new practices must make a commitment to finding and providing resources. Below is a list of some questions that administrators can ask as they plan for the technological infrastructure to support BLEs in their schools:

- How many students do we want to share a device? In what classes do we want them to share? For how long during the day?
- What type of device(s) do we want to use? What will the device(s) or combinations of devices cost per unit to purchase initially?
- What are the technical requirements or constraints must we consider as we plan for every device to access the Internet?
- How do teachers already use Internet and other technologies in their teaching? What are the gaps in knowledge, skills, and dispositions between how they currently teach and how they must teach to be successful in BLEs? What will it cost to close these gaps in instruction?

Once a district decides on the technology they will offer schools, they must next consider how they can support school administrators in its use. Table 5.2 presents resources administrators can consult as they contemplate best practices for implementing BLEs and encouraging their growth.

## MOVING TO ACTION—STRATEGIES AND TOOLS FOR CREATING MIDDLE LEVEL BLEs

So far, this chapter has focused on explaining the critical elements of BLEs, provided examples of how teachers can collaborate in curriculum planning that is *both* blended and responsive to the needs of middle level learners, and how administrators and district leaders can support teacher's efforts in their collaboration to design and implement BLEs. The remainder of this chapter offers strategies teachers can use to promote collaboration within BLEs to meet the unique needs of middle level students.

### What Teachers Can Do

Middle level teachers can do a lot to shape a blended learning initiative within their school and classroom setting. The strategies most helpful to this endeavor is to make curriculum as applicable as possible to students' experiences, foster a culture of collaboration between students, and incorporate pedagogies that build on student strengths.

**Create spaces for sharing students work.** Schools need curriculum that forges stronger connections with students by engaging them in the learning process. Blending learning supports this goal. One blended learning strategy that can increase learner engagement involves sharing and discussing student work in every class. Teachers can share images or text of things students have created, said, or written. Teachers can place student

**Table 5.2.**
**BLE Resources to Support Administrators**

| Resource Name | Support Possible and Link |
| --- | --- |
| Online Learning Consortium (OLC) | A leading professional online learning society devoted to advancing quality e-Education. A search on "blended learning" yielded 3,300 possible resources.  https://onlinelearningconsortium.org/ |
| OLC Future of Blended Learning Blog: Insights from the Field: The Future of Blended Learning | Users can view and interact with posts related to blended learning. Users can also join the blog community and offer their own posts. https://onlinelearningconsortium.org/insights-field-future-blended-learning/ |
| International Association for K–12 Online Learning (iNACOL) | Blended learning is one of main resource topics. They have 76 resources available, including webinars, web resources, executive reports, and handouts. https://www.inacol.org/ |
| Michigan Virtual Learning Research Institute (MVLRI) | Provides access to helpful resources including webinars, podcasts, research reports, and school district blended learning readiness guidelines. In addition, they have established a blog that sorts posts based on relationship building, mentor leaders, and design research. https://mvlri.org/ |

samples in a blog, or other web-based location. The teacher can invite parents to view each new post via an application (app) like Remind. This app allows teachers to send a 140-character text that to notify others that they have posted student work samples on the blog (with a teacher-provided URL shortened link to make access easy). To serve diverse populations, teachers can send this text in any one of 70 different languages. Teachers can also translate the text-based student work samples into other languages using Google Translate. Teachers can access this tool from either a web interface or a mobile app that translates text, speech, images, sites, or real-time video from one language into another. It is also possible to enlist the students in picking examples of their work they would like shared. In allowing them choice, it could prompt engagement as students find their opinions are valued. This proves especially useful to engage students from low socioeconomic and language minority backgrounds who can experience marginalization in educational settings (Ramirez, 2005; Rodriguez, 1993).

**Foster a culture of collaboration.** Truly collaborative cultures at the middle level do not just happen by chance; educators design them purposefully. Instead of hoping collaboration occurs in the BLE, teachers can be proactive by forming collaborative student groups to complete course tasks. This is important because collaboration is an essential skill for all learners, including those in middle level settings (Gilbert, 2016; Partnership For 21st Century Learning, 2015). One specific benefit of collaboration is that learners do more than just share information; rather they teach each other and construct knowledge together (Borup, West, Graham, & Davies, 2014; Gunawardena, Lowe, & Anderson, 1998). Teachers can continually monitor student progress in the BLE by reviewing students' shared work documents online and checking in with them face-to-face. The BLE allows for all kinds of data capture in real time that students deserve to see and to which they are entitled to respond. When students have these chances, they take greater responsibility for their own learning in their school (Moos & Ringdal, 2012).

Teachers can use various applications to empower and enable this collaboration. One approach involves the sharing of any type of document through Google Classroom. Teachers can create assignments that require students to collaborate using this resource, as students can share documents instantaneously among themselves. Students can work simultaneously on the documents, allowing real-time collaboration.

## CONCLUSION

Educators and researchers are doing exciting work informing and guiding the development of high-quality BLEs (Barbour et al., 2013; Graham, 2013; Picciano et al., 2012; Staker, 2011). Drysdale, Graham, Spring, and Halverson (2013) suggested, "research in this context continues to increase, we believe that teachers and administrators will feel more confident in their abilities to establish blended environments and implementation will experience increased growth" (p. 98).

This chapter aimed to provide information that will be valuable to middle level teachers, building-level administrators, and district administrators about the challenges and the possibilities of supporting BLEs in their schools. As we close this chapter, we underscore our faith in middle level teachers; our delight in middle level learners and what they can do; and our respect for the administrators who have an earnest desire to support and enrich the teaching and learning process.

## REFERENCES

Archambault, L. (2011). The practitioner's perspective on teacher education: Preparing for the K–12 online classroom. *Journal of Technology and Teacher Education, 19*(1), 73–91.

Baecher, L., Artigliere, M., Patterson, D. K., & Spatzer, A. (2012). Differentiated instruction for English Language Learners as "variations on a theme." *Middle School Journal, 43*(3), 14–21.

Bailey, J., Schneider, C., & Vander Ark, T. (2013). Navigating the digital shift: Implementation strategies for blended and online learning. *Digital Learning Now!* Retrieved from http://www.gettingsmart.com/publication/navigating-digital-shift-implementation-strategies-blended-online-learning/

Barbour, M., Archambault, L., & DiPietro, M. (2013). K–12 online distance education: Issues and frameworks. *American Journal of Distance Education, 27*(1), 1–3.

Borup, J., West, R. E., Graham, C. R., & Davies, R. S. (2014). The adolescent community of engagement: A framework for research on adolescent online learning. *Journal of Technology and Teacher Education, 22*(1), 107–129.

Brinegar, K., & Bishop, P. A. (2011). Student learning and engagement in the context of curriculum integration. *Middle Grades Research Journal, 6*(4), 207–222.

Clark, P. G., Moore, K. C., & Carlson, M. P. (2008). Documenting the emergence of "speaking with meaning" as a sociomathematical norm in professional learning community discourse. *Journal of Mathematical Behavior, 27*(4), 297–310.

Christensen, C. M., Horn, M. B., & Staker, H. (2013). Is K–12 blended learning disruptive? An introduction to the theory of hybrids. *Clayton Christensen Institute for Disruptive Innovation.* Retrieved from https://files.eric.ed.gov/fulltext/ED566878.pdf

Cuban, L. (2009). *Oversold and underused.* Cambridge, MA: Harvard University Press.

Dallas, F. (2006). Enhancing the 3 R's of resilience, retention, and reform through middle school faculty professional learning communities. *Middle Grades Research Journal, 1*(1), 67–93.

Dawley, L., Rice, K., & Hinck, G. (2010). *Going virtual! 2010 —The status of professional development and unique needs of K–12 online teachers.* Retrieved from http://edtech.boisestate.edu/goingvirtual/goingvirtual3.pdf

Drysdale, J. S., Graham, C. R., Spring, K. J., & Halverson, L. R. (2013). An analysis of research trends in dissertations and theses studying blended learning. *Internet and Higher Education, 17,* 90–100.

DuFour, R. (2007). Professional learning communities: A bandwagon, an idea worth considering, or our best hope for high levels of learning? *Middle School Journal, 39*(1), 4–8.

Edutopia. (2017). *Blended learning.* Retrieved from https://www.edutopia.org/blogs/tag/blended-learning

Farkas, G. (2011). Middle and high school skills, behaviors, attitudes, and curriculum enrollment, and their consequences. In C. Duncan & R. J. Murmane (Eds.), *Whither opportunity? Rising inequality, schools, and children's life chances* (pp. 72–89). New York, NY: Russell Sage Foundation.

Ferdig, R. E., Cavanaugh, C., DiPietro, M., Black, E., & Dawson, K. (2009). Virtual schooling standards and best practices for teacher education. *Journal of Technology and Teacher Education, 17*(4), 479–503.

Garcia, C., & Chun, H. (2016). Culturally responsive teaching and teacher expectations for Latino middle school students. *Journal of Latina/o Psychology*, *4*(3), 173–187.

Garrison, D. R., & Kanuka, H. (2004). Blended learning: Uncovering its transformative potential in higher education. *Internet and Higher Education*, *7*(2), 95–105.

Gilber, A. D. (2016). The framework for 21st century learning: A first-rate foundation for music education assessment and teacher evaluation. *Arts Education Policy*, *117*(1), 13–18.

Graham, C. (2013). Emerging practice and research in blended learning. In M. G. Moore (Ed.), *Handbook of distance education* (3rd ed., pp. 333–350). New York, NY: Routledge.

Grover, S., Pea, R., & Cooper, S. (2015). Designing for deeper learning in a blended computer science course for middle school students. *Computer Science Education*, *25*(2), 199–237.

Gunawardena, C. N., Lowe, C. A., & Anderson, T. (1998). Transcript analysis of computer-mediated conferences as a tool for testing constructivist and social-constructivist learning theories. *Proceedings of the Annual Conference on Distance Teaching and Learning* (pp. 139–144). Madison: University of Wisconsin-Madison.

Horn, M. B., & Staker, H. (2014). *Trends in digital learning: empowering innovative classroom models for learning*. Retrieved from http://www.tomorrow.org/speakup/2015_ClassroomModels.html

Hutchison, A., & Henry, L. A. (2010). Internet use and online literacy among middle grade students at risk of dropping out of school. *Middle Grades Research Journal*, *5*(2), 61–75.

Kennedy, K., & Archambault, L. (2012). Offering pre-service teachers field experiences in K–12 online learning: A national survey of teacher education programs. *Journal of Teacher Education*, *63*(3), 185–200.

Kim, S., & Chang, M. (2010). Does computer use promote the mathematical proficiency of ELL students? *Journal of Educational Computing Research*, *42*(3), 285–305.

LaFrance, J. A., & Beck, D. (2014). Mapping the terrain educational leadership field experiences in K-12 virtual schools. *Educational Administration Quarterly*, *50*(1), 160–189.

Moos, D. C., & Ringdal, A. (2012). Self-regulated learning in the classroom: A literature review on the teacher's role. *Education Research International*, *2012*, 1–15. Retrieved from https://www.hindawi.com/journals/edri/2012/423284/

National Middle School Association. (2010). *This we believe: Keys to educating young adolescents*. Westerville, OH: Author.

Owen, S. (2014). Teacher professional learning communities: Going beyond contrived collegiality toward challenging debate and collegial learning and professional growth. *Australian Journal of Adult Learning*, *54*(2), 54–77.

Partnership For 21st Century Learning. (2015). *P21 framework definitions*. Retrieved from http://www.p21.org/our-work/p21-framework

Parks, R. A., Oliver, W., & Carlson, E. (2016). The status of middle and high school instruction: Examining professional development, social desirability, and teacher readiness for blended pedagogy in the Southeastern United States. *Journal of Online Learning Research, 2*, 79–101.

Picciano, A. G., Seaman, J., Shea, P., & Swan, K. (2012). Examining the extent and nature of online learning in American K-12 education: The research initiatives of the Alfred P. Sloan foundation. *Internet and Higher Education, 15*(2), 127–135.

Positive Learning. (2016, February 11). 7 ways to get funding and grants for your classroom [Web log post]. Retrieved from https://positivelearning.com/blog/2016/2/11/7-ways-to-get-funding-and-grants-for-technology-in-your-classroom

Rahman, S. M. H. (2011). Influence of professional learning community (PLC) on secondary science teachers' culture of professional practice: The case of Bangladesh. *Asia-Pacific Forum on Science Learning and Teaching, 12*(1), 1–23.

Ramirez, A. Y. F. (2005). Esperanza's lessons: Learning about education through the eyes of the innocent. *Multicultural Education, 13*(2), 47–52.

Reidel, M., & Draper, C. A. (2011). Reading for democracy: Preparing middle-grades social studies teachers to teach critical literacy. *The Social Studies, 102*(3), 124–131.

Repetto, J., Cavanaugh, C., Wayer, N., & Liu, F. (2010). Virtual high schools: improving with disabilities. *Quarterly Review of Distance Education, 11*(2), 91–104.

Rice, M., & Stevens, M. (2016). Online learning. In S. B. Mertens, M. M. Caskey, & N. Flowers (Eds.), *Encyclopedia of middle level education* (2nd ed.). Charlotte, NC: Information Age.

Rodriguez, L. J. (1993). *Always running—La Vida loca: Gang days in L.A.* New York, NY: Touchstone.

Sandoval, W. A., & Harven, A. M. (2011). Urban middle school students' perceptions of the value and difficulty of inquiry. *Journal of Science Education and Technology, 20*(1), 95–109.

Sims, R. L., & Penny, G. R. (2014). Examination of a failed professional learning community. *Journal of Education and Training Studies, 3*(1), 39–45.

Staker, H. (2011). *The rise of K-12 blended learning: Profiles of emerging models.* Retrieved from http://www.christenseninstitute.org/wp-content/uploads/2013/04/The-rise-of-K-12-blended-learning.emerging-models.pdf

Stevens, M. (2016). Space for all: Middle level students in blended learning environments. *Voices from the Middle, 24*(2), 50–55.

Stevens, M. & Rice, M. (2016a). A case study of a professional learning community in a highly diverse blended school. In *Proceedings of the E-Learn: World Conference on E-Learning* (pp. 485–495). Washington, DC: Association for the Advancement of Computing in Education. Retrieved from https://www.learntechlib.org/p/173975/

Stevens, M., & Rice, M. (2016b). Inquiring into presence in a middle level blended learning classroom. *Journal of Online Learning Research, 2*(4), 447–473.

U.S. Department of Education. (2015). *Table 218.20. Percentage of public school districts with students enrolled in technology-based distance education courses and number of enrollments in such courses, by instructional level and district characteristics: 2002–03, 2004-05, and 2009-10.* Washington, DC: National Center for Education

Statistics. Retrieved from https://nces.ed.gov/programs/digest/d15/tables/dt15_218.20.asp

Watson, J., & Murin, A. (2014). A history of K-12 online and blended instruction in the United States. In R. Ferdig & K. Kennedy (Eds.), *Handbook of research on K–12 online and blended learning* (pp. 1–23). Pittsburgh, PA: ETC Press.

# SECTION III

## COMMUNITY

CHAPTER 6

# FOSTERING COMMUNITY IN THE MIDDLE LEVEL VIRTUAL CLASSROOM

**Jillian L. Wendt**
*University of the District of Columbia*

**Amanda J. Rockinson-Szapkiw**
*University of Memphis*

**Kyleigh B. Harrell**
*Odyssey Online Learning*

Secondary distance education enrollment continues to increase steadily as technology advances and stakeholders seek to prepare secondary students for online post-secondary learning (Archambault, DeBruler, & Freidhoff, 2014; Watson, Murin, Vashaw, Gemin, & Rapp, 2012). Because of this increase, educators and researchers seek to establish evidence-based practices to support learner achievement and meaningful knowledge building in virtual classrooms. Within the literature on distance education, community influences the quality of online interaction (McIsaac & Gunawardena, 1996) and promoting higher-order thinking (Tu & Corry, 2002; Tu &

*The Online Classroom:*
*Resources for Effective Middle Level Virtual Education,* pp. 99–120
Copyright © 2018 by Information Age Publishing
All rights of reproduction in any form reserved.
99

McIsaac, 2002). Sense of community includes a sense of belonging and commitment to a group and the group members (McMillan & Chavis, 1986) and has been identified as necessary for academic achievement and learning at all levels within virtual environments (Rockinson-Szapkiw & Wendt, 2015; Rovai & Jordan, 2004; Schulte, Shanahan, Anderson, & Sides, 2003; Wendt & Rockinson-Szapkiw, 2015), including the virtual middle level.

Drawing from peer-reviewed literature and the authors' personal research on community in the middle level, a discussion ensues on the evidence-based and empirically supported practices for instructional design and instruction that support a sense of community for middle level virtual classrooms (Buraphadeja & Kumnuanta, 2011; Chauhan, Naseem, & Rashwan, 2016; Drysdale, 2013). This chapter provides resources that support these suggested practices, as well as offering those who are responsible for instructional design and instructional implementation in virtual classrooms resources in maintaining conditions suitable for increased levels of sense of community in the middle level virtual classroom.

## THE IMPORTANCE OF COMMUNITY

Before we can offer resources to virtual teachers regarding the building of community in the middle level virtual classroom, we must first discuss why doing so is imperative. The importance of developing community in classrooms is well supported in the research, for community improves motivation, knowledge creation, and persistence (Abfalter, Zaglia, & Mueller, 2012; Rovai, 2002). McMillan and Chavis (1986) defined sense of community as "a feeling that members have of belonging, a feeling that members matter to one another and to the group, and a shared faith that members' needs will be met through their commitment to be together" (p. 9). Drawing upon the work of McMillan and Chavis and others (e.g., Royal & Rossi, 1997), Rovai (2002) contextualized community in the classroom and developed the construct of classroom community, noting that classroom community has two underlying dimensions: social community and learning community. Social community consists of a learners' spirit, cohesion, trust, trade, and belonging, whereas learning community is the degree to which community members share group norms and values and group members are satisfied. This construction of classroom community, both social and learning, is not limited to brick-and-mortar classroom walls, as building a sense of community does not require geographical proximity (Rheingold, 1993). Therefore, community can be, and needs to be, transferred to the virtual classroom.

Critical lines of research have consistently identified classroom community as associated with quality, effective virtual education (Rovai, 2002). The literature supports community as necessary and foundational to higher-order thinking and learning. However, some recognized that community is not sufficient to develop critical discourse in the virtual classroom (Garrison & Cleveland-Innes, 2005). Thus, Garrison, Anderson, and Archer (2000) expanded the notion of classroom community in the virtual environment and purported that a community of inquiry (CoI) is necessary for quality, effective virtual design, and instruction to take place. Their assumption is that for effective teaching and learning to occur in a virtual classroom, three elements must be present and intersecting: teaching presence, social presence, and cognitive presence. Teaching presence is the design and the facilitation that guides the cognitive and social presence with the aim of obtaining learning outcomes (Garrison et al., 2000). Social presence is "the ability of participants in the Community of Inquiry to project their personal characteristics into the community, thereby presenting themselves to the other participants as *real people*" (Garrison et al., 2000, p. 89). Cognitive presence is "the extent to which the participants in any particular configuration of a community of inquiry are able to construct meaning through sustained communication" (Garrison et al., 2000, p. 89). Because research has shown that a CoI model is useful in providing insight into virtual education (Akyol, Garrison, & Ozden, 2009; Garrison & Arbaugh, 2007), we are drawing on its tenets as a foundation for this chapter and the design and instructional resources we offer for virtual learning at the middle level. Moreover, a sense of "connectedness" (Resnick et al., 1997) or community is fundamental to middle level learners' learning and development, and a community of inquiry is ideal for their construction of deep and meaningful knowledge (Drysdale, 2013).

## THE ROLE OF PRESENCE

The quality of the instructor directly influences the virtual learning experiences for middle level learners (Archambault et al., 2014). While Garrison et al. (2000) referred to teaching presence as the binding element of virtual higher education learning communities, this is even more true with middle level virtual learning environments, where learners are less autonomous than adult learners (Borup, Graham, & Drysdale, 2014). Teaching presence is the design, facilitation, and direction of cognitive and social developments for worthwhile and meaningful learning outcomes (Anderson, Rourke, Garrison, & Archer, 2001). In other words, the teacher fosters quality learning by designing and organizing the learning experience, facilitating learning activities, and contributing academic knowledge by way of direct instruction. The role of teaching presence aligned with cognitive presence and social presence harmonizes learner needs, learner abilities, and learning outcomes (Kozan & Richardson, 2014). Learners will acclimate their cognitive and social performance based on the components of teaching presence—instructional design, instruction, and facilitation (Ke, 2010). Middle level learners will place more value on instructional design and organization and direct instruction, the more objectivist elements, than learners who have advanced in their academic career. Therefore, these elements have a greater effect on middle level learners' success (Kupczynski, Ice, Wiesenmayer, & McCluskey, 2010).

Instructional design and organization begins prior to the start of the course as the instructor plans and designs the learning process, interactions, and evaluation components of the online course (Garrison & Arbaugh, 2007). At this stage, teachers choose technologies to facilitate discourse (Garrison & Arbaugh, 2007). Examples of such technology include discussion forms (such as those available in Blackboard) and web conferencing (such as Blackboard Collaborate, Adobe Connect, and Cisco Telepresence).

While teaching presence begins before the course, as the teacher acts as instructional designer, planner, and preparer of the course of studies, it continues during the course as the instructor facilitates the discourse and provides direct instruction (Anderson et al., 2001). Direct instruction, used during the implementation of the course, is described as providing intellectual and scholarly leadership from a subject matter expert (Anderson et al., 2001) to analyze comments for correct understanding, inject sources of information, direct useful discussions, and scaffold learner knowledge to a higher level (Swan et al., 2008). Direct instruction can be implemented through recorded lectures (through the use of narrated PowerPoint or creation of YouTube videos), providing timely and detailed feedback (through the grading feature in Blackboard), engaging in discussion forums and web conferencing with students, and providing additional resources to support student learning as needed. In the following sections, we discuss specific strategies for creating teaching presence and for establishing and maintaining community.

## CREATING PRESENCE THROUGH INSTRUCTIONAL DESIGN

Fink (2005) said instructors need to answer three questions when designing a course: (a) What do I want students to learn? (goals), (b) How will students demonstrate these goals are being accomplished? (assessment), and (c) What learning activities and technology are needed for students to achieve the goals? In answering the first question, community and interactivity need to be key considerations in the design of virtual classes for middle learners. Effective instructional design contributes to higher levels of sense of community and deep learning (Garrison & Arbaugh, 2007; Shea, Li, & Pickett, 2006; Zhang, Lin, Zhan, & Ren, 2016), therefore, as the virtual instructor plans and prepares the course design, they must pay close attention to process, interaction, and evaluation components (Garrison & Arbaugh, 2007). Activities involved with instructional design and organization include developing curriculum, designing methods, and providing guidelines on utilizing medium effectively (Anderson et al., 2001).

## Welcome Messages

As a course begins, virtual instructors could establish presence through the creation of audio and video welcome messages to promote learners' comfortability with their instructor as they see their instructor as a real person (Kupczynski et al., 2010). Learners feel a strong sense of connection to the instructor when given the opportunity to see photos or a video of the instructor and hear the instructor's voice before or at the beginning of a virtual course (Jones, Naugle, & Kolloff, 2008; Russo & Campbell, 2004). The instructor's welcome message needs to provide introductions to both the course and the instructor. In addition to sharing course information such as course goals, expectations, and requirements, the welcome message needs to include information about the instructor. The instructor could share about their work experience, reasons for enthusiasm about the course topic, family information, and personal interests. When possible, the welcome message needs to include video of the instructor so the learners can hear the instructor's tone and can see the instructor's body language. Because the goal of the video is to welcome the students and develop a sense of connection and presence, it is imperative the instructor comes across as warm, approachable, and genuine. For learners believe that instructors with warm personalities are better, more effective teachers (Dulaney, 2013). Creating a good impression also includes the instructor's consideration of the lighting, audio, and video quality.

Several current tools are available for creating these welcome messages. For instance, teachers can convert narrated PowerPoint presentations to video format and upload them to popular video hosting sites such as YouTube. A free Office Mix add-in is available to provide enhanced online interactive videos using PowerPoint. Thus, instructors can create new or modify existing PowerPoint presentations and easily convert these presentations to video file format. Screen capture software with audio capability, such as Camtasia or Animoto, provides instructors with the capability of creating video presentations with narration and sound as well as the ability to add images directly from a computer, laptop, or mobile device screen.

Finally, accessible and available tools for creating welcome videos also include audio and video recording via smartphone, laptop, or other mobile devices. Most popular smartphones, for instance, have apps included for video recording and uploading to popular video hosting sites.

## Ice Breaker Activities

Planning and integrating icebreakers or introductory activities during the first few days of a course sets a climate of trust and safety and assists the class in forming a sense of belonging (Hung & Chou, 2015). Icebreaker activities need to be aimed at humanizing the virtual environment and be learner focused, non-threatening, and require learner-learner interaction. These activities need to focus on building trust and belonging so learners feel safe to create meaning and test ideas as they progress in the course. For example, icebreakers may include asking learners to introduce themselves by responding to probes such as:

- If you were a candy bar, what candy bar would you be? Why?
- If you were on a deserted island and could bring one book, what book would you bring?
- If you had to describe yourself as an animal, which animal matches your personality?
- Make a list of your top five interests.
- Think about how you would describe yourself. Think about your culture and heritage. Create a bumper sticker that captures who you are.
- Choose an image from our class photo galley that best describe you. Explain why you choose the image.

Effective icebreakers also require learners to respond. So, an instructor may state, "Respond to your peers using the following prompts:"

- Find a peer that chose a candy bar that you did not. Explain how you are different, yet similar to that peer.
- Who choose a book that you have never read? Tell a peer why you may be interested in reading the book they choose.
- Who choose an animal similar or the same to you? Respond to the peer who choose the same or similar to you and explain how you are similar and different.
- Find a peer with similar interests and list the things you have in common.

- Tell a peer what you find interesting about the bumper sticker and ask a question to inquire about something in which you are curious.

The virtual instructor can facilitate Icebreakers on discussion or social media forums, or through collaboration tools. A few include Slack, VoiceThread, Google Communities, Yammer, Vyew, Wikispaces, and Edmodo. Learners can interact via text, video, or audio within these apps.

Learners can also be encouraged by the instructor to use a variety of tools to create their initial posts and responses. For example, learners can use:

- Easel.ly to create an infographic or a visual depiction of information that the learner wants to share about him or herself;
- BigHugeLabs to create colorful posters and trading cards;
- Thinglink to create images and add texts and other items to photos; or
- WeVideo as a web-based tool for video editing.

As an aside, in choosing a tool for icebreakers or any class activity, it is always important that the instructor knows and understands the school policy about technology usage. The instructor must also consider the security of the tool to ensure that he or she is upholding the Family Educational Rights and Privacy Act of 1974 regulations (FERPA).

## Setting Parameters for Interaction

Creating a safe community for learners also requires instructional designers and instructors to establish parameters for interaction, including "rules for interaction" (e.g., be respectful, respond to at least two peers by Wednesday) and an introduction to the places and technologies that enable interaction (e.g., Word documents or YouTube video explaining how to use discussion board, synchronous chat, video conferencing). Because social cues of the traditional face-to-face classroom are absent, it is important for instructors to be more transparent and explicit in how to interact (Kupczynski et al., 2010). Teachers need to establish and sustain expectations for learners to develop sense of community (Hung & Chou, 2015). Instructors can do this by intentionally providing instruction on web-etiquette (also known as netiquette). Web-etiquette guidelines may include:

- Always greet your peer and identify yourself. Begin messages with a salutation with your peer's name and end them with your name.

- Be concise in your responses. A good rule of rule of thumb is a 100-word initial post and a 50-word response.
- Observe good grammar and spelling.
- Use emoticons to help convey meaning. For example, use "smileys" to convey happiness about a peer's comment.
- Never use "flaming" or "screaming" (all caps).

Soliciting learner input on what are acceptable and unacceptable interactions online might look like would also assist in building community, specifically in the areas of connectedness, belonging, and trust.

## Clear Structure and Timelines

From a more academic standpoint, middle level virtual learners also need lessons organized in short segments with concrete deadlines (Borup et al., 2014; Weiner, 2003). For example, a clear structure and timetable is important in improving the quality of the virtual course and creating a positive learning experience (Hung & Chou, 2015). Instructors can chunk information in virtual presentations in more manageable and digestible amounts to reduce the potential of cognitive overload for middle learners, keeping text and graphics to a minimum and reducing presentations to shorter timespans (Nelson & Erlandson, 2008). For example, instructors can produce videos that are no more than 5 to 10 minutes in length. Nelson and Erlandson (2008) argued, "When a student is faced with a large number of elements to process at the same time, she experiences cognitive overload and fails to effectively use all essential elements necessary to form mental models" (p. 627). As aforementioned, instructors can use narrated and converted PowerPoint presentations or screen capture software with audio capability such as Camtasia or Animoto to produce instructor videos. VoiceThread is a useful tool for chunking and presenting information. Articulate has a series of tools teachers can use to create professional, interactive, chunked instruction.

## Collaborative Learning Activities

As the course progresses, teachers can plan student-to-student learning, or collaborative learning activities, to support meaning construction and knowledge creation. Collaborative learning activities, where learners work "in a group of two or more to achieve a common goal, while respecting each individual's contribution to the whole" (McInnerney & Roberts, 2004, p. 205), provide learners with the opportunity to interact with and participate in a community to construct their own knowledge and develop skills by observing, learning from, and negotiating meaning with others. Collaborative learning encompasses a wide range of activities. Web quests, role-plays, case simulations, collaborative discussions, structured synchronous chats, dyad or triad debates, and team problem solving are all collaborative learning activities designers and instructors can plan in designing virtual instruction for middle learners. Teachers can easily implement collaborative learning in the middle level virtual classroom through most learning management systems and learning platforms' discussion forums, group features, and file sharing features. Collaboration tools or social media forums are also useful for collaboration. Example tools include, but are not limited to, Slack, Twiddla, VoiceThread, Padlet, Google Communities, Vyew, and Wikispaces.

## Instructor Modeling and Intervention

Vital to middle level learners' academic growth and community building, however, is the instructor's intentional modeling and intervention (Wendt & Rockinson-Szapkiw, 2014). The instructor cannot leave the learners to fend for himself or herself, the instructor must model collaborative behavior and be involved in the entire collaborative activity, guiding learners' interactions to provide confidence and instruction as needed. In course design, the instructor can outline and explain his or her involvement so learners know what to expect. Instructors can model social presence cues in discussion activities, welcome videos, and instruction by addressing learners by name, describing personal or professional experiences relevant to the learning objectives, and sharing personal evaluations. Modeling social cues is likely to encourage learners to do the same. An effective teaching presence strategy to guide cognitive presence is the use of audio feedback in discussions, within collaborative activities, and on assignments. Teachers can create audio files in a variety of ways including the use of Audacity freeware. Teacher can also embed audio files created with Audacity as attachments to the discussion board, emails, documents, and so on. Many collaboration tools, such as VoiceThread, have audio tools that enable instructors to leave a voice comment through their computer microphone or calling in via telephone.

## CREATING COMMUNITY IN THE VIRTUAL CLASSROOM THROUGH DELIVERY

During course delivery, instructor's actions have power for building and sustaining of community that promulgates positive learner outcomes.

Instructor immediacy is foundational to evidence-based practices in instructional delivery and strategies. While teaching presence supports the design and facilitation of cognitive presence and social presence to meet learning outcomes, instructor immediacy refers to "nonverbal and verbal behaviors, which reduce psychological and/or physical distance between instructors and students" (Christophel & Gorham, 1995, p. 292) and is very similar to the idea of social presence in the CoI framework. High levels of instructor immediacy, therefore, relate to a decreased distance between instructors and learners and, thus, brings a more human and relatable characteristic to the classroom. While researchers have not studied instructor immediacy extensively in the K–12 environment, or in the online context, research is beginning to suggest that the style in which instructors interact with learners may influence perceptions of instructor immediacy (Giles et al., 2012).

## Strategies for Verbal and Nonverbal Immediacy Behaviors

In traditional classrooms, verbal teacher behaviors—characterized by speaking—include feedback, humor, and addressing learners by name; nonverbal teacher behaviors include eye contact, smiling, and body language (Gorham, 1988). While application of nonverbal immediacy behaviors may be limited in asynchronous virtual environments, the implementation of verbal immediacy behaviors is more feasible (Arbaugh, 2001).

A middle level virtual instructor can easily practice verbal immediacy by addressing learners by name in discussion forums, incorporating developmentally appropriate uses of humor in classroom interactions, asking questions that solicit learners' feedback in nonjudgmental ways, and engaging in informal dialogue with learners. Additionally, virtual instructors can be cognizant of the use of body language, for example, smiling, using eye contact, and using mild gestures when engaging in synchronous video communication with learners and when creating video recordings for students—nonverbal behaviors. For instance, instructors need to refrain from body language such as arm crossing or frowning and instead display a relaxed posture and a smile. Instructors need to look directly into the camera rather than off screen and use small, mild gestures rather than large, flamboyant ones.

## Direct Instruction

Another important aspect to consider is that of direct instruction and facilitation, as each are essential in the implementation of a virtual course—especially when employing collaborative learning activities. Direct instruction is valuable and necessary in developmentally and systematically building a learning experience aimed at helping learners achieve higher-order outcomes. Instructors can implement direct instruction in the virtual environment to meet a wide range of learner needs, including those of learners with disabilities and English language learners (Flores & Kaylor, 2007). Direct instruction could be the sharing of subject matter content, enhanced by personal interest, excitement, and in-depth knowledge (Anderson et al., 2001). An important and traditional role of the instructor is the presentation of content and direction of questions. Videos or synchronous video communications are appropriate resources to present content in the virtual classroom. The instructor could also focus discussions on specific issues by providing grading rubrics, exemplary learner samples, and deadline reminders (Chen, deNoyelles, Zydney, & Patton, 2017). Rubistar.4teachers.org, for instance, is a website that instructors can use to create grading rubrics. Rubrics communicate the expectations for an assignment. With Rubistar.4teachers.org, instructors have access to an abundance of already crafted rubrics or they may customize a rubric to fit their needs.

## Feedback

Instructors need to ensure they are not only present and showing a high level of attentiveness and involvement, but also providing immediacy in feedback to further facility student learning. Teachers can support immediacy in feedback by providing in-depth and timely responses to learner interactions in discussion forums and chats and on graded assignments, and keeping an attentive eye on learner-to-learner interactions so they can intervene to guide learners towards accurate conceptions in the virtual environment when needed. Teachers can provide feedback on assignments using audio, video, and text inserted into documents. For instance, teachers can use Microsoft Word Comments and Track Changes features or Adobe Acrobat Pro's comment and mark up feature to provide text feedback throughout the documents. The instructor can also provide a summary and list of needed areas of improvement in audio format at the end of the document. If students submit their assignments as Microsoft Word documents, the instructors can create .mp3 audio files using Audacity freeware and insert the audio file directly into the document. If students submit assignments as PDFs, the instructor can use Adobe Acrobat Pro's record audio comment tool to provide audio summary comments. Real-time discussions and debriefings using videoconferencing systems such as Adobe Connect and Google Hangout may be appropriate for middle level learners they may require more immediate feedback based on the complexity of the task and on their developmental level. With Adobe Connect and Google Hangout, the instructor is in an online conferencing room with the learner, just as if they were sitting in a class together. For example, if a learner incorrectly solves an algebraic equation, the instructor can immediately walk the learner through how to find the correct answer. The learner can see and hear the instructor and can see what the instructor is writing on the virtual whiteboard (e.g., within the videoconferencing tool or via an online collaborative whiteboard such as Vyew, or Twiddla).

## Facilitating Communication and Collaboration

Wendt and Rockinson-Szapkiw (2015) studied middle level learners' collaboration experiences and found that when comparing face-to-face collaborative learning and online collaborative learning, learners involved in virtual collaborative learning demonstrated lower overall community than those involved in face-to-face collaborative learning. The findings suggest that some activities may be better suited for the face-to-face environment than the virtual environment, as activities that rely heavily on nonverbal cues may not facilitate the building of community in the virtual environment as effectively as the face-to-face environment. Thus, virtual instructors need to select technologies that facilitate communication and building of community while also being task-specific. For instance, if a task requires learners to collaborate for a group project, selecting a collaborative tool that facilitates anytime, anywhere interaction among learners, such as Google Docs, would be most appropriate.

Importantly, middle level learners may not possess the self-regulation strategies that some collaborative activities require in the virtual environment. Thus, it is also important that instructors remain present during the activities. Instructors can do so by checking in on learner progress by monitoring written correspondence (such as through Google Docs where instructors can see who is participating in creating and editing documents and in what ways this participation is occurring) or attending synchronous discussion sessions (such as through Google Hangouts or Apple FaceTime where instructors can see and hear learners interact) so that learners can be redirected as needed. However, teachers need to be cautious that they are not to so present that learner autonomy suffers and discourse is stifled.

Key to building community is remembering that instructors need to implement instructional activities that require collaborative critical thinking and discourse in the virtual environment. For example, virtual middle level instructors can develop and present case studies and questions on discussion forums that middle learners cannot easily explain using existing knowledge and beliefs; thus, requiring collaborative critical thinking and brainstorming in the online discussion. Discussions that require critical thinking can also take on the form of collaborative learning activities (such as structured controversy) and creative thinking activities (such as topical discussions and case-based discussions) (Richardson & Ice, 2010). Virtual instructors instruct students to view specific content from one of the many online content providers and critically analyze it. Some excellent examples of this at multiple grade levels and content levels are available through the National Board for Professional Teaching Standards Accomplished Teaching, Learning, and Schools (ATLAS) video library. This video library is an online repository of master teachers' video-recorded teaching practices, linked to national learning standards, with detailed commentary and instructor resources. YouTube channels provide instruction on a variety of topics. For example, Crash Course is a YouTube channel that provides well-researched, engaging lectures and courses on topics such as world history and astronomy. PanOpen is another platform for easily accessing, evaluating, and adapting open educational resources (OERs); PanOpen enables instructors to adapt a content by adding videos and PowerPoint slides and using drag-and-drop tools to rearrange content within resources. Wolfram Alpha is a useful search engine that organizes learning material via visual representations. Finally, Khan Academy offers self-paced, interactive learning videos.

Instructors can ask middle learners to participate in and even create videos of themselves doing familiar tasks but thinking about them in a critical manner, perhaps while talking through their thoughts to assist peers in understanding their unique creative process. For example, an instructor can introduce the idea of aerodynamics by asking students to video themselves making and attempting to fly various paper airplane designs (e.g., flat paper, with wings, with flat nose, and so on). Then during a videoconferencing session, learners can examine videos and engage in discourse regarding the activity, content, and new knowledge learned. Thus, it is important that instructors select technology that best facilitates the given activity rather than integrating technology for the sake of technology integration alone. This assists in facilitating learning opportunities that mimic those that would occur in the face-to-face environment, providing a level of equivalency in instruction. Learners can easily utilize smartphones and mobile devices to record their activities and most learning management systems have videoconferencing capabilities, such as those offered through Blackboard Collaborate, Google Hangout, and Adobe Connect. These videoconferencing tools also offer a recording feature that would enable instructors and learners to view the interaction later for grading or self-reflective purposes.

## TECHNOLOGIES FOR CREATING COMMUNITY IN THE VIRTUAL CLASSROOM

While the use of technology in a virtual classroom is secondary to well-designed learning and instruction (Berge, 1995), it is a vital component in the formation of community for virtual middle level learners (Buraphadeja & Kumnuanta, 2011; Edwards & Rule, 2013; Pope, 2013). Asynchronous and synchronous technologies create a virtual learning community (Akyol & Garrison, 2011). Synchronous technologies enable learning in real-time communication between learners and instructors, while asynchronous technologies occur in delayed time and do not depend on simultaneous contact (Oztok, Zingaro, Brett, & Hewitt, 2013). Examples of asynchronous and synchronous technologies for middle level learners include discussion boards, computer-supported collaborative learning tools, social-networking technologies, and web-conferencing tools.

### Asynchronous Technologies

Asynchronous technologies are technologies that assist students in completing coursework outside of a pre-established moment in time. Such technologies provide flexibility by allowing learners the opportunity to participate in classroom instruction and learning with fewer time constraints. For instance, because asynchronous technologies occur in delayed time, learners are able to absorb content, consider new material, formulate responses, and revise responses prior to synchronous participation. This has been shown to be beneficial in (a) providing enhanced opportunities for critical thinking, (b) alleviating anxiety regarding 'getting the right answer,' and (c) supporting enhanced communication as learners are able to revise thoughts and participate more confidently and introspectively. Several forms of asynchronous technologies benefit the middle level virtual classroom, including discussion forums, collaborative learning tools, and social-networking technologies.

**Discussion forums.** Discussion forums are one example of asynchronous technologies used to create community as students exchange ideas interactively as they might do in face-to-face communication and thoughtfully as might occur in activities that provide extended time for response (Grisham & Wolsey, 2006). The ability to engage in reflection can assist learners with special needs, English language learners, and struggling learners by providing them the opportunity to participate in ways that are equitable to their more advanced peers (Dunn, 2012; Rachels & Rockinson-Szapkiw, 2017). Discussion forums also provide a written record of communication to assist instructors in identifying where additional interventions and instruction are needed (such as in identifying misconceptions) and to more fully understand learners' prior experiences, perspectives, and thought processes. In implementing discussion forums in the middle level virtual classroom, instructor participation, however, is critical in setting tone and increasing the complexity of learner response (Grisham & Wolsey, 2006). Thus, instructors need to set clear expectations, actively monitor discussion forums, and practice teacher presence by participating in discussion. Text-based discussion forums are typically available in learning platforms such as Blackboard, Edmodo, and Moodle. With Blackboard, the instructor provides a prompt for discussion. Each learner creates a new discussion thread to respond to the prompt. Following the creation of these discussion threads, learners may respond to different learners' discussion posts. In Edmodo, instructors may post a discussion prompt and the learners respond to it in one thread.

Discussion in virtual environments is not limited to text. VoiceThread is a cloud-based tool that allows learners to integrate voices, images, and responses on one digital platform, facilitating asynchronous discussions between the author and readers (Parenti & Chen, 2015). In a middle level environment specifically, Wood, Stover, and Kissel (2013) found that the alternative, digital approach of VoiceThreads increased learner interest and engagement. VoiceThread fosters sense of community by providing a platform for learners to express their ideas and communicate with a genuine audience and creating a "personal experience that extends beyond traditional writing activities" (Stover, Kissel, Wood, & Putman, 2015, p. 345). Voice Thread allows middle level learners to interact around images, documents, videos, and audio (Brunvard & Byrd, 2011; Millard, 2010).

**Collaborative learning tools.** Teachers can use computer-supported collaborative learning (CSCL) tools for asynchronous collaboration (Clark & Mayer, 2008). Examples of CSCL tools include blogs, wikis (e.g., Wikispaces), and collaborative, cloud-based tools such as GoogleDocs (Clark & Mayer, 2008; Hughes, Read, Jones, & Mahometa, 2015). The key elements of these tools are collaboration and communication (DiBlasi, 2010). Virtual instructors can ask students to use CSCL tools to debate, analyze, create multimedia products, create collaborative texts and papers, and complete group work through several mediums, that is, text, graphics, audio, and video (McCoy, 2014; Pope, 2013). These elements create active learning (DiBlasi, 2010) while also strengthening sense of community and promoting critical thinking (Blau & Caspi, 2009; Herro, 2014; Zheng, Lawrence, Warschauer, & Lin, 2015).

**Social-networking technologies.** Social-networking technologies such as Facebook and Twitter are an additional option for facilitating learner-to-learner and learner-to-instructor interactions and supporting community asynchronously (Pope, 2013). More than 70% of 9 to 17-year-old learners utilize social networking sites weekly and are adept in using social media technologies to interact with others (Pope, 2013). In reference to secondary learners, Pope (2013) stated:

> These web-based environments provide promise as a space where learners have the opportunity to work together to form communities which can make learner's virtual experiences richer as they feel membership in a scholastic network that satisfies their need to socialize while learning from others. (p. 2)

Based on their research, Rockinson-Szapkiw, Heuvelman-Hutchinson, and Spaulding (2014) found that learners who used social-networking technologies to interact with fellow learners outside of the classroom demonstrated a higher sense of connectedness than those who did not interact using these technologies outside of the classroom. Moreover, social networking technologies have been shown to promote discourse, create learner networks, provide a means for sharing information globally (thus, outside of the classroom walls), support global citizenship, and to provide multiple avenues for learners to communicate in ways that are socially comfortable (Subramony, 2017). As such, social networking tools cross the invisible barrier of academic versus social communication and provide a means for learners to communicate about academic content that also aligns with how learners communicate in their daily lives. Learners can therefore discuss ideas, share information, and engage in ongoing discourse that transcends the walls of the classroom.

## Synchronous Technologies

Synchronous technologies enable learners to interact with others in real time with a richness of communication provided by social and language cues (Hrastinski, 2008; Rockinson-Szapkiw & Wendt, 2015). Media richness theory proposes that communication is better and clearer in face-to-face communication (Trevino, Lengel, & Daft, 1987). While increasing sense of community, synchronous technologies can be used to decrease feelings of isolation and encourage learner confidence (Wang & Chen, 2007), both important to the success of middle level virtual learners (Edwards & Rule, 2013). At the middle level, web conferencing software has proven to be an effective synchronous technology tool to create a sense of community (Pope, 2013). Providing opportunities for learners to hear and see their classmates and instructors reduces feelings of distance and increases learner interaction and satisfaction levels (Pope, 2013) and, thus, community. With the adoption of Google Apps and Google Classroom within many secondary schools, Google Hangouts are a common way to facilitate web conferencing. Web conferencing can also occur through Blackboard Collaborate, Adobe Connect, and Cisco Telepresence, which offer recording functionality to extend conversations, enable reflection, facilitate monitoring of participation, and to facilitate grading.

## CONCLUSION

A sense of community is fundamental to middle level learners' learning and development, and creating a sense of community for virtual middle level learners is crucial in the promotion of critical discourse and deep learning in the classroom (Edwards & Rule, 2013; Garrison & Cleveland-Innes, 2005; Pope, 2013). Situated within Garrison et al.'s (2000) CoI framework, this chapter offers virtual teacher evidence-based and empirically supported practices for instructional design and delivery to create teaching, social, and cognitive presence in their virtual classrooms. This chapter also provides tools to implement these practices; thus, creating a community of inquiry for middle learners construction of deep and meaningful knowledge (Drysdale, 2013) in the virtual classroom.

## REFERENCES

Abfalter, D., Zaglia, M. E., & Mueller, J. (2012). Sense of virtual community: A follow up on its measurement. *Computers in Human Behavior, 28*(2), 400–404.

Akyol, Z., & Garrison, D. R. (2011). Understanding cognitive presence in an online and blended community of inquiry: Assessing outcomes and processes for deep approaches to learning. *British Journal of Educational Technology, 42*(2), 233–250.

Akyol, Z., Garrison, D., & Ozden, M. (2009). Online and blended communities of inquiry: Exploring the developmental and perceptional differences. *International Review of Research in Open and Distance Learning, 10*(6), 65–83.

Anderson, T., Rourke, L., Garrison, D. R., & Archer, W. (2001). Assessing teaching presence in a computer conference environment. *Journal of Asynchronous Learning Networks, 5*(2), 1–17.

Arbaugh, J. B. (2001). How teacher immediacy behaviors affect student satisfaction and learning in web-based courses. *Business Communication Quarterly, 64*(4), 42–54.

Archambault, L., Debruler, K., & Freidhoff, J. R. (2014). K–12 online and blended teacher licensure: Striking a balance between policy and preparedness. *Journal of Technology and Teacher Education, 22*(1), 83–106.

Berge, Z. L. (1995). Facilitating computer conferencing: Recommendations from the field. *Educational Technology, 35*(1), 22–30.

Blau, I., & Caspi, A. (2009, October). *Sharing and collaborating with Google Docs: The influence of psychological ownership, responsibility, and students' attitudes on outcome quality*. Paper presented at the World conference on E-learning in Corporate, Government, Healthcare, and Higher Education. Vancouver, Canada. Retrieved from https://www.learntechlib.org/primary/p/32961/

Borup, J., Graham, C. R., & Drysdale, J. S. (2014). The nature of teacher engagement at an online high school. *British Journal of Educational Technology*, *45*(5), 793–806.

Brunvard, S., & Byrd, S. (2011). Using VoiceThread to promote learning engagement and success for all students. *Teaching Exceptional Children*, *43*(4), 28–37.

Buraphadeja, V. & Kumnuanta, J. (2011). Enhancing the sense of community and learning experience using self-paced instruction and peer tutoring in a computer laboratory course. *Australasian Journal of Educational Technology*, *27*(8), 1338–1355.

Chauhan, S., Naseem, A., & Rashwan, E. (2016). Developing a quality checklist for designing blended learning course content. *International Journal of Information and Education Technology*, *6*(3), 224–227.

Chen, B., deNoyelles, A., Zydney, J., & Patton, K. (2017). Creating a community of inquiry in large-enrollment online courses: An exploratory study on the effect of protocols within online discussions. *Online Learning*, *21*(1), 165–188.

Christophel, D. M., & Gorham, J. (1995). A test-retest analysis of student motivation, teacher immediacy, and perceived sources of motivation and demotivation in college classes. *Communication Education*, *44*(4), 292–306.

Clark, R. C., & Mayer, R. E. (2008). *E-Learning and the science of instruction*. San Francisco, CA: Pfeiffer.

DiBlasi, H. (2010). Tools for schools: What's new with web 2.0. *Middle Ground*, *13*(3), 8–9.

Drysdale, J. S. (2013). *Online facilitators and sense of community in K–12 online learning*. (Doctoral dissertation). Retrieved from ProQuest Dissertations & Theses Global. (Order No. 3613327)

Dulaney, E. (2013). Does the credibility of the presenter influence acceptance of content in the classroom. *American International Journal of Social Science*, *2*(4), 14–20.

Dunn, M. (2012). *The effect of Voice Thread® integration on high school students' anxiety and oral proficiency in the foreign language classroom*. (Doctoral dissertation). Retrieved from ProQuest Dissertations & Theses Global. (Order No. 3546182)

Edwards, C., & Rule, A. (2013). Attitudes of middle school students: Learning online compared to face to face. *Journal of Computers in Mathematics and Science Teaching*, *32*(1), 49–66.

Fink, L. D. (2005). *A self-directed guide to designing courses for significant learning*. Retrieved from http://www.niu.edu/facdev/_pdf/icd/selfdirectedguide.pdf

Flores, M. M., & Kaylor, M. (2007). The effects of a direct instruction program on the fraction performance of middle school students at-risk for failure in mathematics. *Journal of Instructional Psychology*, *34*(2), 84–94.

Garrison, D. R., Anderson, T., & Archer, W. (2000). Critical inquiry in a text-based environment: Computer conferencing in higher education. *The Internet and Higher Education*, *2*(1), 87–105.

Garrison, D. R., & Arbaugh, J. B. (2007). Researching the community of inquiry framework: Review, issues, and future directions. *Internet and Higher Education, 10*(1), 157–172.

Garrison, D. R., & Cleveland-Innes, M. (2005). Facilitating cognitive presence in online learning: Interaction is not enough. *American Journal of Distance Education, 19*(3), 133–148.

Giles, S. M., Pankratz, M. M., Jackson-Newsom, J., Hansen, W. B., Bishop, D., Dusenbury, L., & Gottfredson, N. (2012). The role of teacher communicator style in the delivery of a middle school substance use prevention program. *Journal of Drug Education, 42*(4), 393–411.

Gorham, J. (1988). The relationship between verbal teacher immediacy and student learning. *Communication Education, 37*(1), 40–53.

Grisham, D. L., & Wolsey, T. D. (2006). Recentering the middle school classroom as a vibrant learning community: Students, literacy, and technology intersect: Threaded discussion groups were used in middle school classrooms to facilitate literature study and build a sense of community. *Journal of Adolescent & Adult Literacy, 49*(8), 648–660.

Herro, D. (2014). Techno savvy: A web 2.0 curriculum encouraging critical thinking. *Educational Media International, 51*(4), 259–277.

Hrastinski, S. (2008). The potential of synchronous communication to enhance participation in online discussions: A case study of two e-learning courses. *Information & Management, 45*(7), 499–506.

Hughes, J. E., Read, M. F., Jones, S., & Mahometa, M. (2015). Predicting middle school students' use of web 2.0 technologies out of school using home and school technological variables. *Journal of Research on Technology in Education, 47*(4), 211–228.

Hung, M. L., & Chou, C. (2015). Students' perceptions of teachers' roles in blended and online learning environments: A comparative study. *Computers & Education, 81*(1), 315–325.

Jones, P., Naugle, K., & Kolloff, M. (2008, March). Teacher presence: Using introductory videos in hybrid and online courses. *Learning Solutions Magazine*, 1–3.

Ke, F. (2010). Examining online teaching, cognitive, and social presence for adult students. *Computers and Education, 55*(2), 808–820.

Kozan, K., & Richardson, J. C. (2014). Interrelationships between and among social, teaching, and cognitive presence. *Internet and Higher Education, 21*(1), 68–73.

Kupczynski, L., Ice, P., Wiesenmayer, R., & McCluskey, F. (2010). Student perceptions of the relationship between indicators of teaching presence and success in online courses. *Journal of Interactive Online Learning, 9*(1), 23–43.

McCoy, L. P. (2014). Web 2.0 in the mathematics classroom. *Mathematics Teaching in the Middle School, 20*(4), 237–242.

McInnerney, J. M., & Roberts, T. S. (2004). Online learning: Social interaction and the creation of a sense of community. *Educational Technology & Society, 7*(3), 73–81.

McIsaac, M. S., & Gunawardena C. N. (1996). Distance education. In D. H. Jonassen (Ed.), *Handbook of research for educational communications and technology: A project of the Association for Educational Communications and Technology* (pp. 403–437). New York, NY: Simon & Schuster Macmillan.

McMillan, D. W., & Chavis, D. M. (1986). Sense of community: A definition and theory. *Journal of Community Psychology, 14*(1), 6–23.

Millard, M. (2010). Analysis of interaction in an asynchronous CMC environment. In W. Hall, J. Hendler, C. Lagoze, C. Pope, & A. T. Schreiber, A. T. (Eds.), *Proceedings of the Web Science Conference WebSci10: Extending the Frontiers of Society*. Raleigh, NC: OnLine. Retrieved from http://citeseerx.ist.psu.edu/viewdoc/download?doi=10.1.1.468.5655&rep=rep1&type=pdf

Nelson, B., & Erlandson, B. (2008). Managing cognitive load in educational multi-user virtual environments: Reflection on design practice. *Educational Technology Research & Development, 56*(5/6), 619–641.

Oztok, M., Zingaro, D., Brett, C., & Hewitt, J. (2013). Exploring asynchronous and synchronous tool use in online courses. *Computers & Education, 60*(1), 87–94.

Parenti, M. A., & Chen, X. (2015). Growing reading fluency: Engaging readers with technology and text. *I-Manager's Journal on School Educational Technology, 10*(4), 1–6.

Pope, C. (2013). *Digital distance learning communities: Teachers' beliefs about community in K–12 online education* (Doctoral dissertation). Retrieved from ProQuest Dissertations & Theses Global. (Order No. 3559853)

Rachels, J., & Rockinson-Szapkiw, A. J. (2017). The effects of a mobile gamification app on elementary students' Spanish achievement and self-efficacy. *Computer Assisted Language Learning, 31*(2), 72–89.

Resnick, M. D., Bearman, P. S., Blum, R. W., Bauman, K. E., Harris, K. M., Jones, J., … Udry, J. R. (1997). *Protecting adolescents from harm: Findings from the National Longitudinal Study on Adolescent Health*. Boston, MA: McGraw-Hill College.

Rheingold, H. (1993). *The virtual community: Homesteading the electronic frontier*. Reading, MA: Addison-Wesley.

Richardson, J. C., & Ice, P. (2010). Investigating students' level of critical thinking across international strategies in online discussions. *Internet and Higher Education, 13*, 52–59.

Rockinson-Szapkiw, A. J., Heuvelman-Hutchinson, L., & Spaulding, L. S. (2014). Connecting online: Can social networking and other technology support doctoral connectedness? *Journal of University Teaching & Learning Practice, 11*(3), 1–13.

Rockinson-Szapkiw, A. J., & Wendt, J. L. (2015). Technologies that assist in online group work: A comparison of synchronous and asynchronous computer mediated communication technologies on learners' learning and community. *Journal of Educational Media and Hypermedia, 24*(3), 263–279.

Rovai, A. P. (2002). Development of an instrument to measure classroom community. *Internet & Higher Education, 5*(3), 197–211.

Rovai, A. P., & Jordan, H. M. (2004). Blended learning and sense of community: A comparative analysis with traditional and fully online graduate courses. *International Review of Research in Open and Distance Learning, 5*(2), 1–12.

Royal, M. A., & Rossi, R. J. (1997). *Schools as communities. Eric Digest. Number 111*. Retrieved from ERIC database. (ED405641)

Russo, T. C., & Campbell, S. W. (2004). Perceptions of mediated presence in an asynchronous online course: Interplay of communication behaviors and medium. *Distance Education, 25*(2), 215–232.

Schulte, L. E., Shanahan, S., Anderson, T. D., & Sides, J. (2003). Student and teacher perceptions of their middle and high schools' sense of community. *School Community Journal, 13*(1), 7–33.

Shea, P., Li, C. S., & Pickett, A. (2006). A study of teaching presence and student sense of learning community in fully online and web-enhanced college courses. *Internet and Higher Education, 9*(1), 175–190.

Stover, K., Kissel, B., Wood, K., & Putman, M. (2015). Examining literacy teachers' perceptions of the use of VoiceThread in an elementary, middle school, and a high school classroom for enhancing instructional goals. *Literacy Research and Instruction, 54*(4), 341–362.

Subramony, D. P. (2017). Revisiting instructional technologists' inattention to issues of cultural diversity among stakeholders. In A. D. Benson, R. Joseph, & J. L. Moore (Eds.), *Culture, learning, and technology: Research and practice* (pp. 28-43). New York, NY: Routledge.

Swan, K., Shea, P., Richardson, J., Ice, P., Garrison, D. R., Cleveland-Innes, M., & Arbaugh, J. B. (2008). Validating a measurement tool of presence in online communities of inquiry. *E-Mentor, 2*(24), 1–12.

Trevino, I. K., Lengel, R. K., & Daft, R. I. (1987). Media symbolism, media richness and media choice in organizations. *Communication Research, 14*(5), 553–574.

Tu, C. H., & Corry, M. (2002, April). *Social presence and critical thinking for online learning.* Paper presented at the annual meeting of the American Educational Research Association, New Orleans, LA.

Tu, C. H., & McIsaac, M. (2002). The relationship of social presence and interaction in online classes. *American Journal of Distance Education, 16*(3), 131–150.

Wang, Y., & Chen, N. S. (2007). Online synchronous language learning: SLMS over the Internet. *Innovate, 3*(3), 1–7.

Watson, J., Murin, A., Vashaw, L., Gemin, B., & Rapp, C. (2012). *Keeping pace with K–12 online and blended learning: An annual review of policy and practice.* Evergreen, CO: Evergreen Education Group. Retrieved from https://www.inacol.org/wp-content/uploads/2015/03/KeepingPace2012.pdf

Weiner, C. (2003). Key ingredients to online learning: adolescent students study in cyberspace–the nature of the study. *International Journal on E-Learning, 2*(3), 44–50.

Wendt, J. L., & Rockinson-Szapkiw, A. J. (2014). The effect of collaboration on middle school student science misconceptions as an aspect of science literacy. *Journal of Research in Science Teaching, 51*(9), 1103–1118.

Wendt, J. L., & Rockinson-Szapkiw, A. J. (2015). The effect of online collaboration on adolescent sense of community in eighth-grade physical science. *Journal of Science Education and Technology, 24*(5), 671–683.

Wood, K. D., Stover, K., & Kissel, B. (2013). Using digital VoiceThreads to promote 21st century learning. *Middle School Journal, 44*(4), 58–64.

Zhang, H., Lin, L., Zhan, Y., & Ren, Y. (2016). The impact of teaching presence on online engagement behaviors. *Journal of Educational Computing Research*, *54*(7), 887–900.

Zheng, B., Lawrence, J., Warschauer, M., & Lin, C. H. (2015). Middle school students' writing and feedback in a cloud-based classroom environment. *Technology, Knowledge and Learning*, *20*(2), 201–229.

CHAPTER 7

# CREATING A COMMUNITY OF CARE IN THE MIDDLE LEVEL VIRTUAL CLASSROOM

**Brooke B. Eisenbach**
*Lesley University*

**Paula Greathouse and Mary Kirk**
*Tennessee Tech University*

Louis, Murphy, and Smylie (2016) posited the concept of caring in educational contexts is "powerful in terms of addressing the immediate needs of students, teachers, and families, and may also promote the longer term outcomes of belonging and engagement, a sense of personal well-being, and academic success" (p. 312), thus making the nature of teacher-student relationships a critical component in the academic and personal success of students. Because the absence of caring in the classroom can be detrimental to a student's academic success and well-being (Rodriguez, 2008), caring teachers are fundamental to any learning context (Anderson, Standerford, & Imdieke, 2010; Louis et al., 2016; Murphy & Torres, 2014), as they help students discover the drive to succeed in their education (Cassidy & Bates, 2005; Dillon, 1989; Garza, 2009) and assist students in developing a

*The Online Classroom:*
*Resources for Effective Middle Level Virtual Education*, pp. 121–136
Copyright © 2018 by Information Age Publishing
All rights of reproduction in any form reserved.

sense of belonging (Cassidy & Bates, 2005; Rovai, 2007), well-being (Garza, 2009) and moral development (Alder, 2002), regardless of content or grade level. Most teachers have been equipped with the tools and strategies to create these caring relationships, which lays the foundation for communities of care (Roth & Brooks-Gunn, 2003). Drawing on theories of care, education programs introduce teacher candidates to strategies that build positive teacher-student relationships and ways in which this relationship can foster students' self-efficacy, all in an effort to maximize student learning (Rovai, 2007). While the strategies and approaches taught within these programs are effective in creating a community of care in the brick-and-mortar classroom, in what ways do they translate to the virtual classroom?

Enhanced use of modern technology and an increase in online learning environments does not change the basic nature and developmental needs of our middle level students. If anything, the growing trend in online student learning and attrition lends itself to the need for online classrooms that foster student empowerment through autonomy and sense of self-efficacy (Baran, Correia, & Thompson, 2011). So then, how do teachers meet these needs within the online middle level classroom? One way teachers may accomplish is by drawing on relational care theory (Noddings, 2012). In doing so, virtual teachers can work to address the individual needs of each student, thereby possibly decreasing online attrition and promoting student success through the creation of a virtual community of care.

In the end, middle level students desire unique and genuine relationships with others. According to Richardson and Swan (2003), "The model (classroom) should not only present the information and materials to students, but also incorporate the social aspects of learning in both the design and instruction of online courses" (p. 81). In other words, it is necessary that the act of caring for students reach farther than academics; it must also reach the early adolescent on a social and emotional level. A caring classroom community must include knowing and showing interest in students' experiences, as well as encouraging and instilling confidence, competence, and care. This chapter offers resources for virtual teachers on how to create a community of care in the virtual classroom. Through Noddings's relational care theory, we present resources and strategies that will equip teachers to better define and execute care in the virtual classroom.

## A REVIEW OF RELATIONAL CARE THEORY

Before we can offer virtual stakeholders resources and strategies for creating a community of care in the virtual context, we must first discuss the theory from which these suggestions stem. The term *care* can be tricky. When asked, most teachers would say they care for their students. What exactly does that mean? What does this care actually look like? Noddings (2012) suggested that to answer these questions we need to begin by examining the teacher-student relationship itself. In relational care ethics, there are two individuals—the "carer" and the "cared-for." The carer first devotes attention to the cared-for, making sure to listen to their individual needs, desires, and concerns. The carer then extends what Noddings referred to as "motivational displacement" (p. 53) upon the cared-for. Motivational displacement exists when the carer is motivated and is moved to action in an effort to "care" or meet the needs of the individual. For the interaction to be complete, the cared-for must receive the care. Teachers could demonstrate this reception in several different ways, such as a smile, a word of gratitude, or simply in having their expressed need met. Figure 7.1 demonstrates the cycle noted in (Noddings, 2012) relational care theory.

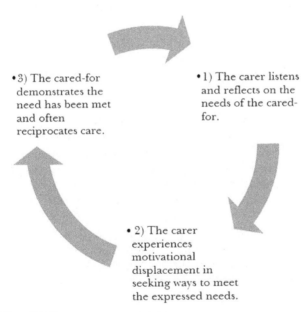

- 3) The cared-for demonstrates the need has been met and often reciprocates care.

- 1) The carer listens and reflects on the needs of the cared-for.

- 2) The carer experiences motivational displacement in seeking ways to meet the expressed needs.

*Source:* Noddings (2012).

**Figure 7.1.**   Relational care theory demonstrating cyclical process and reciprocity.

So, what does it mean to be a "caring teacher" through this theoretical framework? When one examines the tenets of a caring teacher with a focus on relational care, one begins by describing the teacher's willingness to listen. Unlike virtuous care, or assumed care, in which the teacher gives attention to what they or the institution believes to be the needs of the student, relational care involves listening to the expressed needs of the individual student, whether those needs are institutional in nature or other (Noddings, 2012). For instance, a "virtuous carer" might examine a student's grade, note a need to see them excel in the course, and choose to focus attention on the student's academic needs and progress claiming she would "thank me for this later" (Noddings, 2012). Whereas, a "relational carer" takes the time to talk with the student and listen to what it is they have to say. Why are they failing the course? What circumstances have led them here? What is it they *need* from me at this time? While both aspects of care address a focus on academics and academic needs, relational care provides opportunity to reflect on the expressed need, rather than an assumption of need.

Relational carers are willing to set aside their own interpretations and conclusions so they may focus on the needs expressed by the cared-for. Once the cared-for has expressed a need, relational carers take time to think (Noddings, 2012). Their goal is to achieve empathetic accuracy (Icckes, 1997; Noddings, 1992, 2012; Stueber, 2006). Rather than ask, "How would *I* feel if *I* were in this situation," relational carers strive to think and understand what the cared-for is currently experiencing. They could accomplish this through reflection, a necessary tenet of relational care (Noddings, 2012). Rather than jump to unwarranted conclusions, one must be willing to digest what they have learned and experienced and consider the avenues of action one might take in working to meet the expressed needs of their students. Upon reflecting, the teacher finds themselves motivated to take action. They consider the expressed need, the potential avenues for addressing the need, and they take steps to address the need. In doing so, they maintain a focus on reflecting and observation to ensure their action affected and met the needs of the student.

What sets Noddings's theory of relational care apart from many of the others, such as Mayeroff (1971), Tronto (1993), and Gilligan (1982) is Noddings's attention to the recipient's demonstration that the caring cycle is complete. It is not enough for the teacher to take action and assume the action has worked. Rather, it is important that the student demonstrate they have, in fact, had their expressed need noted and addressed.

The final tenet of a caring teacher is one who extends a moral climate in the classroom and beyond (Noddings, 2012). This means working to promote the moral development of each student so that we each learn to listen and care for one another. As students witness the teacher's attempts to listen and act on their expressed needs, it can encourage them to think outside themselves and take note of the needs of those around them.

Noddings's (2012) theory of relational care assists teachers in addressing the social, psychological, and educational needs of today's adolescent learners (Cassidy & Bates, 2005; Rivera-McCutchen, 2012). When experiencing relational care, students are more motivated to learn when they acquire a sense of confidence in their academic ability (Bandura, 1997; Eccles, Wigfield, & Schiefele, 1998) and forge a positive relationship with the teacher (Cassidy & Bates, 2005; Darling-Hammond & Bransford, 2005; Goodenow, 1993; Ryan & Powelson, 1991).

Demonstrating care in the classroom can assist students in furthering their motivation and academic engagement (Alder, 2002; Cassidy & Bates, 2005; Garza, 2009; Noddings, 1992, 2012). As we listen to their expressed needs and strive to meet those needs, students can grow in their feelings of safety, trust, and belongingness (Garza, 2009). In this way, they will be more inclined to take academic risks and engage in pro-active academic and social behavior (Noddings, 2012).

## TRADITION TO INNOVATION—TRANSITIONING RELATIONAL CARE TO THE VIRTUAL CLASSROOM

Noddings's (2012) theory of relational care ethics promotes the idea that while care is a global need and moral obligation, such care extends to those who surround us on a personal level. She holds lesser hope for our ability to extend immediate care on a wider, global level (Noddings, 1984, 2012). In other words, we are not capable of caring for those outside our personal context and connection as we are for those within our immediate vicinity. Although virtual teachers have the opportunity to interact with online learners within the technological context, it is not often that they have the chance to encounter students on a face-to-face level. Teachers cite a lack of personal connection with virtual learners as a key deficit to online instruction (Hawkins, Graham, & Barbour, 2012). Virtual teachers must make the effort to establish a social presence and sense of immediacy to encourage student motivation and course success (Hawkins et al., 2012; Murphy & Rodriguez-Manzanares, 2009; Picciano, 2002; Richardson & Swan, 2003). If this is the case, in what ways might relational care theory translate within the online classroom? The separation of space and time between teacher and student might hinder the forging and maintaining of relational care. In what ways can teachers establish a strong, intimate connection with students despite the apparent distance? What follows are strategies and suggestions for striving to enact relational care in the virtual middle level classroom.

### Relational Care Through Teacher Presence

To begin, it is important to establish presence with and between students. By teacher presence, we refer to the need for the teacher to be available and accessible to students as they work within the virtual course. Ideally, virtual learners need someone available for regular assistance in the course. Online learners often need a teacher available to assist them with coursework in a regular and timely manner. While some students take the initiative to reach out for assistance on a regular basis, others do their best to navigate the course independently, often striving to avoid contact or communication with the course instructor. A teacher with presence will make contact with each and every student throughout the course. What follows are some strategies the virtual teacher can implement as a means of establishing teacher presence.

**Greeting call.** At the start of the course, it is important to establish communication with the student and family. A great method for opening the line of communication is through an introductory greeting call (e.g., phone, text, e-mail, video chat). During this initial contact, take time to introduce yourself, your course and expectations, and get to know a little about the student and their family. What are their interests? What brings them to the course? Where and when do they plan to engage in the class? How can you, as their instructor, meet their needs in the class? Is there anything you should know as you strive to guide them through the course and content?

Find out more about the student's current knowledge and experience with online learning. Take time to walk them through the software and technological aspects of the class. Ensure they understand how to log into the course, access course content and assignments, submit coursework, and navigate the virtual space.

Some students might prefer contact through phone while others request communication via text, e-mail, or video chat. In following the understanding that relational care requires the carer take the time to listen, reflect, and act on the expressed need (Noddings, 2012), teacher presence provides teachers with opportunities to listen to the expressed needs of their students. A teacher's presence, though not physical in nature, provides students opportunity to express an immediate need and establish open communication. For this reason, be sure to ask about the student and family's preferred method of contact and availability throughout the week.

Teachers may reach out to offer a student assistance and find themselves speaking to a voicemail, rather than the student. For this reason, it is important for virtual teachers to continue in their attempts to connect with students and families and establish classroom expectations, parameters, and scheduling needs from the start. During initial communication, speak with the student and family regarding communication and contact expectations—expectations of the teacher as well as those of the student and family. What are the teacher's hours of availability? When does the student expect to log in to work in the course? When are the guardians available for assistance and contact? Setting a general schedule and guidelines for course interactions can further help reduce the tendency of miscommunication and failure to establish consistent presence within the online environment.

While presence is key to establishing a connection with students and families, it is important to be realistic in your general expectations and availability. As time and space separates teachers and students, some students may prefer to work online in the morning hours, while others sign-in throughout the evening. Teachers cannot be available to assist students 24 hours a day, just as students cannot be accessible for communication every hour of the day. For this reason, it is important to be clear in sharing your expectations, open to the needs of the student, but also honest in setting guidelines that promote student learning and each individual's outside needs and schedule.

**Introductory e-mail.** Follow up your greeting call with an introductory e-mail. In your e-mail, be sure to reiterate the process, expectations, and contact information for the student and family. In addition, share some information about yourself, including a photograph. Let the student see that there is a person on the other side of the computer screen. In addition, share what you learned and heard from the greeting call. Reiterate what the family shared with you to further ensure you heard and understood what they intended for you to understand.

You might also request a response from students and families. Confirm that they received your correspondence and see if they are willing to share a photograph and information about their own experience, culture, and home. This will help you ensure that you are reaching out to the correct e-mail addresses, and that you are establishing an open line of communication.

## Relational Care Through Dialogue

Once the teacher has established presence, it is important to establish relational care by initiating dialogue, maintaining clarity and quality during teacher to student communication, being prompt in providing a response to student contact or request for support, being accessible to students, and engaging in self-disclosure. In this way, the teacher is able to note expressed needs, and reflect on ways to respond (Noddings, 2012). Whether the teacher is reaching out in an attempt to encourage student work, or simply to catch up on student experiences outside of school, successful attempts at establishing dialogue provide virtual teachers the opportunity to learn more about students, and in turn, find additional ways to assist them in the course. In addition, such dialogue can make teachers aware of outside demands for student time and attention—demands that might affect their ability to work in the course in a given week. For instance, just as middle level learners in the brick-and-mortar school engage in activities, sports, hobbies, and familial engagements outside of the classroom, middle level virtual learners engage in activities like these outside of school. Yet, unlike the traditional classroom setting in which students and teachers interact daily, absences are obvious, and conversation can flourish, the distance associated with virtual learning can impede a teacher's ability to identify student needs and interests. Dialogue via channels such as phone, text, or online communication can help the virtual teacher maintain contact with online learners and engage in conversation that provides information regarding the student's time away from the course, and students' interests that teachers can use within the course curriculum and discussions.

In addition to providing academic assistance, continuous dialogue can also result in discussions that encourage personal disclosure and relationship building. Dialogue provides opportunity to establish a personalized approach to the course that can ease student stress, and provide the individualized scaffolding necessary for student success. Just as a traditional middle level teacher might share some aspects of their life outside of the classroom to encourage a sense of safety and belonging in the classroom, it is important for virtual teachers to share their own humanity and personality with online learners. Online learning has the capability to become an isolated event. It is easy to forget there is a face and personality on the other side of the computer screen. By engaging in self-disclosure, and encouraging students to do the same, virtual teachers and students can become "real" and further set out to establish and maintain caring relationships.

However, just as in a traditional brick-and-mortar setting, some students do not seek a personal bond or relationship with the teacher. As educators, we may not connect with every student who passes through our classroom door. The online world is no different. Some students simply want to move forward in the class, complete their work, and earn the credit necessary for graduation. Such students often neglect to answer teacher calls, respond to e-mails, or reach out for communication unless they have a specific question concerning a lesson or assignment. Because the first tenant of relational care is to listen to the expressed need of the learner, in this case, the learner seeks a teacher who is available to discuss course assignments. For this reason, it is important to be available for such communication, and find effective ways of translating course material and content in a manner that is accessible for the individual student. What follows are strategies that virtual teachers can implement to accomplish this goal.

**Good News—Bad News.** In a traditional classroom setting, teachers can hold weekly class meetings and provide students opportunity to share out information and experiences of personal significance. Opening the classroom to such meetings allows middle level students the opportunity to further the connections and relationships that are vital to their social and emotional development. The same connections and relationships can occur in the virtual setting.

For "Good News—Bad News," take time during your established conversations to learn more about the experiences and day-to-day lives of your virtual learners. Perhaps they recently won an award or tournament. Maybe they have an upcoming recital or performance. Or, perhaps they have recently suffered a traumatic loss or witnessed the end of a significant relationship. Ask, listen, and reflect on what your students share with you. If appropriate, ask your student if they mind that you share their news with the class. If they give their approval, consider creating a distinct section of your outgoing correspondence that highlights student news. In this way, they see the significance of their story, and feel a stronger connection to peers they might not otherwise have the opportunity to get to know.

**Weekly newsletters.** Another strategy for maintaining strong communication in an effort to establish caring connections is the establishment of a weekly newsletter. Several websites offer free newsletter templates that allow you the opportunity to create and e-mail a regular newsletter containing information important to the course. For example, Constant Contact, Mail Chimp, and Canva. Canva is extremely easy to use, as the program walks you through every step of the process. It allows you to not only select the layout and colors, but also upload your own photos or images to include, which can make a newsletter more personal. If you prefer something simpler, or already have a design in mind, Microsoft Publisher serves as a viable option. Take into account your opening conversations and the knowledge you have acquired through student and family communication to identify the information you should share out in your weekly newsletters. You might remind students of approaching deadlines, online gatherings, or live lessons. You could personalize each newsletter to provide students and families with updates on the learner's course progress and course engagement. In addition, you could use this opportunity to continue to connect and share more of your own experiences and the experiences of your students outside of the virtual classroom. Newsletters provide opportunity to share academic expectations and progress, as well as maintain personal connections with students and families.

## Relational Care Through Observation

After establishing one's presence and means of open dialogue, it is important to remain observant of student behavior and demonstrated needs as a means of consideration and reflection on student needs. Unlike the traditional classroom, in which teachers can observe student behavior, body language, facial expressions, and open expression of emotion, virtual teachers must find ways to observe student needs via voice and written communication. Take notes and reflect on what students and families share in phone conversations. Read student texts and e-mails to identify the message and tone of the student's communication efforts. Examine student work submissions and feedback to gain a clear perspective of the student's ability, strengths, and areas of need. In addition, be sure to examine the silences. What is it the student is not saying? What appears to be missing from communication and dialogue?

For example, it is important to take note of students who struggle in particular lessons, and strive to identify ways to assist students in not only mastering course material, but finding confidence in their abilities as learners. Online teachers can use what they observe to tailor their communication and instructional attempts to meet the needs of virtual students. Whether this means implementing and utilizing a "student of the week" incentive to encourage a struggling student, or sending a personalized video e-mail to encourage students in their weekly effort, it is important to take time to observe and reflect on student communication each week. Observations of student work, contact, and correspondence provide insight into student lives outside of the classroom, and enhance the virtual teacher's ability to reflect on expressed needs. A virtual teacher can implement several strategies as a means of observation.

**Teacher notes.** In the traditional classroom, teachers have the opportunity to see and chat with students daily. The same is not always true for virtual teachers. In fact, when teaching in an asynchronous classroom, students and teachers can spend days—maybe even weeks—without direct contact. For this reason, it is even more necessary for teachers to maintain detailed anecdotal notes of student interactions.

In an effort to really listen to the expressed needs of the student, be sure to maintain notes concerning the student's academic progress, engagement with the course (e.g., how often they sign into the class, frequency of coursework submission, strengths and areas of demonstrated need), as well as notes regarding conversation and outside experiences. In addition, try to focus in on the silences. Are there particular things that are not being said or shared? Are there aspects of the course that the student seems to avoid more so than others?

Then, reflect on your notes. Read your notes multiple times and see if themes begin to emerge. Keep your notes available, and when you see things change, consider what this might mean for the student's current needs and how they have changed over time.

**Family connection calls.** Another great way to observe and thereby listen to the students' expressed needs is through regular family connection and communication. Keeping in mind the family's preferred method of contact, try to reach out at least once a month, if not more often, to keep family members abreast of course and student progress. In today's traditional middle level classrooms, teachers and parents occasionally engage in parent teacher conferences. When students need additional support or assistance at home, the teacher might make a phone call to reach the guardian. The same is important for online middle level learners.

Online learning can be very isolating. When middle level learners sign in and participate in a virtual course on their own time and pace, many struggle to maintain active engagement and motivation to move forward. Students who lack an internal drive to succeed often disengage and fall behind. In addressing this particular need, as well as expressed needs observed in communication and course effort, it is important to maintain contact with family. Connection calls, texts, e-mails, or online correspondence can help guardians keep aware of student progress and offer additional support in motivating and engaging the virtual learner.

In addition, communicating with guardians and family members can provide the virtual teacher additional insights regarding the life and experiences of the student. When engaging in family communication, approach the connection with an openness to learning more about the student, the student's culture, and the student's home life experience. The connection call should reach beyond simply relaying information concerning the student's academic progress, and engage in an open dialogue regarding other aspects of the student's life.

## Relational Care Through Tailored Instruction

After listening, and reflecting on expressed needs, tailored instruction provides a means of addressing the expressed need of the student. The teacher strives to structure the course, coursework, content, or instructional methods to address the individual student needs. While there is variety in terms of the virtual teacher's flexibility within course structure and content, it is important for the teacher to identify ways in which they can adjust the course to meet the needs of the individual learner. What follows are strategies that can assist virtual teachers in tailoring instruction.

**Live lessons.** Some middle level virtual learners might demonstrate a need for more personalized, individual attention. For example, students who struggled to find success in the course without weekly support and course assistance. Perhaps they demonstrate a need for assistance in navigating the online platform. They might communicate a need for scaffolded instruction as they strive to master course material. In this case, the virtual teacher can work with the student through synchronous channels such as a phone call or online discussion space (e.g., Blackboard Collaborate,

Skype, or Zoom) to assist the student in understanding course material and skills. Such students might benefit from synchronous lesson sessions, or elect to meet with the instructor one-on-one in a virtual classroom for direct instruction and collaboration with peers. The live lesson structure provides the teacher opportunity to adapt the instruction, and encourage peer-to-peer collaboration on challenging concepts and ideas. If the online course permits customization, the teacher can adjust the course material or assigned reading to meet the individual needs of the student. If this is not the case, the teacher can identify supplemental material or online tools that can further assist the student in striving toward mastery.

At times, virtual middle level students might demonstrate a need for confidence and autonomy. In striving to address such expressed needs, it is important to further the teacher-to-student relationship, and communicate a belief in the student's ability to press forward and reach success. Online learning can be challenging for students, especially those new to this ever-growing educational landscape. Finding ways to communicate a growth mindset—one that promotes continued effort and personal development—can help middle level virtual learners further their sense of self-efficacy.

## Relational Care Through Personalized Learning

"Personalized learning" represents the virtual teacher's ability to attend to the overall education and well-being of their virtual students. It is important to take action to address expressed needs through adjusted instruction, regular and consistent attempts at communication, and expressed concern for students beyond the scope of their academics. Virtual teachers should consider the current living or personal conditions that might affect a student's sense of well-being and ability to thrive within the course. Today's online students come from a variety of backgrounds, cultures, and experiences. While some students log into class as they sit in a traditional classroom setting, surrounded by fellow students, others might log in while at home, while confined in a detention center, or while seeking treatment for personal physical or mental needs. It is important to consider the student's overall well-being and personal needs in your communication and attempts at establishing a connection with the student. Utilize this information in your attempts to assist the student in the course, at times extending your conversation to a more personalized connection and self-disclosure. The following strategies can help you keep in mind their current experience.

**Teaming.** Unlike the traditional classroom, there is no guidance counselor office down the hall, no administrator roaming the classrooms, and no regular peer-to-peer interactions taking place within the virtual setting.

For this reason, it is important that virtual teachers use what they observe and learn to find outlets for student assistance and growth. Maintaining communication with families, virtual colleagues, and virtual support systems can help online educators personalize learning in a way that meets the academic and social emotional needs of students. In addition, finding support through teaming structures—working with colleagues and sharing knowledge of student needs—can further assist virtual educators in terms of time management and ability to address individual learner needs. In working together to assist students in the virtual class, teachers are able to learn about the needs of one another's students, and might be more apt to address individual needs in a timely manner, all the while also having the time necessary to attend to our personal obligations outside of work. For instance, while one teacher is taking time to grade course assignments or focusing attention on non-school related needs, a teaming colleague can be accessible for student phone calls, e-mails, and text messages. Working with a fellow colleague provides opportunity to achieve not only a stronger work-life balance, but it also affords students the chance to gain the attention and assistance they need.

## Relational Care Through Recognition

Finally, Noddings's (2012) relational care theory identified the need for recognition of care. The cared-for must demonstrate that they received care for care to be complete. Unlike the traditional classroom, in which the teacher has opportunities to see and identify when they met a student's need, virtual educators must often look a bit deeper to see if they addressed a student's expressed need. Students might express their need has been met through e-mails, calls, or texts. At times, students respond to successful efforts at care with a "thank you," thereby demonstrating they received care. Other times, they respond by returning to work or demonstrating added effort on course assignments. It can be challenging to identify the caring act is complete, furthering the need to continue consistent dialogue and reflection.

## CONCLUSION

Creating a community of care in the classroom is essential to reach students. Yet, is it possible to generate relational care in virtual environments? Yes. However, there are limitations put in place by the educational organization, individual student, and the individual teacher— limitations that teachers need to consider and place in perspective if we hope to encourage relational care within the online classroom. Because attempts to know and care for students is fostered through the quality of interactions and not, necessarily, by the number of interactions (Rovai, 2007), it is important that virtual middle level teachers implement strategies that cultivate quality interactions if they are to truly create a community of care in the virtual classroom.

In the end, middle level students seek unique, genuine relationships and affirmation. Therefore, a caring classroom community must include knowing and showing interest as well as encouraging and instilling confidence in students. It is necessary that this level of care reach beyond academic needs; it must also reach the social and emotional needs of the students. Caring teachers possess the opportunity to create virtual spaces for middle level learners that allow them to grow academically as well as socially and emotionally. To accomplish this, virtual teachers must strive to establish and maintain open communication and reflect on the information shared by students and families. In other words, given the complexity of virtual school environments and the varying needs of the virtual middle level learner, it is imperative that virtual teachers create and maintain communities of care because it is these contexts that students will thrive the most.

## REFERENCES

Alder, N. I. (2002). Interpretations in the meaning of care. *Urban Education, 37*(2), 241–266.

Anderson, D. L., Standerford, N. S., & Imdieke, S. (2010). A self-study on building community in the online classroom. *Networks, 12*(2), 1–10.

Bandura, A. (1997). *Self-efficacy: The exercise of control.* New York, NY: W.H. Freeman and Company.

Baran, E., Correia, A., & Thompson, A. (2011). Transforming online teaching practice: Critical analysis of the literature on the roles and competencies of online teachers. *Distance Education, 32*(3), 421–439.

Cassidy, W., & Bates, A. (2005). "Drop-outs" and "push-outs": Finding hope at a school that actualizes the ethic of care. *American Journal of Education, 112*, 66–102.

Darling-Hammond, L., & Bransford, J. (Eds.). (2005). *Preparing teachers for a changing world: What teachers should learn and be able to do.* San Francisco, CA: Jossey-Bass.

Dillon, D. R. (1989). Showing them that I want them to learn and that I care about who they are: A microethnography of the social organization of a secondary low-track English reading classroom. *American Educational Research Journal, 26*(2), 227–259.

Eccles, J. S., Wigfield, A., & Schiefele, U. (1998). Motivation. In N. Eisenberg (Ed.), *Handbook of child psychology: Social, emotional, and personality development* (Vol. 3) (5th ed., pp. 1017–1095). New York, NY: Wiley.

Garza, R. (2009). Latino and white high school students' perceptions of caring behaviors: Are we culturally responsive to our students? *Urban Education, 44*(3), 297–321.

Gilligan, C. (1982). *In a different voice: Psychological theory and women's development.* Cambridge, MA: Harvard University Press.

Goodenow, C. (1993). Classroom belonging among early adolescent students: Relationships to motivation and achievement. *Journal of Early Adolescence, 13*(1), 21–43.

Hawkins, A., Graham, C. R., & Barbour, M. K. (2012). Everybody is their own island: Teacher disconnection in a virtual school. *The International Review of Research in Open and Distance Learning, 13*(2), 123–144.

Icckes, W. (1997). *Empathetic accuracy.* New York, NY: Guildford Press.

Louis, K. S., Murphy, J., & Smylie, M. (2016). Caring leadership in schools: Findings from an exploratory analysis. *Educational Administration Quarterly, 52*(2), 310–348.

Mayeroff, M. (1971). *On caring.* New York, NY: Harper & Row.

Murphy, E., & Rodriguez-Manzanares, M. A. (2009). Teachers' perspectives on motivation in high school distance education. *Journal of Distance Education, 23*(3), 1–24.

Murphy, J., & Torres, D. (2014). *Creating productive cultures in schools for students, teachers, and parents.* Thousand Oaks, CA: Corwin Press.

Noddings, N. (1984). *Caring: A feminine approach to ethics and moral education.* Berkeley, CA: University of California Press.

Noddings, N. (1992). *The challenge to care in schools.* New York, NY: Teachers College Press.

Noddings, N. (2012). The language of care ethics. *Knowledge Quest, 40*(4), 53–56.

Picciano, A. G. (2002). Beyond student perceptions: Issues of interaction, presence, and performance in an online course. *Journal of Asynchronous Learning Networks, 7*(1), 170–182.

Richardson, J., & Swan, K. (2003). An examination of social presence in online learning: Students' perceived learning and satisfaction. *Journal of Asynchronous Learning Networks, 7*(1), 68–88.

Rivera-McCutchen, R. L. (2012). Caring in a small urban high school: A complicated success. *Urban Education, 47*(3), 653–680.

Rodriguez, L. (2008). Teachers know you can do more: Understanding how school cultures of success affect urban high school students. *Educational Policy, 22*(5), 758–780.

Roth, J. L., & Brooks-Gunn, J. (2003). Youth development programs: Risk, prevention and policy. *Journal of Adolescent Health, 32*(3), 170–182.

Rovai, A. P. (2007). Facilitating online discussions effectively. *Internet and Higher Education, 10*(1), 7–88.

Ryan, P. L., & Powelson, C. L. (1991). Autonomy and relatedness as fundamental to motivation and education. *Journal of Experimental Education, 60*(1), 49–66.

Stueber, K. (2006). *Rediscovering empathy: Agency, folk psychology, and the human sciences*. Cambridge, MA: MIT Press.

Tronto, J. (1993). *Moral boundaries: A political argument for an ethic of care*. New York, NY: Routledge.

CHAPTER 8

# MENTORING VIRTUAL MIDDLE SCHOOLERS THROUGH THE USE OF A GUIDED ONLINE MENTORING LOOP

**Natalie Duvall**
*Johns Hopkins University*

**Matthew Duvall**
*Drexel University*

The thought of mentoring students probably conjures up images of lunch meetings, job shadowing, and huddling at tables in the library discussing issues and post-graduation goals. None of these images fit within the online environment that many middle schoolers find themselves in today. For this reason, some might doubt the mentorship's ability to effect change and growth in the life of a cyber-schooled adolescent. Yet a strong mentor/mentee relationship is possible and beneficial in today's educational landscape, using online tools (Duvall, 2016).

Research has shown that the middle school is an important time in determining a student's trajectory through the educational system. Middle

*The Online Classroom:*
*Resources for Effective Middle Level Virtual Education,* pp. 137–149
Copyright © 2018 by Information Age Publishing
All rights of reproduction in any form reserved.

school presents students with the opportunity for greater autonomy, but also offers new challenges. By the time students reach high school, they have largely developed their sense of what is possible—and impossible—for them to achieve. For example, a student might decide in middle school that she is not good at math or that becoming an engineer is an impossible career choice. While it is possible to overcome these perceptions, it becomes harder. Developing a mentoring relationship, particularly with a caring and capable adult, is important to help students recognize the challenges they are facing and develop realistic strategies for dealing with their issues. Such mentorships sometimes happen fortuitously, by accident, but schools can and should, also be proactive by fostering these relationships. It is especially important to adopt a system for matching students with mentors in a virtual setting, where the physical distance reduces the likelihood of such a relationship occurring by happenstance.

In this chapter, we detail why a strong mentorship program is essential to modern schools—including cyber schools—and how online learning organizations can develop and facilitate programs with the potential to be even more beneficial than standard and traditional face-to-face programs, especially in middle school, when effort and persistence begin to wane (Pajares & Graham, 1999). Through Relate to Motivate, a virtual mentoring loop, we offer virtual teachers and online schools with a framework for implementing a mentorship program.

## THE NEED FOR MENTORSHIP AT THE MIDDLE LEVEL

America's neediest youth, both socially and economically, face more barriers for academic success than their peers do (Becker & Luthar, 2002; Burris & Welner, 2005; Darling-Hammond, 2004). They have an increased risk of dropping out of school (Becker & Luthar, 2002) and demonstrate lower rates of academic achievement (Lareau, 2011; Rury & Mirel, 1997). Both of these risks can be linked to a lack of school engagement or academic motivation (Deci, Vallerand, Pelletier, & Ryan, 1991), poor, nonworkable visions of possible future selves (Cadely, Pittman, Kerpelman, & Adler-Baeder, 2011), and a lack of appropriate strategies for overcoming obstacles (Gollwitzer, Oettingen, Kirby, Duckworth, & Mayer, 2011). Online education compounds these factors for students. In some cases, researchers estimated that students are twice as likely to drop out of online courses as traditional classes (Willging & Johnson, 2009).

When entering middle school and rising through high school, students' motivation drops (Otis, Grouzet, & Pelletier, 2005). This is most likely due to the very nature of schools themselves (Ryan & Deci, 2000). The transition from elementary school to middle school includes an emphasis on specific curricula and standardized core-based testing, as well as a transition in how schools handle things such as school absenteeism. The nature of high stakes testing deters internally regulated motivation (Stevens, Olivárez, & Hammond, 2006), as well as the way that students are disciplined for various school offenses like tardiness or absenteeism (Farkas, Grobe, Sheehan, & Shaun, 1990). Educators must counter this drop in motivation, because motivation is a predictor of academic success. In online education, student self-efficacy, which helps determine motivation, relates to dropout rate (Willging & Johnson, 2009). The less efficacious a student feels, the more likely they are to leave online education. One thing that research has shown to counter this limited motivation is a positive connection with an adult. To make this connection in an online setting is especially necessary when students and teachers are separated by distance and do not have similar face-to-face interactions as those in brick-and-mortar contexts.

Positive mentoring relationships are essential for fostering academic motivation in students. Relationships with teachers who demonstrate high expectations can increase internally regulated motivation (Jodry, Robles-Piña, & Nichter, 2004). However, sometimes students do not feel as if their schools and teachers hold the same values as their families and communities. When students believe that their home values do not mesh with those promoted by the school, academic motivation decreases (Flouri & Buchanan, 2002; Tanaka & Watanabea, 2012). If a student's home environment is not conducive to academic motivation, it is possible that appropriate mentorship can mediate this motivation, which is helpful for online learners who do not have the motivational stimulus found when surrounded by teachers and peers.

Research shows that mentorship programs can increase motivation, and enhance college and career readiness (Bierema & Merriam, 2002). Teachers who participate in these programs also benefit. They find more satisfaction in their jobs (Archambault & Crippen, 2009), which is especially helpful for teachers serving students from backgrounds of poverty because they are especially susceptible to feelings of burnout and a loss of efficacy (Hoy & Spero, 2005; Tucker et al., 2005). In virtual settings, where teachers might feel disconnected due to the daily face-to-face interaction found in brick-and-mortar schools, a mentorship program allows for increased relationship building. Additionally, while studies have shown that middle school students can lack focus in online learning when on their own, when teachers build in scaffolded supports within online tools, student focus improves (Zhang & Quintana, 2012).

While some might predict online programs would have more difficulty building mentoring relationships, the opposite can be true. The walls of race and class can stymy traditional face-to-face mentorship programs. However, an online format can transcend these barriers (Bierema

& Merriam, 2002). In some instances, students might find it easier to approach and engage with an adult virtually. Today, young people are very comfortable with online interactions. As of 2015, 92% of teenagers reported going online daily, while only 8% reported going online weekly or less frequently (Lenhart, 2015). In addition, nearly 75% of teenagers own or have access to a smartphone (Lenhart, 2015).

Unfortunately, in a study of online programs in 25 states, only 2% of virtual educators consider mentoring part of their job requirements (Archambault & Crippen, 2009). Of those teachers surveyed, many said their main goal was to help coach students within the content areas. Because the goal of the school system is to impart content knowledge, teachers should not consider mentoring to be a fringe or extra role, because mentoring not only has the ability to improve relationships but improve content delivery (Archambault & Crippen, 2009). School systems can rest assured that the time and resources invested in a mentoring program not only benefit students' long-term success, but also improve the content knowledge upon which states evaluate schools.

Connecting students with professional adult mentors, like teachers, provides a way to treat the student as a whole person with many different concerns and interests, rather than merely an empty vessel waiting for teachers to fill them with knowledge. It also provides teachers in virtual middle school settings the ability to better understand and address the social/emotional needs of their students, which can be difficult outside of face-to-face contact.

## RELATE TO MOTIVATE—
## AN ONLINE MENTORING RESOURCE

Relate to Motivate is an online application that was designed to foster mentoring relationships between adults and students. In this section, we provide a brief overview of the application functionality, and then describe why we designed it the way it is—key principles for making a virtual mentoring relationship successful.

Relate to Motivate provides students with sample scenarios and questions to answer. Students receive an e-mail when a new prompt is available. They log into the system, read the scenario or question, and then reply to the prompt (see Tables 8.1 & 8.2). If they do not respond within a set period—the default is a week—then the system e-mails them again, as well as alerting the administrator that their response is overdue. Mentors, who the system administrator matches with the students, receive an e-mail whenever a student responds to a prompt. They log into the system and then review the student's response. Then, they reply to the student. The application provides starter prompts for the mentor, to ensure that they do three things: respond specifically to the student's response, provide specific advice, and share a story about a time they were in a similar situation. The teacher can save their response as a draft. Once they mark it as completed, Relate to Motivate e-mails the student so they can review the teacher's response. Like the students, the teacher has a week to respond. This loop can continue indefinitely, with as many prompts and responses as desired. Next, we explain the key underlying principles that guided our design.

## Principle 1: Accessibility

Relate to Motivate is web-based, making it accessible from any device with a web browser. In our pilot study of the program, students most often used smartphones to access it, while the adults were more likely to use computers or laptops. The design was flexible enough that screens, lists, buttons, and so on were easy to identify and use, regardless of the device. This is important because the mentors and mentees need to be able to focus on relationship building, not how they can (or cannot) access the application.

## Principle 2: Timeliness

Relate to Motivate e-mails students and mentors to notify them when they need to check the application. The system sets a time limit on how long students could take to respond to tasks. In the pilot study, there was never a need for an administrator to follow up with students or mentors, but having an automatic report for overdue responses is important because the system will only work if users are using it actively.

## Principle 3: Effective Feedback

The application uses response stems to help mentors create research-based responses that help students with motivation, self-efficacy, and problem-solving skills. These are important factors in helping students see their future selves and the ways they feel about their ability to deal with school and life issues.

## Principle 4: Fostering Relationships

After the student responds to a prompt, the teacher provides feedback, and the student reviews that feedback, they can continue their conversation either through the application interface or by e-mail. In our pilot study, we paired students with teachers who had taught them in at least one class. We matched one student with a teacher she did not especially like, but after using the application, she reported that she was glad that teacher was her mentor because the advice she received was very valuable.

In our pilot study, we used four prompts. Even if the student and mentor only completed the assigned prompts/feedback, with no additional interaction, we found that by the fourth interaction, both the student and the teacher were writing more text and sharing more of their feelings with each other. One reason for this change is the nature of the feedback prompt for the mentor. Structuring the feedback in the specific way (i.e., acknowledgement, specific strategy, and shared story) builds trust and makes the student realize that the teacher is actually reading his or her response and providing personalized, relatable feedback.

## Principle 5: Using Data to Improve the Process

The final principle, and a key reason why we developed Relate to Motivate rather than using some other system, is to ensure the collection as much data as possible. First, you need to know how/where/when users are logging into the system. This can provide insight into what additional features/resources you might need. It is also important to be able to track the activity of the students and mentors to make sure they are participating actively. Finally, saving this data provides a way to identify high quality responses that administrators can use to refine the feedback prompts to improve mentor comments.

## DESIGNING AN ONLINE MENTORING SYSTEM

The design of Relate to Motivate implements a simple feedback loop and requires little student preparation, other than an explanation on how students need to proceed through the process. In using this program in the virtual context, virtual teachers/administrators need to allow for a pre-activity period where teachers get to know their students to pair them with a mentor. To begin, those in charge of administering the program could develop prompts that relate specifically to their students, whether it be helping them with their transition to the middle school or planning for their future. For a virtual setting, having students complete a short survey with both fixed choice and open-ended questions about challenges and goals could provide a base for creating prompts that would be relevant. Table 8.1 provides example prompts.

Teachers need to give students a short amount of time to respond to a single prompt—no more than a week. Teachers do not need to worry about

**Table 8.1.**
**Example Prompts**

| Situation | Prompt |
|---|---|
| Students are transitioning to an online environment or to middle school. | What part of cyber-school or middle school do you think will be most difficult for you to handle? How can you overcome those difficulties? |
| There is concern about students' retention. | Why is completing middle school important to your future? What could stop you from completing middle school? |
| Students seem disengaged from school. | What might keep you from doing your schoolwork? What strategies do you have for completing your schoolwork? |
| A student is disengaged from school, and educators know the reason for the disengagement. | Because you have to help with household chores, you do not often complete your coursework on time. What makes it most difficult to complete coursework? How could you overcome that obstacle? |
| Teachers are worried that a student has no workable school goals. | Imagine a future where you are about to drop out of school. What has happened to get you to that spot? What can you do to stay and finish? |

the length or presentation of these responses. Remember, it is thinking about the answers that matters most! No matter the length or material in the response, teachers need to answer by using all response stems and giving thorough feedback.

There are three parts to each teacher response. The first part deals specifically with the prompt and asks teachers to react to the content. The second portion asks teachers to provide specific advice to students. The third portion wraps up by discussing a time they were in a similar situation. Table 8.2 provides sample teacher feedback and possible student responses.

Relate to Motivate provides a structured, research-based framework to connect students and adult mentors in a way that improves student motivation and enables better problem-solving by using targeted feedback based on research around intrinsic motivation and possible selves theory. This targeted feedback is created by ensuring that the mentor's responses include specific elements (acknowledgement of the mentee's concerns, a specific and realistic strategy for dealing with the problem, and a shared story of a similar situation the mentor faced) to empower the mentee in

**Table 8.2.**
**Sample Prompts and Responses**

| Prompt | Student Response | Teacher Feedback |
|---|---|---|
| What part of cyber school do you think will be most difficult for you to handle? How can you overcome those difficulties? | I think it'll be hard for me to handle setting my own work schedule. I could overcome this by logging in every morning at 9 A.M. | Starting cyber-school can be difficult because there are no bells to tell you when to switch classes or teachers making sure you show up to class at a certain time. |
| | | When beginning a new cyber-school, it is helpful to think about how you will manage your time before you start classes. If you have a smartphone, you need to program reminders into it. You can set an alarm for every day at 10 A.M. that says, "Work on math lessons." The school's online calendar also has features you can use to map out due dates. |
| | | When I started teaching at Online Cyber School, I had to get used to working on various schedules. In fact, one time I missed responding to Principal Smith's e-mail because I had a week to do it and forgot about it! When I talked to Principal Smith about it, she suggested I schedule an hour every Wednesday for responding to emails. I have done this ever since and found it super helpful! |

Even though doing chores takes time and makes me tired, I could stay up late to finish.

Because you have other responsibilities, such as mowing the lawn and helping with household chores, you do not often complete your homework. What makes it most difficult to complete homework on the nights you have to work? How could you overcome that obstacle?

It is often difficult to manage both a job and school. School is like a job in itself, and I could imagine having two responsibilities would be overwhelming and very tiring.

Have you thought about working on your schoolwork for short periods when you have time? For example, set a timer for 15 minutes and do as much work as you can get done. Sleep is very important, especially when you are young, so is it possible to go to bed when you get home and then do work in the morning when you wake up? Online Cyber School has study counselors who can help you map out assignments. Have you talked to them about possible options?

When I was in high school, I worked every weekend. I had trouble completing the larger assignments because I never had more than an hour to work on them. What I ended up doing was dividing the larger assignments into smaller pieces and telling myself it was okay to only do portions of work a night. It was not the easiest thing to do, but with the help of some of my teachers, I was able to pull my grades up and graduate.

developing his or her own strategies. As described previously, a mentoring system of this type needs to include a number of prescribed prompts and accompanying feedback—the minimum we recommend is four. The system also provides a way for students and mentors to continue interacting through the system. Obviously, the predesigned prompts will not address every single issue for every single student. However, what the system does is aid in developing relationships. In our pilot study, teachers and students continued to interact with each other using e-mail even after the study was finished. Several students remarked that they felt the mentor really cared about their success, and they looked to them as valuable resources for advice about issues they encountered throughout the school year.

## STRATEGIES THE FOSTER THE MENTOR RELATIONSHIP BEYOND RELATE TO MOTIVATE

After the initial communication through Relate to Motivate or a similar system, there are additional ways to continue building the relationship between the mentor and the mentee. In an online environment, technology can be useful in facilitating these conversations. It is important for the mentor and mentee to stay in contact and communicate about what challenges the mentee is encountering and how he or she is handling those. The mentor needs to respond to these communications in a thoughtful and caring way, and, when possible, to follow the same pattern of responses as specified by Relate to Motivate. Some suggestions include:

- Weekly video chats;
- Weekly e-mails or phone calls;
- Virtual attendance to online events followed by a one-on-one discussion of topic;
- Development of online creative projects like art, text, video games, and so on by the mentee with input from the mentor; and
- Input from other mentors, which shows that the school is a community.

## KEY CONSIDERATIONS IN IMPLEMENTING A MENTORING PROGRAM IN THE VIRTUAL MIDDLE SCHOOL

Integrating a mentorship program into online middle school education is simple and effective. Using human resources already available, virtual schools can connect with students in a way that prepares them for future obstacles and improves academic and career outcomes. The Relate to Motivate system is a cost-effective and simple way to enhance student success. Those looking to implement the program in their virtual school need to make several considerations as they construct a successful program. To begin, it is important that virtual schools assign a staff member(s) to oversee mentor matching, creation of prompts, and completion of prompts. Next, after the staff leaders decide on the length of program and frequency of prompts, it is necessary to train staff members in the feedback loop and importance of change-oriented feedback. Feedback needs to be prompt, considerate, nonaccusatory, offer suggestions, and allow for student autonomy.

Matching students and staff is a crucial step in any mentoring program, including Relate to Motivate. To keep staff members' hands-on time manageable, we recommend assigning no more than ten students to each staff member. This number will require about an hour's worth of time for each prompt. If needed, allow for an introductory period between staff and students to help match mentor/mentee.

After pairing the mentors and mentees, students need to become aware of the program and how it works. To accomplish this, provide training for both students and staff on the software. Once all are versed in how the system works, teachers can deploy the first prompt. Keep a watchful eye on initial submissions from both students and staff to make sure they understand how to respond. Send reminders when students or staff members have not completed responses.

At the conclusion of the program, include reflection meetings with students and staff, in an effort to evaluate the effect of the program. Also, encourage the mentor/mentee relationship to continue through fun and off-program interactions. For example, have a time when students can ask mentors about their own educational stories. Incorporate games like mentor/mentee challenges and competitions across the school. Such activities support the continued communication between mentors and mentees.

## CONCLUSION

As middle schools seek to address the academic, social, and emotional development of middle school students, the National Middle School Association (2010) posited strong mentoring programs might be beneficial in meeting this goal. Komosa-Hawkins (2012) stated this is especially true for students who are at-risk for school failure. While some might predict that virtual schools would have more difficulty building mentoring relationships, the opposite can be true. In this chapter, we demonstrated that a strong mentor/mentee relationship in a virtual school is possible and beneficial in today's educational landscape. Such a relationship can further motivate and engage online middle school learners as they connect and relate to virtual instructors and advisors. Mentoring can add a layer of connection necessary for online learners to see they are not operating in isolation, and to see the humanity that exists on the other side of the computer screen. Through an examination of the Relate to Motivate program, we provided a framework for virtual schools and educators to begin constructing and fostering mentor/mentee relationships.

## REFERENCES

Archambault, L., & Crippen, K. (2009). K–12 distance educators at work: Who's teaching online across the United States. *Journal of Research on Technology in Education, 41*(4), 363–391.

Becker, B. E., & Luthar, S. S. (2002). Social-emotional factors affecting achievement outcomes among disadvantaged students: Closing the achievement gap. *Educational Psychologist, 37*(4), 197–214.

Bierema, L. L., & Merriam, S. B. (2002). E-mentoring: Using computer mediated communication to enhance the mentoring process. *Innovative Higher Education, 26*(3), 211–227.

Burris, C. C., & Welner, K. G. (2005). Closing the achievement gap by detracking. *The Phi Delta Kappan, 86*(8), 594–598.

Cadely, H. S., Pittman, J. F., Kerpelman, J. L., & Adler-Baeder, F. (2011). The role of identity styles and academic possible selves on academic outcomes for high school students. *Identity, 11*(4), 267–288.

Darling-Hammond, L. (2004). The color line in American education: Race, resources, and student achievement. *Du Bois Review, 1*(2), 213–246.

Deci, E. L., Vallerand, R. J., Pelletier, L. G., & Ryan, R. M. (1991). Motivation and education: The self-determination perspective. *Educational Psychologist, 26*(3/4), 325–346.

Duvall, N. (2016). *Relate to Motivate: An investigation of an online intervention geared toward increasing motivation and college and career readiness in students from backgrounds of poverty* (Unpublished doctoral dissertation). Johns Hopkins University, Baltimore, Maryland.

Farkas, G., Grobe, R. P., Sheehan, D., & Shuan, Y. (1990). Cultural resources and school success: Gender, ethnicity, and poverty groups within an urban school district. *American Sociological Review, 55*(1), 127–142.

Flouri, E., & Buchanan, A. (2002). What predicts good relationships with parents in adolescence and partners in adult life: Findings from the 1958 British birth cohort. *Journal of Family Psychology, 16*(2), 186–198.

Gollwitzer, A., Oettingen, G., Kirby, T., Duckworth, A., & Mayer, D. (2011). Mental contrasting facilitates academic performance in school children. *Motivation & Emotion, 35*(4), 403–412.

Hoy, A. W., & Spero, R. B. (2005). Changes in teacher efficacy during the early years of teaching: A comparison of four measures. *Teaching and Teacher Education, 21*(4), 343–356.

Jodry, L., Robles-Piña, R. A., & Nichter, M. (2004). Hispanic academic advancement theory: An ethnographic study of urban students participating in a high school advanced diploma program. *The High School Journal, 88*(2), 23–31.

Komosa-Hawkins, K. (2012). The impact of school-based mentoring on adolescents ' social-emotional health. *Mentoring & Tutoring: Partnership in Learning, 20*(3), 393–408.

Lareau, A. (2011). *Unequal childhoods: Class, race, and family life.* Berkley, CA: University of California Press.

Lenhart, A. (2015). *Teen, social media and technology overview 2015.* Washington, DC: Pew Research Center. Retrieved from http://www.pewinternet.org/2015/04/09/teens-social-media-technology-2015/

National Middle School Association, (2010). *This we believe: Keys to educating young adolescents.* Westerville, OH: Author.

Otis, N., Grouzet, F. M. E., & Pelletier, L. G. (2005). Latent motivational change in an academic setting: A 3-year longitudinal study. *Journal of Educational Psychology, 97*(2), 170–183.

Pajares, F., & Graham, L. (1999). Self-efficacy, motivation constructs, and mathematics performance of entering middle school students. *Contemporary Educational Psychology, 24*(2), 124–139.

Rury, J. L., & Mirel, J. E. (1997). The political economy of urban education. *Review of Research in Education, 22*(1), 49–110.

Ryan, R. M., & Deci, E. L. (2000). Self-determination theory and the facilitation of intrinsic motivation, social development, and well-being. *American Psychologist, 55*(1), 68–78.

Stevens, T., Olivárez, A., & Hamman, D. (2006). The role of cognition, motivation, and emotion in explaining the mathematics achievement gap between Hispanic and White students. *Hispanic Journal of Behavioral Sciences, 28*(2), 161–186.

Tanaka, M., & Watanabea, Y. (2012). Academic and family conditions associated with intrinsic academic motivation in Japanese medical students: A pilot study. *Health Education Journal, 71*(3), 358–364.

Tucker, C. M., Porter, T., Reinke, W. M., Herman, K. C., Ivery, P. D., Mack, C. E., & Jackson, E. S. (2005). Promoting teacher efficacy for working with culturally diverse students. *Preventing School Failure: Alternative Education for Children and Youth, 50*(1), 29–34.

Willging, P. A., & Johnson, S. D. (2009). Factors that influence students' decision to dropout of online courses. *Journal of Asynchronous Learning Networks, 13*(3), 115–127.

Zhang, M., & Quintana, C. (2012). Scaffolding strategies for supporting middle school students' online inquiry processes. *Computers & Education, 58*(1), 181–196.

# SECTION IV

## STRATEGIES

CHAPTER 9

# MAKING THE LEAP FROM TRADITIONAL TO VIRTUAL

## Resources and Strategies for Teaching Middle Level Learners Online

**Jeremy Wendt and Jason Beach**
*Tennessee Tech University*

Although the concept of online teaching and virtual learning has existed in various formats for many years, the evolution of technology and resources have created educational avenues for students of all ages. As students have unique intellectual and developmental needs (Bloom, Engelhart, Furst, Hill, & Krathwohl, 1956; Gardner, 2011), educators continually innovate and explore ways to guide every student to success. Middle level learners and teachers are no different. In their vision statement, *This We Believe*, the Middle School Association (NMSA, 2010) sets forth their agenda for supporting the individual and unique needs of middle level learners. Outlined within their vision are reminders that the implementation of digital tools and strategies open new pathways and opportunities to provide an education that can adapt to the needs of every learner. Throughout this chapter,

*The Online Classroom:*
*Resources for Effective Middle Level Virtual Education*, pp. 153–166
Copyright © 2018 by Information Age Publishing
All rights of reproduction in any form reserved.

we provide tools and resources that will aid in the search for the best strategies to teach middle level learners within the virtual classroom. As new applications (apps), websites, and tools appear daily, it is important to keep in mind the big picture and focus on the overall concepts presented here to select the tools appropriate to meeting each student's individual needs.

## THE ONLY CONSTANT IS CHANGE

With more than 20 years of teaching experience, Mr. Jackson has been a consistently successful teacher in his science courses. However, over the past few years, he has observed a shift in learning styles and interests in his courses, but he has not been able to nail down the discrepancy. When his principal first approached him with the opportunity to teach two of his sections online and make them available to other middle schools in the district, he was not onboard. Watching other teachers in his district struggle, while trying to implement the latest technologies into their pedagogy, made him very apprehensive about trying something new. After all, he had seen new strategies and technologies come and go through the years with varying levels of success and failure. After hearing from his principal that over 5.8 million postsecondary students participated in some form of distance education, he knew it was only a matter of time before secondary schools would start participating in this approach to learning (Allen & Seaman, 2016). When a professional development opportunity focusing on teaching using digital tools cycled through his inbox, he saw it as a sign that he should explore new ways to reach the students in his classroom. Given the purpose of this handbook, to provide resources for middle level virtual educators in the teaching of virtual middle level students, we draw on Mr. Jackson's experiences in this chapter to provide readers with tools and strategies to accomplish this goal. Therefore, what follows are discussions of approaches, resources, and technological tools that he found useful as he began to build and adapt into a new style of teaching.

## WHERE TO START

The first step in crafting an effective online middle level classroom is researching platforms and tools available to virtual teachers and students, along with taking time to seek out experts and supportive networks for online teaching. With more than a million applications (apps) at your fingertips, it is nearly impossible to sort and filter the good and the bad apps without a little guidance. The websites, Commonsense.org and TeachersWithApps.com, are two excellent resources to assist educators in narrowing down the most useful apps and sites for teachers and students. These sites provide expert ratings and advice that will increase the chances of finding the perfect set of apps for a classroom's needs. The experts develop ratings through several methods including practicing educator reviews, input, rubrics, and independent sources to avoid influence by commercial developers.

While the resources above provide virtual teachers with a place to start, there may still be an uncertainty as to how the virtual tools and strategies work. Seeking out teachers who are experienced with virtual teaching, or who have experimented in implementing enhanced curriculum with digital tools, is a logical next step. Novice virtual teachers should be sure to join an online community focused on virtual teaching, essentially creating an instant support network. But, where can they find these? Edutopia's online-learning community group has hundreds of pages of resources, blogs, discussions, and videos to support teaching online and in hybrid contexts. Additionally, becoming members of groups such as Edutopia, International Society for Technology in Education, or International Association for K–12 Online Learning, or following content-specific professional organizations such as the National Council for Teachers of Mathematics, the National Council of Teachers of English, or the National Science Teachers Association on Twitter can be extremely helpful in providing a network of support and information. Teachers who participate in these groups find that they feel less isolated when implementing technology and are often more willing to take risks (Johnson, Lucas, & Lucas, 2014). Finally, organizations and experts coordinate and host #EdChat and #EdTech sessions—synchronous online Twitter gatherings—that can garner several hundred participants sharing best practices from around the world. Many times, the chats will coincide with conferences or initiatives from a state or federal educational organization, which generates many resource links and ideas.

Identifying thought-leaders that aid with implementing new ideas can be daunting. Richard Byrne (n.d.) maintains a website called Free Technology for Teachers that is dedicated to helping teachers with everything technology related. Podcasts, PDFs, learning guides, and app recommendations are a few of the tools found in his series of resource sites. His anecdotal writing keeps the information interesting, and his consistent updates provide teachers productive tips and ideas for virtual teaching.

Kathy Schrock is another insightful educational technology driver. Her website, Guide to Everything (Schrock, 2017), and the resources within it, are beneficial when designing and implementing digital tools and strategies in the middle school classroom. She provides videos that train, direct, and steer teachers toward all areas of educational technology integration. She updates her website continually updated and includes a compilation of resources for topics such as virtual reality, virtual learning, apps, creating and learning with online tools, and student learning strategies.

In their report, Adams Becker, Krueger, and Cummins (2016) examined and reviewed current information and communication technology trends expected to change K–12 education. This report is also an excellent resource to provide insight from many movers, shakers, and forward-thinkers in the educational technology realm. Understanding the trends of today and tomorrow are helpful in fueling ideas and collaborations with colleagues in the field of virtual education. They publish their report annually with editions for classrooms, libraries, museums, and even higher education.

## FROM RESEARCH TO IMPLEMENTATION

After research comes implementation. The first step in building a digital curriculum is engaging with the school district's adopted learning management system (LMS). Because an LMS is versatile, teachers can host a variety of digital documents, assessment tools, forums, positive behavior support systems, and learning paths within a single system. Learning paths are the advanced features in an LMS that allow teachers to design a digital road map of sequenced learning objectives (De Smet, De Wever, Schellens, & Valcke, 2016). Students accomplish the learning objectives as they complete teacher-generated tasks. These tasks can range from an organized order of lessons—spiral curriculum where students will see the same topics that reinforce understanding and increase in complexity—to custom completion rules that allow students to determine when, how much, and in what order they want to complete course objectives.

Regardless of which LMS a district chooses to adopt, there are digital tools a virtual teacher can use to improve the LMS's functionality, and ensure they are able to meet the diverse needs of middle level virtual learners. Many of the digital tools referenced in this chapter can be resources in an LMS. The current top learning management systems in K–12 are Google Classroom, Edmodo, Schoology, and Canvas. Google Classroom is free and works best with the G Suite (Gmail, Google Drive, and Google Docs). Edmodo is also free for single use, but requires a school license to gain access to all of the features. These features include connecting with the district's gradebook program, attendance program, and proficiency reporting programs. Schoology and Canvas use the same model; they are free for a single use. However, a school district will need to purchase a license to unleash all the functionality of the programs. The company manages the servers and software associated with these systems; therefore, the company can provide the latest software upgrades and add new features as they become available.

## SEARCHING, LEARNING, AND SHARING ONLINE

It can be difficult to help students filter through the abundance of information available online to determine which information is relevant and educational. To increase productivity, teachers need to introduce students to alternative search engines and resource sites as part of a larger virtual learning toolkit. Middle level learners are very accustomed to devices and online interactions, but often require guidance and support to transition common virtual tools into tools for learning (Beetham & Sharpe, 2013). Many web-based tools and apps are more powerful and information-rich than the traditional textbook. Billed as a computational knowledge engine, the WolframAlpha site has many strengths that move it well beyond a typical search engine. With the ability to solve equations, graph statistical data, or calculate how many babies named Frederick were born in 1968 (2,614), the uses are seemingly endless and can truly inform the curious learner.

PanOpen is an open source educational content platform that fills a unique niche by gathering and assembling open source resources. Designers built the platform to be functional and user-friendly on any device. Once instructors select the information within the system, users are able to interact, take notes, highlight text, and watch videos. Instructors are able to set calendar dates, assign grades, and track student progress.

ExplainEverything functions similarly to a small dry erase board common to the brick-and-mortar classroom. Conceptually, a great way to demonstrate understanding is through explanation by writing, drawing, or simply talking through a concept aloud. The ExplainEverything app provides teachers and learners opportunity to accomplish all three modes of explanation simultaneously, providing the teacher with a full view of the students' thought processes. Students can also collaborate across devices and show the work they have completed together.

## RESOURCES FOR STUDYING AND LEARNING IN THE VIRTUAL MIDDLE LEVEL CLASSROOM

Today's virtual middle level learners face an unprecedented number of technological distractions. Rosen, Carrier, and Cheever (2013) found that most students engage in online interactions for just 6 minutes before a technological related distractor such as a social media site like Facebook distracts them. However, students who employ some type of study strategies are more likely to stay on task when engaged in virtual learning.

One way virtual teachers can help curb online distraction is by limiting online advertisements and external commentary. For instance, when students engage in lessons that require them to view a YouTube video, teachers can utilize resources that filter out advertisements, video suggestions, and comments to help students remain on track when completing an assignment. YouTube Kids provides additional controls and content tailored for a younger audience. ViewPure is not specifically an app, but rather a web site that works well to filter videos on mobile devices or computers. Many video providers such as Amazon and Netflix have moved towards stronger controls for adults that give options based on rating scales for content.

Quizlet is another resource that can assist virtual middle level students in their study habits. Quizlet has compiled flash card study sets for nearly every topic imaginable, from life cycles to complex physics. As a great addition to traditional note cards, the designers have created hundreds of sets based on the most common concepts students want help studying. Users can also create and upload their own study topics and card sets to study and share. Built-in features assist with motivation and rewards to keep users focused. Checkpoints, reminders, and updates motivate students to move forward despite the challenges of studying.

Gamification of content is commonplace and threaded throughout the tools shared in this chapter and handbook. Middle level learners are a prime target of the gaming industry as well as the educational gaming industry. Researchers (Hamari, Koivisto, & Sarsa, 2014) have found that gamification does provide positive effects in general, but there are wide variations depending on the context and the user. With this in mind, Brainscape comes from a company that has a history of creating educational games and continues to expand that presence. This particular app is an online flashcard style system of learning that incorporates some interesting methods of "confidence-based repetition" that attempt to have a greater impact on learning a concept than typical studying methods. In addition to being able to upload original course content, the site contains pre-made learning modules available for purchase.

Kahoot is another educational gaming app that engages students through fun, competitive, simple-to-build learning games. The teacher creates the quiz questions or selects them from a preset question bank through the Kahoot website. As students answer questions, individually or as a team, the timer runs down and feedback is immediate. Points are awarded and the winner is celebrated before moving along to the next set of questions. The simplicity and accessibility of the site is appealing to teachers and students of all subjects and grade levels.

## GOOGLE APPS FOR EDUCATION

Google has entered the education market in a big way, filling the void left by Apple. Since Apple has shifted its focus to consumer devices, and away from creative applications and hardware, Google is quickly replacing Apple as the go-to company supporting K–12 education. Beyond Chromebooks, Google offers software that fills the need for flexibility and collaboration in the virtual classroom. The G Suite for education core services include Gmail, Calendar, Classroom, Contacts, Drive, Docs, Forms, Groups, Sheets, Sites, Slides, Talk/Hangouts and Vault. G Suite services are in compliance with the Children's Online Privacy Protection Act (COPPA, 1998) and the Family Educational Rights and Privacy Act (FERPA, 1974) and do not use information for advertising purposes and the software contains no advertising (Barlow & Lane, 2007).

Google Classroom is an LMS that works well with other G Suite products. The user interface is simple and Google is always adding new features for students and teachers to explore. Drive is the "cloud hard drive," storing G Suite content. Google Docs is a simplified text editor that allows students to collaborate in real-time. Like Docs, Google Sheets is a simplified spreadsheet program that provides most of the functions that the average student needs. Google Forms is an online form generator used to create sign-up sheets or to create quizzes that are graded automatically once the student is finished. Google Slides is a simplified presentation program that has built-in audience response capabilities.

Finally, Talk/Hangouts offer video conferencing capability that allows students to share their screen with other students on the video conference. Currently, up to 15 people can participate in a video conference and interact with each other (Conner, 2008). Using the G Suite tools provides middle level learners opportunities to create their own projects, which promotes student buy-in. When students have an opportunity to collaborate with others in class or internationally, they can develop their self-identity and socialize with their peers (Armstrong, 2016).

The app Remind has grown from a small fan base to reported implementation in approximately half of all U.S. schools (Konrad, 2016). The easy interface enables educators to preset reminders or send them out on the fly, while maintaining the ability to receive responses without sharing a private cell number. While e-mail communication can be problematic, today's middle school students often connect to mobile devices personally or through a family member at all times. With the virtual or hybrid environment, the ability to reach students is vital and needs exploration through apps like Remind to find the most effective tools for students.

Socrative is an interactive tool that has found a space to thrive in many traditional classrooms. By applying the interactive nature of the face-to-face environment to the virtual world, students can respond and share their ideas, answers, and thoughts with each other as a class. The service has interactive feedback, charts, and graphs for teachers to conduct formative and summative assessments in the virtual classroom. Socrative's grading tools, learning reports, and learning communities can fill gaps where a school-based learning management system is lacking. This simple, yet powerful question and answer system can flourish outside the constraints of some school-mandated systems.

PlayPosit is a forward-thinking tool for interactive video that is a great addition to any virtual classroom content management system. The simplicity of taking an educational video and making it much more interactive should be a standard part of a typical learning management system. The instructor can select a video for student viewing, and then partition the video into sections with questions and interactive elements. Once the instructor creates the interactions, students can view the video independently or collaboratively. Instructors can save the video for future student viewing.

## CONTENT SPECIFIC STRATEGIES

Educators can use some strategies and technological tools across all virtual curriculums. However, there are several strategies and tools that virtual educators can utilize which are specific to certain content areas. While the resources we outline below may change with time, the general ideas of identifying and utilizing online sources that engage the interest and strengths of middle level virtual learners in specific content areas is essential to helping them grow as learners. For this reason, in addition to the following resources, it is important for virtual teachers to maintain a focus on researching and learning more about content-specific strategies and tools to meet the academic needs of the online learner.

### Mathematics

Khan Academy is foundational for independent learning and creates a new mindset in student support and nontraditional learning. Students who require additional support or supplemental insights regarding a mathematical topic will find the site tremendously useful. The site is very simplistic, with direct explanations and interpretations. While the site includes a variety of topical areas, the author has focused heavily on math and science. The primary offerings consist of custom-created videos that are screen captures of processes, explanations, and concepts.

BetterExplained is a site created in the spirit of Khan Academy, but contains a slightly different interface with more images and graphics than Khan. The founder borrows a philosophy from Einstein, believing the learner should be able to simply explain a concept if they truly have an understanding. This simple idea has developed into a powerful resource of step-by-step articles, interpretations, and graphic explanations over hundreds of difficult math topics that can support a student's path to success.

Desmos is a free, accessible, online graphing calculator interface that rivals many of the expensive desktop calculators. The interface is simple and effective for novice users, while the site's resources are expanding daily into new options for users. With several million users, the site has found a niche in a market still driven by desktop battery-powered calculators. Teachers can take advantage of concepts added for specific courses and environments. For example, the activity builder enables teachers to tailor activities to their specific needs. In a full class setting, the activity builder can function across students to graph and compare data as well as document errors and comprehension. Additionally, with student device policies changing daily, many students can use the site on their laptop, tablet, or smartphone.

## Social Studies

An ongoing area of concern with many middle level learners is conducting credible research. As large portions of the virtual student's work may involve online or guided independent tasks, students need to master research standards. Many variations and interpretations of research exist, but many students struggle to understand the vast differences between variations of primary and secondary sources. Several online resources are available to aid teachers and students: Edutopia.org; TeachingHistory.org; PBS.org; Library of Congress–LOC.org. Each of these sites contains excellent guides, videos, lesson plans, and examples that allow virtual teachers to differentiate research instruction in an effort to address the individual virtual student's diverse needs.

As teachers guide students through the research process, no matter the learning context, they must ensure that students have an understanding of plagiarism. For virtual teachers, straightforward resources such as Plagiarism.org could be required reading for virtual students. Teachers could also utilize the information offered within the site as discussion points for all middle level students. Additionally, several previously mentioned resources (Kahoot, Quizlet, and Socrative) provide practice examples to enhance students' understanding of plagiarism.

The National Archives' "Today's Document" on Facebook, Twitter, and the National Archives' website provide access to a plethora of primary source documents from the past 240 years. Featured items such as the Declaration of Independence, the Emancipation Proclamation, handwritten presidential notes, and photos from different decades will engage the inner historian in everyone, while providing just enough information to pique the interest of a middle level student. This first-hand information can provide a level of reassurance for the student looking to find accurate representations and accounts of moments in history.

The History Project is a multimedia time capsule for online users and for those interested in history in general. Users store, share, and document life moments online, thereby providing increased opportunities for documenting stories of those in their own community, region, and the world at large. Information can be documented through videos, timelines, photos, documents, music, and much more. Providing middle level students a platform to document an important event can stimulate interest in history and produce value in the process.

FieldTripZoom provides an alternative to the traditional field trip experience. This online service contains a calendar of events for schools to join synchronously in on a pre-arranged virtual field trip, or they may choose their own experience from a wide range of topics and experts. Live guided tours can be streamed out one-way for schools to view, or can be set up as a two-way video chat to provide greater interaction. The virtual trips provide online learners question and answer opportunities and the chance to engage actively in content across approximately 500 predetermined programs.

Users can use archival footage to explain thought processes, support written assignments, and share project-based learning failures or successes for virtual learners. When teachers or students find inspiration in historical events, and they are ready to document their own experience, the OurStory app helps them create, edit, and share their personal stories. The interface lends itself to quick story creation with audio, photos, video, and text. If you students utilize a Mac computer, the iMovie app from Apple is a next logical step for upcoming movie producers and documentary creators. A fun middle ground between the two is an app and lesson plan combo titled Stop Motion Studio. The software is fun, providing students options for documenting their learning process and products, and even contains options for Ultra HD filming.

## Science

Project Noah has earned awards and high ratings for its ease of use and push towards creating citizen scientists. Supported by National Geographic and highlighted by *CNN* and the *Wall Street Journal*, the app can easily bring out the otherwise hidden nature explorer within the virtual middle level learner. While the basic idea of documenting a species is not new, a site that provides the capacity to contribute their own nature experience using their smart device is ingenious. The project's goal is to build a go-to platform for documenting all of the world's organisms. Students and teachers can easily snap a picture and then use one of the field guides to identify the organism, which in turn documents the information in the project's central database. If a student or class chooses to participate in a mission, they may opt to document certain species like squirrels, migrating birds, or invasive intruders in their area.

MyNature Animal Tracks is a site that provides virtual learners much needed motivation and engagement in learning more about their local community and natural environment. The site provides resources that assist students in identifying a variety of animals that may be wandering around their neighborhood. The illustrations provided throughout the website help students identify some of the most common signs (e.g., tracks, scat) of animal presence around ponds, parks, and backyards. Students can then extend their curiosity to learn more about their long-distance classmates and teachers' neighborhoods. The wide assortment of nature guides is not only engaging and fun to flip through, but provide a wealth of information at the student's fingertips.

Another excellent informational and conversation-starting website is the free Report Card for America's Infrastructure by the American Society of Civil Engineers. While the title may not catch the attention of the average middle level student, the expert maps, videos, infographics, and interactive content about state and national bridges, water, budgets, and environmental issues will engage virtual learners for hours on end. For example, did you know that 56,000 of the nation's bridges are structurally deficient? The site details this type of information and so much more. Utilizing these resources to engage middle level learners' sense of citizenship is vital to their success in any learning environment.

## Language Arts

Choice and voice are important to middle level learners. Online institutions can connect with local libraries to provide virtual students access to eBooks, audiobooks, and streaming videos using the OverDrive Media Console More than 30,000 libraries worldwide offer titles via OverDrive. This resource makes it easy to find references and books needed for online lessons, projects, and collaborative discussions. Student access to this resource will open doors to volumes of information accessible from their own home or while they are on the go.

The Free Books app from Apple provides students with access to more than 23,000 classic works of literature. The app includes features such as notes, highlights, bookmarks, and dictionary support. Examples of the works include the autobiography of Benjamin Franklin, Abraham Lincoln's writings from Project Gutenberg, letters from historical leaders, collected works of early writers, the plays of William Shakespeare, the philosophy of Seneca, and much more.

Identifying activities that are simple, yet effective for review and conceptual learning can be difficult. Quill has 150 activities built around Common Core standards that include proofreading, sentence correction, and collaborative writing. Instructors can use the activities for warm-up practice at the beginning of a lesson, summative/formative assessment tools, or review at the end. The activities are free and last 10–15 minutes each, but there are also premium features for teachers and schools such as school and class-wide reporting. With premium features, the school district can integrate the system into the school district's software, creating a more robust platform for evaluating mastery of student data.

Google Scholar is another simple, yet powerful tool that is valuable to students and teachers within the language arts virtual classroom. This resource offers students the opportunity to search articles, dissertations, research abstracts, full academic papers, universities, academic websites, and much more for information pertaining to a wide array of topics. Citation options enhance the ease of referencing sources. Author and article metrics enable visibility of information related to each document. For example, users can search and view the top cited documents related to global warming or World War II. The focus on academia helps students in creating works that include reliable and valid topic information.

Finally, NewsEla is a site that seeks to integrate skills within the language arts with current events and news articles. The intent is to enhance student language skills at all levels while increasing comprehension and critical thinking. The site offers predesigned assessments in the form of quizzes, annotations, and writing prompts embedded within each news article. Virtual teachers can utilize this resource as a means of encouraging student reading comprehension and engagement with current events from around the globe.

## THE CHANGING LANDSCAPE OF EDUCATION

As the classroom and the learner changed rapidly around him, Mr. Jackson eagerly adopted the tools and strategies that engaged today's learner. By utilizing the new tools and staying grounded in sound teaching practices, he discovered many new ways to reach students. The educational experience of researching, studying, learning, searching, and sharing were all enhanced, and made meaningful to the students by the integration of technological tools. During his prep time behind the scenes, he is able to pull together a rich new source of data to help strengthen his student's education and create new levels of success that he could not reach before.

As with any body of resources, there are situations and classroom dynamics that dictate methods and materials appropriate for the individual learner. Regardless of the concept or the content area under study, there are tools, instructional strategies, and examples that can help virtual educators reach and teach each middle level student in the virtual context. As a new virtual educator, not knowing what is offered and unfamiliarity with some of the technological tools currently being utilized, can make designing the virtual classroom an overwhelming task. In this chapter, we offered virtual teachers a place to start. Through resources that can guide virtual teachers in their discovery of the latest and greatest resources and tools, and encouragement to forge connections with other virtual teachers, new virtual teachers can rest assured that there are several avenues of support as they transition into the world of online teaching.

## REFERENCES

Adams Becker, S., Krueger, K., & Cummins, M., (2016). *NMC/CoSN Horizon Report: 2016 K12 edition*. Austin, TX: The New Media Consortium. Retrieved from http://cdn.nmc.org/media/2016-nmc-cosn-horizon-report-k12-EN.pdf

Allen, I. E., & Seaman, J. (2016). *Online report card: Tracking online education in the United States*. Retrieved from http://onlinelearningsurvey.com/reports/onlinereportcard.pdf

Armstrong, T. (2016). *The power of the adolescent brain: Strategies for teaching middle and high school students*. Alexandria, VA: Association for Supervision and Curriculum Development.

Barlow, K., & Lane, J. (2007). Like technology from an advanced alien culture: Google apps for education at ASU. *Proceedings of the 35th annual ACM SIGUCCS Fall Conference* (pp. 8–10). ACM Digital Library. doi: 10.1145/1294046.1294049

Beetham, H., & Sharpe, R. (2013). *Rethinking pedagogy for a digital age: Designing for 21st century learning*. London, England: Routledge.

Bloom, B. S., Engelhart, M. D., Furst, E. J., Hill, W. H., & Krathwohl, D. R. (1956). *Taxonomy of educational objectives: The classification of education goals. Handbook I: Cognitive domain*. New York, NY: Longman.

Byrne, R. (n.d.) *Free technology for teachers*. Retrieved from http://www.freetech4teachers.com/

Children's Online Privacy Protection Act (COPPA) of 1998, 15 U.S.C. 6501–6505. Pub.L. 105–277, 112 Stat. 2681-728.

Conner, N. (2008). *Google apps: The missing manual*. Newton, MA: O'Reilly Media.

De Smet, C., De Wever, B., Schellens, T., & Valcke, M. (2016). Differential impact of learning path based versus conventional instruction in science education. *Computers & Education*, *99*, 53–67.

Family Educational Rights and Privacy Act (FERPA) of 1974, 20 U.S.C. § 1232g; 34 CFR Part 99.

Gardner, H. (2011). *Frames of mind: The theory of multiple intelligences*. Philadelphia, PA: Basic Books.

Hamari, J., Koivisto, J., & Sarsa, H. (2014). Does gamification work?—A literature review of empirical studies on gamification. In R. H. Sprague, Jr. (Ed.), *47th Hawaii International Conference on System Sciences* (pp. 3025–3034). Waikoloa, HI: IEEE Computer Society. doi:10.1109/HICSS.2014.649. Retrieved from https://people.uta.fi/~kljuham/2014-hamari_et_al-does_gamification_work.pdf

Johnson, K., Lucas, L., & Lucas, C. (2014). Learning together: A technology professional learning community. In M. Searson & M. Ochoa (Eds.), *Proceedings of Society for Information Technology & Teacher Education International Conference 2014* (pp. 1912–1915). Chesapeake, VA: Association for the Advancement of Computing in Education.

Konrad, A. (2016, September 14). Parent-teacher app remind passes 20 million users, taps former bleacher report boss as new CEO. *Forbes*. Retrieved from https://www.forbes.com/sites/alexkonrad/2016/09/14/remind-passes-20-million-users-appoints-former-bleacher-report-boss-as-ceo/#37fff9091947

National Middle School Association (2010). *This we believe: Keys to educating young adolescents*. Westerville, OH: Author.

Rosen, L. D., Carrier, L. M., & Cheever, N. A. (2013). Facebook and texting made me do it: Media-induced task-switching while studying. *Computers in Human Behavior, 29*(3), 948–958.

Schrock, K. (2017). *Kathy Schrock's guide to everything*. Retrieved from http://www.schrockguide.net/

CHAPTER 10

# MOTIVATING AND ENGAGING LEARNERS IN THE MIDDLE LEVEL ONLINE ENVIRONMENT

**Eve Bernstein and Andrea Mosenson**
*Queens College*

Motivation and engagement are two of the most salient factors driving students' academic success. As young adolescents move from the elementary grades to the middle level, academic interest and motivation begin to wane (Williams & Stockade, 2004) and student engagement becomes challenging (Tadich, Deed, Campbell, & Prain, 2007). Because motivation and engagement are key in promoting student interest and enjoyment of school (Manning, 2000) and academic achievement (Martin & Marsh, 2003), the way educational experiences are structured in the middle level classroom must include a focus on these two tenets (Rhodes, Camic, Milburn, & Lowe, 2009).

Understanding how to motivate and engage students in the online middle level classroom is a key struggle for many of today's virtual educators, as most have only been prepared to address these factors within the brick-and-mortar context. Understanding what motivates online learners is just as important as understanding what motivates traditional students

*The Online Classroom:*
*Resources for Effective Middle Level Virtual Education,* pp. 167–187
Copyright © 2018 by Information Age Publishing
All rights of reproduction in any form reserved.

because student motivation is key to learning (Deci, Koestner, & Ryan, 2001). So how can virtual teachers motivate and engage their online students to learn? This chapter explores a variety of motivational strategies virtual teachers can implement to promote student engagement in online environments. We divided these strategies into the following sections: (a) course structure, (b) content presentation, and (c) student interaction. Incorporating strategies within these three areas into the online environment can improve student motivation to engage in the virtual course (Lister, 2014; Louwrens & Hartnett, 2015).

## DEFINING MOTIVATION AND ENGAGEMENT

Before we can begin to share strategies for motivating and engaging students in the online middle level classroom, we must first define these terms. *Motivation* is the desire to behave in a particular manner to pursue a goal (Ryan & Deci, 2000), while *engagement* is being actively involved in something (Marks, 2000). This means that motivation is a precursor and necessary component to engagement (Saeed & Zyngier, 2012). Motivation can be either intrinsic or extrinsic (Ryan & Deci, 2000). Intrinsic motivation arises from within the student. In this type of motivation, the student focuses their improvement and competence in terms of their own learning goals. An intrinsically motivated student persists through difficult tasks when learning material, increases their feeling of competence, and contributes to long-term participation in learning (Tabernero & Wood, 1999; Wigfield & Wagner, 2005). The extrinsically motivated student seeks to earn a reward (e.g., good grades, praise) or avoid a punishment. As middle level students prepare themselves for future academic challenges, teachers should foster both intrinsic and extrinsic motivation in the classroom.

## MOTIVATION AND ENGAGEMENT THROUGH VIRTUAL COURSE STRUCTURE

Courses—both traditional and virtual—are grounded within a structure. Traditionally, course structure is a way in which the course is laid out, or the expected progression of course content and material. With regard to the virtual classroom, course structure refers to the overall set-up of an online course within a learning management system (LMS). An LMS is a digital platform used by teachers to plan and deliver content, monitor student participation, and assess student performance. Examples of LMSs currently used in education are Moodle, Blackboard, Schoology, and Edmodo (Beatty & Ulasewicz, 2006; Biswas, 2013; Hart, 2015). The advantage of using an LMS is that they provide a platform where the teacher can organize a variety of course materials and download relevant digital resources. Students then have access to all the course content through a single system. Utilizing such a system motivates students through the simplicity of the system and ease in navigating course content and material. These systems also enable teachers to grade submitted assignments and view analytics on student progress, thereby allowing them easy access to information that is key to helping students consistently engage and progress in the online course. After selecting an LMS, it is time for virtual teachers to turn their attention to the design of the course. Strategies in designing an online course should include beginning with an online orientation to assist students in getting started and setting clear guidelines and expectations that help students through the material (Dahalan, Hasan, Hassan, Zakaria, & Noor, 2013; Grant & Thornton, 2007).

## Begin With an Orientation

Students are motivated and engaged when they feel comfortable and knowledgeable of the educational context or environment of the course (Yang, Tsai, Kim, Cho, & Laffey, 2006). Before students begin a course, it is important to provide them guidance and direction in navigating the virtual environment. An orientation that helps familiarize students with course material and how the course is set up is crucial for academic success (Chen, 2007; Dahalan et al., 2013; Miller, 2014). As this is a teacher's first opportunity to grab students' attention, it is important that the teacher show students (not tell them) what and how they will be learning throughout the course. For example, a virtual teacher can share some of the projects students will be completing in a slide show or video as a way of acquainting them with required tasks. It is also important that teachers acclimate students to the course site and take time to introduce students to their classmates (Chen, 2007; Preece, 2001). What follows are several strategies a virtual teacher can use to accomplish these goals.

**Simplify online navigation.** Navigation of the selected LMS must be simple and user-friendly (Storey, Phillips, Maczewski, & Wang, 2002). When learners become frustrated or confused in locating course information and assignments within the LMS, their motivation and engagement are hindered (Urdan & Schoenfelder, 2006). Therefore, the more familiar and comfortable students are with using an LMS, the more confident they will feel in engaging with a virtual class. The following suggestions can help teachers ensure easy navigation for virtual students:

- Use icons or images along with instructions for each new tool. The use of images with text can increase comprehension for middle level students in a subject (Boerma, Mol, & Jolles, 2016), as it allows a visual aid for each tool that the student can use.
- Use simple sans serif fonts that are easy to read on-screen like Arial, Verdana, and Helvetica.
- Course set up should be organized in a logical way—one that makes it easy for students to follow (Cantrell, Pekcan, Itani, & Velasquez-Bryant, 2006). For example, teachers could set up a course by weeks, modules, or topics.
- Organize content into chunks. Having less information on the screen at any given time will prevent students from becoming overwhelmed with too much information to view and take in at once.

**Create an introductory scavenger hunt.** It is important that students are able to navigate through the course sections with ease, so they can focus on engaging with the content rather than trying to find it. A scavenger hunt can help introduce students to the course structure and technology. Students search the online course site to find different content. What follows are some examples of a scavenger hunt to help students locate different areas within the virtual course:

- Go to Module 1 (or Lesson 1). Write down the title and length of the video presented in this module. (This shows students how to access course folders, modules, and materials. It can also assist them in locating and viewing instructional videos related to the course).
- Using the Message function, send me an e-mail titled Course Goal and explain one of your learning goals for taking this course. (This allows students to practice with the e-mail feature.)
- Go to the Introductory Module and read the Getting to Know You assignment. When finished, go to the Discussion Board link and click on the "Getting to Know You" Discussion Forum. Create a thread, following the task directions, and post your assignment. (This allows students to practice navigating the course and the Discussion Forum.)

**Set clear guidelines and expectations.** Teachers can increase student motivation by setting clear expectations of what the students should be accomplishing in the class (Furrer, Skinner, & Pitzer, 2014) because students will then understand what is needed to be successful. One way teachers can do this is by posting an online forum with step-by-step instructions on how to access, use, and save information with a particular technology tool. These step-by-step instructions can guide students and can regulate motivation as the students make progress (Lehmann, Hähnlein, & Ifenthaler, 2014). Teachers might also produce an online tutorial or utilize online tutorials already in place such as YouTube videos. These tutorials may increase learner satisfaction, understanding of the content, and motivation to want to continue with the subject (Hong et al., 2016). After establishing guidelines for the use of the technological platform, teachers should establish expectations for teacher to student, as well as student-to-student communication (Hanna, Glowacki-Dudka, & Conceicao-Runlee, 2000).

**Set netiquette guidelines for online discussions.** It is important to establish a set of guidelines for students to follow when communicating online. By doing so, these guidelines, also known as *netiquette* guidelines, provide students insight into teacher expectations on how to respond to both peers and teachers in an appropriate manner when discussing a topic or issue in the course. Students need to realize they cannot rely on body language or tone of voice in an online discussion. Clear netiquette guidelines can encourage student engagement within a virtual classroom, as students will feel more comfortable and confident to participate (Louwrens & Hartnett, 2015; Urdan & Schoenfelder, 2006). Some example guidelines to consider are:

- Read first, and then respond. Take time to read a peer's comment carefully before responding.
- Be brief and to the point. Be clear in your communication and stick to the subject.
- Use appropriate language. Be respectful to your peers and refrain from using any offensive language. You cannot undo what you have written once it has been posted.
- Use electronic cues to add emotions. Because body language, facial expressions, and tone of voice are not present in online communications, you can use emoticons to help express yourself. Do not use all caps in writing, as it appears you are YELLING at someone.

## MOTIVATION AND ENGAGEMENT
## THROUGH CONTENT PRESENTATION

Presenting content in a variety of ways can stimulate student interest and motivate them to engage with course material (Miller, 2014). Variety can prevent students (and teachers) from getting bored in a course. The more interested a middle level student is in a topic, the more likely they will remain focused (Grisham & Wolsey, 2006) and actively engaged in the work (Louwrens & Hartnett, 2015). Teachers can present content through many mediums in a virtual classroom: videos, multimedia, text, and Web 2.0 sites. In deciding which approach to use, it is important to think first about the learning outcomes of the course. In addition, teachers will want to take into account the preferred learning style and academic needs of the individual learner. They can use several strategies to present students with a variety of content to motivate and engage them in a virtual classroom.

## Use Both Synchronous and Asynchronous Activities

Another way to provide variety in online content presentation is through synchronous and asynchronous activities. Synchronous activities are similar to face-to-face classroom lessons where everyone meets online at the same time. These prescheduled lessons make use of videoconferencing tools such as Google Hangouts, Skype, or Blackboard Collaborate Ultra. Synchronous instruction allows the teacher to gauge if students understand the material as they teach it, and students can receive immediate feedback to questions and concerns (Al-Shalchi, 2009). Students can also collaborate and discuss a project together in real time without having to wait for responses from their peers. The real-time collaborative aspects of synchronous instruction motivate and engage learners so they can work with other students in real time because it helps eliminate feelings of isolation and fosters a sense of belonging to a community (Wang, 2008).

Asynchronous activities provide students with opportunities to learn and work on their own schedule, as they complete course assignments and lessons in isolation. Asynchronous instruction can provide students more time to digest content and reflect on material, which can increase their motivation to participate and learn (Giesbers, Rienties, Tempelaar, & Gijselaers, 2014). Students are welcome to engage in course material at a time and pace that meets their own developmental and academic needs.

While both formats have advantages to motivating students (Murphy, Rodríguez-Manzanares, & Barbour, 2011), they do have some disadvantages. The main drawback to using synchronous activities is the technical difficulties that can arise (Ng, 2007). When technology fails, whether on the teachers end or the students, it can disrupt the purpose of the lesson and become a frustrating experience. The disadvantages to using asynchronous activities are the delay in getting a response from either the teacher or another student. Therefore, by combining a series of synchronous and asynchronous activities into a course, teachers can enhance student motivation and engagement in an online environment as it encourages and fosters student participation throughout a course (Giesbers et al., 2014).

## Use Different Media

Best practice for teaching online is to use a variety of different media to engage students in the learning process (Simonson, Schlosser, & Orellana, 2011). One way to present content is through audio or podcasts, both of which require students to listen to the material. Podcasts can increase both motivation and interest in a subject (Nozari & Siamian, 2015). Audio is most useful for presenting foreign languages, speech development (Ducate & Lomicka, 2009) and music (Tam, 2012). Some recommend presenting audio along with text or visuals, as this combination provides a richer medium in presenting content in online environments (Miller, 2014). Multimedia, like videos, provides students the ability to stop, rewind, and replay the material to gain a better understanding of the information presented (Bates, 2015).

Teachers can utilize a trifold format wherein they present three types of media to students within a single lesson as a means of incorporating a variety of media into the online course. One example of this format is Read-Watch-Do. Students first *read* about a topic, then *watch* a video on it, and lastly *do* an assignment to apply what they have learned. With this format, different media types pique student interest and curiosity about the topic being studied thereby furthering their engagement with course content. A module or lesson using the Read-Watch-Do format in an online environment might look like the example in Figure 10.1.

## Provide Students Choice

One of the easiest ways to incorporate student autonomy over their learning is to allow them choice (Stefanou, Perencevich, DiCintio, & Turner, 2004). Teachers can immerse students in the course content when given an opportunity to decide how they learn and the activities or assessments they use to demonstrate mastery (Kerr, 2011; Urdan & Schoenfelder, 2006). Providing students with choices gives them a sense of control over their learning that can lead to increased student engagement (Louwrens & Hartnett, 2015). Teachers could give students a list of topics to choose from in completing an assignment. For example, in a family and consumer sciences class, students can select an entrepreneur to research from a list provided to them. Teachers could also give the students a choice in how they complete this assignment. Students could demonstrate their understanding of a topic by creating an interactive poster using Glogster, an engaging comic strip using Pixton, or a visual timeline using Timetoast. Offering choice of activities in a course can meet the diverse needs of young adolescents (Kerr, 2011) and foster motivation and engagement (Wallace & Sung, 2017;

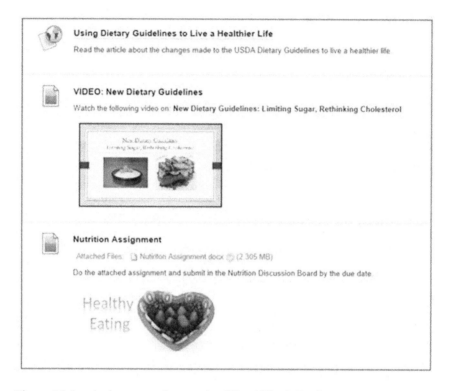

**Figure 10.1.**   Author created example of Read-Watch-Do format.

Williams, Wallace, & Sung, 2016) as it speaks to the developmental need for autonomy and affords learners opportunity flex their skills and see the relevancy of course material to their own experience and strengths.

## Encourage Reflective Thinking

The middle level years are an ideal time for students to reflect on their learning to help them become more aware of how they learn, and what they learn. Reflective thinking can help students develop higher order thinking skills as we ask them to evaluate, critique, and assess the content they are learning (Grant & Thornton, 2007). Students can reflect on an article or book they read, a video they watched, or a project they just completed. Students can also maintain weekly reflections in journals or blogs such as Kidblog or Blogger, as they evaluate what they learned and how they might apply this knowledge to their lives. The key component to effective student reflection is to ask questions or provide prompts that promote critical thinking (Chin & Chia, 2004; Hsieh, Jang, Hwang, & Chen, 2011). Teachers can increase motivation and conceptions of self-efficacy in the middle level when students have opportunities to practice writing and increase their competencies in and skills during the writing task (Pajares & Valiante, 2006). Here are a few examples that any content area teacher can use:

- Describe three things you learned from this week's video. Discuss how you could incorporate one of these ideas into your life.
- After reading the article, how could you use this information to make improvements in our local community (or your family)?
- In your journal (or blog), discuss one thing you found interesting about this week's topic Be sure to include why this topic resonated with you.
- How does this topic relate to the world in which we now live?
- After completing the project, discuss one thing you found fascinating about your topic and one thing you found disappointing.

EdPuzzle is a technology tool that teachers can use to encourage reflective thinking. This Web 2.0 tool allows teachers to insert questions throughout any video to encourage students to think more critically about a topic. EdPuzzle has four editing options: (a) crop a video to focus on the part that best shows what you want students to view, (b) record your own audio to accompany the video, (c) record audio notes to add a personal touch to the video (You can add a comment any time, clarify a point made, and add an introduction or conclusion to the video), and (d) add questions to assess student understanding throughout the video. You can infuse multiple-choice questions or open-ended questions at any point throughout the video. EdPuzzle is not only a great tool to encourage reflection, but it also captures every student's response to the questions posed to help teachers assess students' thinking on the topic presented. Reflection can allow middle level students a chance to examine their thoughts regarding the material, and define what the content means to them. This can increase a sense of autonomy or control over their own learning (Ryan & Patrick, 2001), especially as students make more personal connections to the content being studied. Therefore, using activities for students to reflect upon can stimulate motivation and engagement in a virtual course.

## Make Tasks Relevant

Students view a task as being relevant if they perceive it to be useful in their present lives or in reaching their personal goals. The more you know the students in your class, the more likely you can create authentic learning tasks that they will find meaningful to their lives (Dahalan et al., 2013; Therrell & Dunneback, 2015), thus increasing engagement and motivation to learn. For example, a virtual teacher can include reading material or videos that allow students to identify with characters and noted situations. Here are just a few examples of how to accomplish this:

- Scenarios: Provide students a real-life scenario where they must make decisions about a situation and then explain why they chose that decision.
- Role-playing: Students can create a talking avatar using Voki to role-play a historic figure or book character and record what this person might say in a given situation. Students can save the avatar recording and share it with the class. This web tool is easy to use with step-by-step directions to follow and takes just a few minutes of time to complete a recording. Students will find this technology application (app) engaging, as they are able to select their own character or avatar and either use their own voice or choose one to record a message. Voki is also a great tool for teachers to use to include some interesting tidbits throughout the virtual course.
- Web Quests: These are problem-based, inquiry-oriented online learning experiences. Web quests provide students with valid and reliable research that has been pre-selected by the teacher on a given topic or area of focus. Given a task to complete, students can research a topic online and present their findings toward a solution. Students can work in collaborative teams where each member has a specific role to play or work to complete. Teachers can locate pre-made web quests in a variety of topic areas or create their own at WebQuest, Zunal and Bookwidgets.
- Virtual Field Trips: Teachers can send students on a virtual trip to discover fascinating places and to learn more about topics, people, or time periods being studied in the course. Google Earth or Air Pano—a website that features 360° views of locations around the world—offer virtual educators and students the opportunity to further engage in course material despite their separation through time and location. Teachers can also create their own virtual field trips with any video creator tool.
- Interviews: Have students interview a family or community member to uncover a unique perspective on a topic of study. The results of such interviews could lead to inviting a community member to talk to the class about their experiences using a videoconferencing tool like Google Hangouts. Students could ask

questions and converse with the guest speaker about the discussion topic. Connecting the curriculum to an authentic audience helps motivate students to see that their work matters beyond the classroom (Levy, 2008).

These are just a few examples that teachers can use in a virtual classroom to motivate and engage students through relevant assignments as they connect the course content to the real world. When students feel the online activities are personally relevant, they are more interested and engaged to work on them (Kerr, 2011; Louwrens & Hartnett, 2015).

## MOTIVATION AND ENGAGEMENT THROUGH STUDENT INTERACTION

Positive instructor-to-student interactions and student-to-student interactions are essential to promote motivation and engagement in a virtual class (Dixson, 2010; Louwrens & Hartnett, 2015). It is imperative that during online interactions teachers maintain a social presence and foster a positive connection, as this sets the tone and mood of the online environment (Dixson, 2010; Hostetter & Busch, 2013). Students prefer a teacher who is passionate and caring, and who challenges them to think more deeply about the course material (Therrell & Dunneback, 2015). In an online environment, a teacher can demonstrate a caring attitude toward students by getting to know and understand them through continuous dialogue and shared experiences (Velasquez, Graham, & West, 2013). This is one way that teachers can build their social presence and interactions with others in an online community, so students perceive them as real people (Biocca, Harms, & Burgoon, 2003). In fact, learners view teachers with a high degree of social presence as more positive and effective (Sung & Mayer, 2012). Teachers can accomplish social presence by communicating with students through multiple channels such as announcements, e-mails, discussion boards, and synchronous sessions (Dixson, 2010; Hostetter & Busch, 2013). Maintaining a strong social presence can encourage student motivation and engagement in an online course because it provides a sense of humanity to an otherwise isolated learning event. In the same vein, a lack of social presence will undoubtedly lead to a decrease in student motivation and engagement (Louwrens & Hartnett, 2015) as students fail to establish an essential connection with the course instructor.

Teachers will need to facilitate student-to-student interactions that can help build an online learning community where students feel a sense of belonging, which can further enhance motivation and engagement leading to increased learning (Conrad & Donaldson, 2004). Building a sense of community in a virtual environment is key to a successful online course (Wang, 2008). When students feel part of a community of learners, they are less likely to feel isolated (Rovai, 2002a, 2002b) and more inclined to be motivated to collaborate in group activities and projects (Brook & Oliver, 2003). Additionally, it is suggested that the sooner students get to know their peers in the course, the more likely they will be motivated to focus on the content (Miller, 2014) and begin to develop a sense of belonging in the class (Louwrens & Hartnett, 2015). This is particularly important at the middle level where students seek acceptance by their peers. A virtual teacher can nurture social interaction among middle level students to help meet their needs for relatedness by (a) including getting-to-know-you activities and student profiles to encourage students to learn more about their classmates (Brook & Oliver, 2002; Chen, 2007), (b) utilizing interactive technologies that foster collaboration and communication (Abrami, Benard, Bures, Borokhovski, & Tamin, 2011), (c) fostering an online environment of mutual respect (Patrick, Ryan, & Kaplan, 2007), and (d) encouraging students to engage in self-disclosure with one another (Sung & Mayer, 2012). These strategies will help students build relationships with their peers and feel more comfortable with sharing information with one another. As they grow in their sense of belonging and security in the virtual classroom, they will become more motivated to engage with course content and take part in online discussion.

## Establish a Tone of Excitement From the Beginning

Students make their initial judgements about a virtual course as soon as they log on, so it is important to set a positive, encouraging tone from the beginning. If students perceive a teacher to be caring about them and passionate about the subject they teach, students will be more motivated to learn and more engaged in the class (Therrell & Dunneback, 2015; Velasquez et al., 2013). Here are just a few ideas on how to create a positive environment from the start:

- Create a Welcome Message to post online (in the Announcement section of the LMS) and e-mail to students before the course starts to introduce the course and yourself to the students. The message should reflect your enthusiasm for teaching the course and excitement to meet and get to know the students. One way to accomplish this is to make a short video of yourself talking to the students using a tool like Screencast-o-matic. Another is to create an avatar with Voki to record your welcome message. Providing a positive, energetic welcome message is sure to hook students in from the beginning of the course.

- Set up virtual office hours so students can schedule a time to talk about their progress or any issues they may be experiencing in the course. Most LMS provide a way to host online office hours making it easier for students to access and use because it is within the online system.

- For the more tech-savvy teacher, you can create a Course Trailer video that highlights key aspects of the course for students to watch. Like a movie trailer or book trailer, a brief video (1-2 minutes long) gets students excited about the course they will be taking. You can use any video creator like Animoto or Spark.Adobe.

## Use a "Getting to Know You" Activity

In a traditional classroom, teachers often start the school year with icebreaker activities. In much the same way, one of the first activities to help virtual students interact with their virtual classmates, and to help the teacher get to know more about each student, is to set up a "Getting to Know You" or icebreaker activity. There are numerous activities utilized in traditional classrooms that translate well to an online environment. Below are several examples.

- Name Poem: Write an "I Am" poem or story about yourself. Figure 10.2 is an example of an "I Am" poem.

I am Poem
I am first born in a family of four.
I am the best big brother to my sister.
I am board games with family and video games by myself.
I am skier in the winter and swimmer in the summer.
I am pepperoni pizza and hamburger and fries.
I am reader and writer of fantasy and adventure stories.
I am, and hope to be one day, a famous writer.

**Figure 10.2.**   Example of author-created "I Am" poem.

This is Me Collage: Create a digital collage using images and words that represent who you are. Students can accomplish this with almost any technology tool from Word or PowerPoint to websites like Canva and Photo-Collage. Students can add their own images or find images on the Internet and arrange them into a collage. The collage-maker websites also provide templates where images can be placed along with text to create a personal collage.

- iReflections Digital Story: Create a four-slide digital story that describes who you are. Each slide should complete one of the following "i-statements" with images and words (choose four of the following): iLove, iBelieve, iDream, iHope, iWant, iWonder, iCare, iValue, iAppreciate, iStrive, iDislike, iExcel, or iCreate. Students can create their story using *PowerPoint*, or slideshow programs such as PicoVico or PhotoPeach.
- Students can use these Web 2.0 apps by inserting images and text to each slide and then downloading their work as a video to their computer or YouTube account. Teachers can also create a digital story to share with students. This not only provides students an exemplar, but also helps establish teacher presence in an online environment. Figure 10.3 provides example slides.

**Figure 10.3.**   Author-created example of iReflection slides for a digital story.

## Communicate Through Multiple Channels

Middle level learners often need guidance, support and encouragement to maintain motivation and engagement in an online class (Louwrens & Hartnett, 2015). For this reason, instructors should maintain consistent communication within the online environment. There are multiple ways to communicate with students throughout an online course using asynchronous tools like e-mail, announcements, and discussion boards. For instance, instructors typically display course announcements on the home page or first screen students access when they log into a course and, therefore, located in a prime place to share important information with students. A teacher can post new content, remind students about an upcoming test or project deadline, announce special events or achievements like students' birthdays or sports accomplishments, and direct students to a website with interesting information they are currently studying. To motivate students further through personal connection and authentic audience, teachers can utilize announcements as a space to share student's work or student generated facts that they have gathered in their research.

Virtual teachers can also communicate with the aid of synchronous tools such as videoconferencing, chat sessions, and phone communication. There are even tools that can provide a synchronous-like experience where teacher and students communicate and work together. For example, Google tools (e.g., Google Docs) offers a shared workspace for students and teachers to synchronously or asynchronously access in navigating a common project or assessment. Text messaging is another common tool that young adolescents prefer to use in communicating with others (Velasquez et al., 2013). The key to a successful online course is offering several different channels to initiate and maintain open communication and consistent interaction (Dixson, 2010).

## Provide Meaningful Feedback

Students value feedback on assignments that guides them to improve their work and enhance their learning (Miller, 2014; Therrell & Dunneback, 2015). According to research, meaningful feedback that keeps students engaged in a course includes the following four criteria (Ambrose, Bridges, Lovett, DiPietro, & Norman, 2010; Jonsson, 2012; Morris & Chikwa, 2016):

- Timely: Provide feedback as soon as possible to help students understand what they did correct and what they misunderstood. Delayed feedback is not as useful for student learning and growth.
- Constructive: Identify areas where students failed to meet criteria of an assignment and provide them with suggestions on how to improve their work for the future.
- Balanced: Provide both positive comments and constructive feedback to improve an assignment using the "sandwich" approach. Like a good sandwich, the beginning and end should contain positive comments that support the learner, while the middle hosts comments focused on areas for improvement.
- Focused: Do not overwhelm students with too much feedback. This is particularly important for struggling students to prevent

them from becoming demotivated and detached from the course (Brookhart, 2011).

In line with the four criteria to meaningful feedback, the following strategies and resources will not only target feedback to students, but also help teachers manage their time better in evaluating student work.

- Global feedback: When the majority of students are struggling to complete an assignment or project, it is best to provide global feedback to the entire class. Using a screen capture tool such as Screencast-o-matic, or Screenr, a teacher can record the screen of their computer while explaining and showing students what general issues arose with an assignment and ways to make corrections. This not only saves the teacher time in giving effective feedback, but also targets the main problems students are experiencing with an assignment.
- Rubrics: Most LMSs have rubric tools that teachers can set up to show students how they will evaluate and grade an assignment. The teachers make the rubric available to students when issuing an assignment so they can focus their efforts on meeting the requirements. Students can easily access the graded rubric within the LMS to view teacher feedback.
- Voice message: Another way to provide more personalized feedback to students is to record a voice message. Once a teacher records a response, he or she saves and shares it with a student through a link or an MP3 audio file. Students hear the teacher's voice, thereby providing a more personalized approach to positive feedback (Morris & Chikwa, 2016).
- Grading announcement: Teachers need to post an announcement to students to notify them when they complete reviewing and grading assignments. This allows students to view their graded assignments along with the feedback as soon as possible.

These strategies can provide students with meaningful feedback that encourages and motivates them to continue working in a course to reach their learning goals (Louwrens & Hartnett, 2015). Meaningful feedback can guide students to what they are doing correctly in the course, or what they need to change to make improvements. This guidance can prove motivational as students understand how they are progressing in the course (Kerr, 2011).

## Allow Students to Revise Work

Some recommend that once students receive feedback on an assignment, teachers need to give them the opportunity to use the feedback in subsequent assignments to enhance their achievement (Jonsson, 2012; Morris & Chikwa, 2016). There are also times when students can repeat certain assignments or assessments in their attempt to reach mastery before moving forward in the course. This conveys to students that the teacher values the learning process in developing a set of skills over grades (Urdan & Schoenfelder, 2006), while providing students the opportunity to be more successful in the class. When a student feels more academically successful, they are encouraged to stay engaged in learning the content (Miller, 2014).

Another way to offer students multiple opportunities to practice using their knowledge and skills is through writing. By allowing students to submit multiple drafts of the same paper and receive feedback on their progress, students can refine their knowledge of the content and their writing skills (Ambrose et al., 2010). As students experience opportunity to improve their writing, they can increase competency as their writing skill improves, which in turn increases their motivation (Pajares & Valiante, 2006).

## CONCLUSION

The middle level years are a special time when students are exploring who they are. Teachers can shape part of this experience through their courses as students develop cognitively, socially, and emotionally. To promote this development, it is necessary to offer students opportunities to engage in productive learning experiences, especially in the virtual environment. Teachers can help middle level students create connections in an online course by fostering student motivation and engagement. This is important because the more connections that students make, the more meaningful the material will be in motivating and engaging students in a virtual class. By implementing the motivational strategies presented in this chapter, a virtual teacher can enhance course structure, content presentation, and student interaction in any online course they teach, thus facilitating student enjoyment, motivation, and engagement.

## REFERENCES

Abrami, P. C., Bernard, R. M., Bures, E., Borokhovski, E., & Tamim, R. M. (2011). Interaction in distance education and online learning: Using evidence and theory to improve practice. *Journal of Computing in Higher Education, 23*(2/3), 82–103.

Al-Shalchi, O. N. (2009). The effectiveness and development of online discussions. *Journal of Online Learning and Teaching, 5*(1), 104–108.

Ambrose, S. A., Bridges, M. W., Lovett, M. C., DiPietro, M., & Norman, M. K. (2010). *How learning works: 7 research-based principles for smart teaching.* San Francisco, CA: Jossey-Bass. Retrieved from http://firstliteracy.org/wp-content/uploads/2015/07/How-Learning-Works.pdf

Bates, A. W. (2015). *Teaching in a digital age: Guidelines for designing teaching and learning.* Vancouver, BC, Canada: Tony Bates Associates. Retrieved from https://opentextbc.ca/teachinginadigitalage/

Beatty, B., & Ulasewicz, C. (2006). Faculty perspectives on moving from Blackboard to the Moodle learning management system. *TechTrends, 50*(4), 36–45.

Biocca, F., Harms, C., & Burgoon, J. (2003). Toward a more robust theory and measure of social presence. *Presence: Teleoperators and Virtual Environments, 12*(5), 456–480.

Biswas, S. (2013). Schoology-supported classroom management: A curriculum review. *Northwest Journal of Teacher Education, 11*(2), 187–195.

Boerma, I. E., Mol, S. E., & Jolles, J. (2016). Reading pictures for story comprehension requires mental imagery skills. *Frontiers in Psychology, 7,* 1–10.

Brook C., & Oliver, R. (2003). Online learning communities: Investigating a design framework. *Australian Journal of Educational Technology, 19*(2), 139–160.

Brookhart, S. M. (2011). Tailoring feedback: Effective feedback should be adjusted depending on the needs of the learner. *Education Digest: Essential Readings Condensed for Quick Review, 76*(9), 33–36.

Cantrell, P., Pekcan, G., Itani, A., & Velasquez-Bryant, N. (2006). The effects of engineering modules on student learning in middle school science classrooms. *Journal of Engineering Education, 95*(4), 301–309.

Chen, S. J. (2007). Instructional design strategies for intensive online courses: An objectivist-constructivist blended approach. *Journal of Interactive Online Learning, 6*(1), 72–86.

Chin, C., & Chia, L. G. (2004). Problem-based learning: Using students' questions to drive knowledge construction. *Science Education, 88*(5), 707–727.

Conrad, R., & Donaldson, J. (2004). *Engaging the online learner: Activities and resources for creative instruction.* San Francisco, CA: Wiley.

Dahalan, N., Hasan, H., Hassan, F., Zakaria, Z., & Noor, W. (2013). Engaging students online: Does gender matter in adoption of learning material design? *World Journal on Educational Technology, 5*(3), 413–419.

Deci, E., Koestner, R., & Ryan, R. (2001). Extrinsic rewards and intrinsic motivation in education: Reconsidered once again. *Review of Educational Research, 71*(1), 1–27.

Dixson, M. D. (2010). Creating effective student engagement in online courses: What do students find engaging? *Journal of the Scholarship of Teaching and Learning, 10*(2), 1–13.

Ducate, L., & Lomicka, L. (2009). Podcasting: An effective tool for honing language students' pronunciation? *Language Learning & Technology, 13*(3), 66–86.

Furrer, C., Skinner, E., & Pitzer, J. (2014). The influence of teacher and peer relationships on students' classroom engagement and everyday motivational resilience. *National Society for the Study of Education*, *113*(1), 101–123.

Giesbers, B., Rienties, B., Tempelaar, D., & Gijselaers, W. (2014). A dynamic analysis of the interplay between asynchronous and synchronous communication in online learning: The impact of motivation. *Journal of Computer Assisted Learning*, *30*(1), 30–50.

Grant, M., & Thornton, H. (2007). Best practices in undergraduate adult-centered online learning: Mechanisms for course design and delivery. *Journal of Online Learning and Teaching*, *3*(4), 346–356.

Grisham, D. L., & Wolsey, T. D. (2006). Recentering the middle school classroom as a vibrant learning community: Students, literacy, and technology intersect. *Journal of Adolescent & Adult Literacy*, *49*(8), 648–660.

Hanna, D. E., Glowacki-Dudka, M., & Conceicao-Runlee, S. (2000). *147 practical tips for teaching online groups*. Madison, WI: Atwood.

Hart, J. (2015). 7 best practices for building a multimodal, online elementary curriculum: A course designer shares the process that her virtual school uses to create STEAM and humanities content. *The Journal Technological Horizons in Education*, *42*(1), 9–10.

Hong, J. C., Hwang, M. Y., Szeto, E., Tsai, C. R., Kuo, Y. C., & Hsu, W. Y. (2016). Internet cognitive failure relevant to self-efficacy, learning interest, and satisfaction with social media learning. *Computers in Human Behavior*, *55*(A), 214–222.

Hostetter, C., & Busch, M. (2013). Social presence and learning outcomes. *Journal of the Scholarship of Teaching and Learning*, *13*(1), 77–86.

Hsieh, S. W., Jang, Y. R., Hwang, G. J., & Chen, N. S. (2011). Effects of teaching and learning styles on students' reflection levels for ubiquitous learning. *Computers & Education*, *57*(1), 1194–1201.

Jonsson, A. (2012). Facilitating productive use of feedback in higher education. *Active Learning in Higher Education*, *14*(1), 63–76.

Kerr, S. (2011). Tips, tools, and techniques for teaching in the online high school classroom. *TechTrends*, *55*(1), 28–30.

Lehmann, T., Hähnlein, I., & Ifenthaler, D. (2014). Cognitive, metacognitive and motivational perspectives on preflection in self-regulated online learning. *Computers in Human Behavior*, *32*, 313–323.

Levy, S. (2008). The power of audience. *Educational Leadership*, *66*(3), 75–79.

Lister, M. (2014). Trends in the design of e-learning and online learning. *Journal of Online Learning and Teaching*, *10*(4), 671–680.

Louwrens, N., & Hartnett, M. (2015). Student and teacher perceptions of online student engagement in an online middle school. *Journal of Open, Flexible and Distance Learning*, *19*(1), 27–43.

Manning, M. L. (2000). Child-centered middle schools: A position paper association for childhood education international. *Childhood Education*, *76*(3), 154–159.

Marks, H. M. (2000). Student engagement in instructional activity: Patterns in the elementary, middle, and high school years. *American Educational Research Journal*, *37*(1), 153–184.

Martin, A., & Marsh, H. (2003). Fear of failure: Friend or foe? *Australian Psychologist, 38*(1), 31–38.

Miller, M. D. (2014). *Minds online: Teaching effectively with technology.* Cambridge, MA: Harvard University Press.

Morris, C., & Chikwa, G. (2016). Audio versus written feedback: Exploring learners' preference and the impact of feedback format on students' academic performance. *Active Learning in Higher Education, 17*(2), 1–13.

Murphy, E., Rodríguez-Manzanares, M. A., & Barbour, M. (2011). Asynchronous and synchronous online teaching: Perspectives of Canadian high school distance education teachers. *British Journal of Educational Technology, 42*(4), 583–591.

Ng, K. C. (2007). Replacing face-to-face tutorials by synchronous online technologies: Challenges and pedagogical implications. *The International Review of Research in Open and Distributed Learning, 8*(1). Retrieved from http://www.irrodl.org/index.php/irrodl/article/view/335/764

Nozari, A. Y., & Siamian, H. (2015). The effect of applying podcast multimedia teaching system on motivational achievement and learning among the boy students. *Acta Informatica Medica, 23*(1), 29–34.

Pajares, F., & Valiante, G. (2006). Self-efficacy beliefs and motivation in writing development. In C. MacArthur, S. Graham, & J. FitzGerald (Eds.), *Handbook of writing research* (pp. 158–170). New York, NY: Guilford Press.

Patrick, H., Ryan, A. M., & Kaplan, A. (2007). Early adolescents' perceptions of the classroom social environment, motivational beliefs, and engagement. *Journal of Educational Psychology, 99*(1), 83–98.

Preece, J. (2001). Sociability and usability in online communities: Determining and measuring success. *Behaviour & Information Technology, 20*(5) 347–356.

Rhodes, J. E., Camic, P. M., Milburn, M., & Lowe, S. R. (2009). Improving middle school climate through teacher-centered change. *Journal of Community Psychology, 37*(6), 711–724.

Rovai, A. P. (2002a). Development of an instrument to measure classroom community. *Internet and Higher Education, 5*(3), 197–211.

Rovai, A. P. (2002b). Sense of community, perceived cognitive learning, and persistence in asynchronous learning networks. *The Internet and Higher Education, 5*(4), 319–332.

Ryan, A. M., & Patrick, H. (2001). The classroom social environment and changes in adolescents' motivation and engagement during middle school. *American Educational Research Journal, 38*(2), 437–460.

Ryan, R. M., & Deci, E. L. (2000). Intrinsic and extrinsic motivations: Classic definitions and new directions. *Contemporary Educational Psychology, 25*(1), 54–67.

Saeed, S., & Zyngier, D. (2012). How motivation influences student engagement: A qualitative case study. *Journal of Education and Learning, 1*(2), 252–267.

Simonson, M., Schlosser, C., & Orellana, A. (2011). Distance education research: A review of the literature. *Journal of Computing in Higher Education, 23*(2/3), 124–142.

Stefanou, C. R., Perencevich, K. C., DiCintio, M., & Turner, J. C. (2004). Supporting autonomy in the classroom: Ways teachers encourage student decision making and ownership. *Educational Psychologist, 39*(2), 97–110.

Storey, M. A., Phillips, B., Maczewski, M., & Wang, M. (2002). Evaluating the usability of web-based learning tools. *Educational Technology & Society, 5*(3), 91–100.

Sung, E., & Mayer, R. E. (2012). Five facets of social presence in online distance education. *Computers in Human Behavior, 28*(5), 1738–1747.

Tabemero, C., & Wood, R. E. (1999). Implicit theories versus the social construal of ability in self-regulation and performance on a complex task. *Organizational Behavior and Human Decision Processes, 78*(2), 104–127.

Tadich, B., Deed, C., Campbell, C., & Prain, V. (2007). Student engagement in the middle years: A year 8 case study. *Issues in Educational Research, 17*(2), 256–271.

Tam, O. C. (2012). The effectiveness of educational podcasts for teaching music and visual arts in higher education. *Research in Learning Technology, 20*(1), 1–13.

Therrell, J., & Dunneback, S. K. (2015). Millennial perspectives and priorities. *Journal of the Scholarship of Teaching and Learning, 15*(5), 49–63.

Urdan, T., & Schoenfelder, E. (2006). Classroom effects on student motivation: Goal structures, social relationships, and competence beliefs. *Journal of School Psychology, 44*(5), 331–349.

Velasquez, A., Graham, C. R., & West, R. E. (2013). An investigation of practices and tools that enabled technology-mediated caring in an online high school. *The International Review of Research in Open and Distance Learning, 14*(5), 277–292.

Wallace, T. L., & Sung, H. C. (2017). Student perceptions of autonomy-supportive instructional interactions in the middle grades. *The Journal of Experimental Education, 85*(3), 425–449.

Wang, S. K. (2008). The effects of a synchronous communication tool (Yahoo messenger) on online learners' sense of community and their multimedia authoring skills. *Journal of Interactive Online Learning, 7*(1), 59–74.

Wigfield, A., & Wagner, A. L. (2005). Competence, motivation, and identity development during adolescence. In A. Elliot & C. Dwerk (Eds.), *Handbook of competence and motivation* (pp. 222–239). New York, NY: Guilford Press.

Williams, J. D., Wallace, T. L., & Sung, H. C. (2016). Providing choice in middle grade classrooms: An exploratory study of enactment variability and student reflection. *The Journal of Early Adolescence, 36*(4), 527–550.

Williams, R. L., & Stockdale, S. L. (2004). Classroom motivation strategies for prospective teachers. *The Teacher Educator, 39*(3), 212–230.

Yang, C. C., Tsai, I. C., Kim, B., Cho, M. H., & Laffey, J. M. (2006). Exploring the relationships between students' academic motivation and social ability in online learning environments. *The Internet and Higher Education, 9*(4), 277–286.

CHAPTER 11

# EMPLOYING CULTURALLY RELEVANT PEDAGOGY IN MIDDLE LEVEL BLENDED AND VIRTUAL CLASSROOMS

**Ebony Terrell Shockley and Cachanda Orellana**
*University of Maryland, College Park*

**Arquimen Chicas**
*Montgomery County Maryland Public Schools*

Classrooms in the United States have become increasingly diverse (National Center for Education Statistics, 2015; U.S. Census Bureau, 2015). In response to these demographic changes, teachers can become aware of the cultural differences that may exist among their students. These cultural differences include tapping into students' prior knowledge and acquiring an awareness of the similarities and differences that students bring to classrooms.

Cultural awareness extends to practices of student's culture that influences their academic experiences. Culture is "language, symbols, and artifacts; customs, practices and interactional patterns; and shared values,

*The Online Classroom:*
*Resources for Effective Middle Level Virtual Education,* pp. 189–203
Copyright © 2018 by Information Age Publishing
All rights of reproduction in any form reserved.
189

norms, beliefs, and expectations" (Moule, 2012, p. 310). Cultural awareness is a critical component of pedagogical practice in blended and virtual settings. The pedagogical practices that center culture is referred to as culturally relevant pedagogy (Ladson-Billings, 1995). Given the increase of diverse learners in virtual classrooms, it is imperative for virtual teachers to help these students achieve academically by aligning pedagogy in culturally relevant ways.

Culturally relevant pedagogy (CRP) is a pedagogical approach that "draws on the cultural characteristics, experiences, and perspectives of students as conduits for teaching them more effectively" (Ladson-Billings, 1995, p. 382). This approach recognizes that students learn differently and that these differences relate to background, language, and other identify forms (Gay, 2000; Howard & Rodriguez-Scheel, 2017; Ladson-Billings, 1995). Through CRP, it is argued that diverse students will achieve academically when teachers fashion instruction through these cultural filters (Gay, 2000; Ladson-Billings, 1995). Additionally, CRP is said to empower "students intellectually, socially, emotionally, and politically by using cultural referents to impart knowledge, skills, and attitudes" (Ladson-Billings, 1995, p. 382). Teachers enact CRP when they analyze and prioritize students' cultural experiences and incorporate those experiences into their instruction. By doing so, there is an opportunity to not only learn about the cultures of their students, but the approach also becomes an avenue in helping students find their strengths and build upon them to be successful both in and out of school.

CRP is an integral component of teaching culturally diverse learners. In the traditional classroom, it is easy for a teacher to recognize cultural diversity, as they can "see" their students. But what if teachers are teaching in a virtual context? How can they develop their knowledge of the diverse students they teach and use this knowledge to implement CRP? This chapter offers resources and tools for virtual teachers in developing their funds of knowledge of diverse students and how drawing on this new knowledge can help them employ CRP in the virtual middle level classroom.

## DEVELOPING FUNDS OF KNOWLEDGE OF DIVERSE VIRTUAL STUDENTS

Before teachers can employ CRPs, they must first develop their funds of knowledge (FoK) of the diverse students they teach. FoK are "historically accumulated and culturally developed bodies of knowledge and skills that students hold" (Moll, Amanti, Neff, & González, 1992, p. 133). These bodies of knowledge are considered resources for teachers when planning for culturally responsive instruction. Through the development of FoK, teachers come to learn about diverse students through the student themselves, rather than drawing on the perceived understandings that teachers may hold. Therefore, it is critical that the virtual teacher take steps in first developing this knowledge.

A shared FoK and CRP offers culturally and linguistically diverse learners the opportunity to not only learn about their teacher and the cultures that exist in the virtual classroom from other students, but also a chance to highlight the cultural practices of their own families. The reason that a joint approach in a virtual classroom is critical, is because virtual middle level classrooms can be difficult to navigate when the facilitator or teacher aims to build rapport with learners without having physical contact (Posey, Burgess, Eason, & Jones, 2010). As such, there are boundaries that exist because of the limits of virtual spaces; boundaries between the knowledge that is shared and valued by the teacher and that of the middle level student and the boundaries between diverse learners and nonminority groups. Virtual educators can integrate CRP and FoK into their classroom to cross these boundaries.

## Getting to Know Learners in Virtual Classrooms

Using CRP and FoK to cross the boundaries of potentially unshared knowledge between teacher and student begins with getting to know the learner through identifying similarities, differences, and interests (Robinson, Wolffe, Hunt, & Hoerr, 2002; Terrell Shockley, 2017). One way that a virtual teacher could develop FoK of their students is through the implementation of an introductory activity at the beginning of a course that asks students to represent their interests and their culture through the sharing of key words and phrases. Users with Java installed on their computers can use Wordle.net and users without Java can refer to WordItOut.com to generate an image that shares words the student feels represent who they are culturally.

Another way that virtual teachers could develop their FoK could be through the students' use of an avatar for introductory coursework. For example, students could choose to include a photo of themselves, their country's flag (cultural heritage), their favorite author or artist of their culture, or their family coat of arms. Understanding the meaning of symbols and pictures in an avatar begins to illuminate the personalities, culture, and interest of students. Additionally, "students take pride in seeing their heritage and culture taught in the classroom" (Gonzalez, Pagan, Wendell, & Love, 2011, p. 180). Learning management systems such as Blackboard and Canvas offer an opportunity to create avatars as images. Instead of uploading pictures of themselves, students may decide to add an image that reflects his or her culture as described above. Additionally, students may create a Voki character, that includes an option for audio recordings, or computerized recordings that offer the option of an introduction. A Voki character is an avatar-like image that the student creates. Voki currently offers free options and those are the options referenced. Voki Classroom allows users to create avatar-like characters of their choice. Once students log on to Voki and create an account, they can choose their character (e.g., humans, animals, famous person). They select their character's attire (including makeup and jewelry for some characters) and then students may either record their own voice, or they can use an automated voice from Voki (which is created by typing in the message). Students can use the image as their avatar by taking a screenshot of the image that they created, or by participating in an opportunity in your class for learners to get to know each other. Voki offers a possibility for leaners to interact with each other and with their teacher by creating a character that represents them that they can post to a learning management system, send via e-mail, or upload into an avatar space (see Figure 11.1).

**Figure 11.1.**    Example of an avatar using Voki.

## Understanding Student Interests in Virtual Classrooms

It is important for virtual teachers to develop an understanding of their students' interests. One manner in which virtual teachers can accomplish this is to present students with an interest inventory to collect specific information about each learner and what they value (Terrell Shockley, 2017). Interest inventories provide teachers with insight on what students want to learn and how teachers may want to spend their instructional time. Teachers can learn about their students prior to the first official day of class by sending an interest inventory to collect specific information about each learner and what they value. Interest inventories can be created by the teacher based on a list of anticipated outcomes, such as favorite books to determine reading material, favorite sports teams to provide group names to students, and favorite subject to gain an understanding about how to integrate topics into a lesson. Students engaging in topics of interest generally have higher achievement in those topics, particularly with respect to texts (Johns & Lenski, 2001). Interests may change over time, therefore, including multiple ways to gauge students' interests (e.g., surveys, questionnaires, interviews) keeps the teacher informed.

Teachers can also present an inventory of experiences to learn about facets of students' lives (Johns & Lenski, 2001). These experiences include a list that students generate or teachers generate that can evolve into a collaborative game, such as bingo. Students identify their interests and their experiences and the students or the teachers place them onto a bingo board. As the experiences are called at random, students can mark the corresponding squares. If teachers want to know more about genres of interest, they may want to try incorporating Genre Bingo, which is a form of a bingo game in which teachers prepare the various bingo sheets with genres in the different blocks (Johns & Lenski, 2001). The teacher and/or the students can mark the squares as the different genres they have read or genres of interest are called throughout the game. In a virtual classroom, the teacher can create the bingo board using a site like BingoBaker.com. The site allows users to create text in each bingo cell. Once the creator of the board selects 'generate' on the BingoBaker website, the site populates a URL to share with students. As the students play using BingoBaker, the box the teacher calls will turn yellow. The instructor selects 'play online' to begin the game with students. Teachers can also include different disciplines and topics prior to presenting a unit or as an option to better understanding student's perspectives on a topic.

## INCLUDING CULTURALLY DIVERSE CONTENT IN THE VIRTUAL CURRICULUM

As teachers begin to understand their learners and their learners' interests, and consider ways to cross boundaries across differences, they must continue to develop their CRP and FoK by considering the curricula. The rationale for considering multiple perspectives for learners is to include learners whose stories may be otherwise omitted. Tapping into students' FoK includes extending and inviting their knowledge as part of the classroom discourse. Historically, text content may have changed over time for a variety of audiences, and these audiences may or may not represent the perspectives and the experiences of the learners in today's classrooms (Moule, 2012). This is not to suggest that current curricular content is not relevant or accurate. However, a current and accurate curriculum may not include perspectives of multiple groups. Does the textbook include a wide range of ethnic groups? Are the same few minorities represented repeatedly? For example, do historical texts present multiple positions when land is conquered or a war is won? What was it like for the individuals that took land compared to those who lost land? Are both perspectives presented? How does the text describe these groups? Gay (2002) maintained that CRP "deals directly with controversy; studying a wide range of ethnic individuals and groups; contextualizing issues of race, class, ethnicity, and gender; and including multiple kinds of knowledge and perspectives" (p. 108).

## Bringing in Student's Perspectives

Students are our greatest resource and including student voice in the curriculum allows a space for dialogue that teachers can connect to content (Erlandson & McVittie, 2001). Teachers can include student perspectives by offering them the opportunity to share their perspectives on a topic through a cultural lens. Depending on students' FoK, positions on topics can vary from what is traditionally incorporated in the curriculum or in texts (Moule, 2012), as both are often limited in cultural perspectives (Adams & Bell, 2016; Gay, 2002). Therefore, inviting student perspectives into the classroom is an opportunity to draw on the experiences of diverse learners, which expands CRP and develops both the teacher and students' FoK. For example, a virtual teacher can utilize online platforms such as Blackboard Collaborate or Google Hangouts to invite students to share their stories, experiences, and perspectives with one another. Teachers can create multiple discussion rooms, and have students work in small online groups to interview one another on topics of personal interest, or share links and documents that further develop and share their funds of knowledge. While student voice might be limited to the virtual context, it does not mean it must be stifled. Rather, online teachers can harness the power of the Internet and technology to open the curriculum and instruction to student-led research and discussion.

## Local and Global Perspectives

In addition to the student perspective, acquainting students with cultures from around the world is a way for teachers to implement CRP. Teachers can draw upon student interest and select cultures that students are not as familiar with so that the class can learn about these cultures together. The teacher could also choose to highlight a region that is well known by a student, either due to a previous visit, prior residence in the location or due to ancestry and history of a region from the family's funds of knowledge. There are a several ways to explore new places depending on the content area.

One example of how to virtually "explore" with your students is through the online content from the Smithsonian Institution's education website (https://learninglab.si.edu/). With the website, students can explore collections from the National Museum of African American History and Culture, opened in 2016. Teachers can obtain resources for students that help describe historical contexts through current contexts as part of the African American experience, including resources for participants to trace their genealogy and the history of culture for enslaved Africans. The historical components provide information beginning in the 15th century and make connections to Africans in other countries, African American inventors, explorers, and advocates. Teachers can reference sources that present stories from the perspectives of African Americans.

More than likely, few, if any students have had the privilege of traveling outside of the United States. However, there is a way for virtual teachers to make this happen. On a global perspective, teachers can take their students on virtual field trips to explore cultures outside their immediate country. ProjectExplorer.org is a resource that houses over 400 videos centered on cultures from 14 different countries; students can explore the culture and history of places like Thailand and Azerbaijan. Students are able to develop understandings of the similarities and differences between cultures and traditions. Developing this level of global awareness addresses misconceptions students may have about other peoples and cultures. Google Earth is another online resource that enables students to virtually visit and explore cities, historic landmarks, landforms, or areas that would otherwise be impossible to visit.

## Inclusion of Social Justice Themes

Incorporating resources that offer diverse perspectives by incorporating a social justice lens to an issue, text, or instructional unit is not only a CRP, but it can be beneficial to all involved (Toppel, 2015). While there are several definitions and frameworks focusing on social justice, we draw on Adams and Bell's (2016) definition that justice is the "recognition and respect of marginalized or subjugated people" (p. 3). Adams and Bell further posited:

> Social justice must address both resources and recognition. Resources include fair distribution of social, political and symbolic, as well as economic, assets. Recognition and respect for all individuals and groups requires full inclusion and participation in decision-making and the power to shape the institutions, policies, and processes that affect their lives. (p. 3)

One way to incorporate social justice themes into the virtual middle level classroom is to encourage conversations and discussions on current and past issues that present inequity in the world. Teachers may decide to follow an advocate, activist, or politician on social media and have students share what they learned in a whole class discussion. For example, students could follow the voting trends of Supreme Court Justice Sonia Sotomayor, uncovering the perspectives that informed her voting decisions. Through this examination, students are afforded opportunities to debate her decisions and discuss their perspectives.

By actively engaging students in conversations centered on social justice issues, and encouraging students to compose written narratives regarding issues of social inequity, teachers can contribute to cultivating a classroom with CRP, gain greater insight into students' perspectives, and strengthen opportunities to foster connection within the virtual classroom.

## Counternarratives

To diversify content, teachers can incorporate counternarratives into their courses. Counternarratives are the presentation of images and accounts that are not widely captured in mainstream society. They counter the general narrative, particularly for underrepresented groups, by including culturally and linguistically diverse people and topics in areas where they are otherwise excluded. Kee (2015) defined counternarratives as "stories told by marginalized people and communities themselves to interrogate and resist dominant narratives" (p. 17). When minority groups, or subgroups about whom there are negative dispositions, can navigate academic spaces (Khalifa & Briscoe, 2015) and succeed, they counterbalance the negative dispositions about their ability to perform.

Teachers should seek to provide resources, images, and texts that include or represent narratives to counter the deficit views that exist about minority groups. Strategies to incorporate counternarratives in content areas may include accessing the resources from the Smithsonian Institute's National

Museum of African American History and Culture, as well as the National Museum of American History, which documents resources on ethnic groups and indigenous groups in the United States, their history, and their stories. Or, virtual teachers could tap into the power of online connection, and invite community members, or people from around the world to speak with students about their unique experiences. Literature often explores the counternarratives missing from much of today's classroom texts and dialogue. A quick search of authors with Skype accounts can provide virtual teachers with a wealth of information regarding ways to reach and schedule Skype visits with authors in their classroom.

## CULTURALLY RELEVANT PEDAGOGY
## THROUGH COMMUNICATION

Toppel (2015) suggested that "culture strongly influences communication styles and how people convey understanding to others" (p. 556). This culture includes that of the teacher and the student. The ways that teachers communicate with students are likely to depend on the teacher's background or prior experiences (Moule, 2012). Considering ways that students communicate based on their FoK is important to engage in healthy dialogue in the virtual classroom.

Diverse learners bring a range of experiences, dialects and language to the classroom. A consideration for communicating within these ranges is important. Effective cross-cultural communication is critical for a teacher who is implementing CRP (Gay, 2002). A teacher engaging in CRP is potentially navigating conversations from different linguistic patterns. In a virtual classroom, applications that provide a space for communicating by reading, writing, speaking, listening and/or viewing are domains that support various forms of communication (Chen, Zhang, & Liu, 2014; Garrett, 2009). For students to communicate with teachers in multiple forms, teachers may decide to use online resources they can reference regularly either for each class or for each student. The app Padlet is an option that offers different language domains for teachers and students to communicate. Padlet is a tool that offers an option for written text, audio, video, and attachment in multiple languages. Joining Padlet allows the instructor or administrator to customize features linguistically.

Another resource for students to engage in communication using various domains of language is Mic Note. Students listen to statements in English, and potentially other languages, and answer a question or respond to a statement. Listening tasks can be made across levels, so it is a good practice for native speakers and speakers of other languages. Teachers can record themselves or students for the listening portion of Mic Note, which is an option for instruction and for assessment. After a teacher models how to use the app for listening, students can apply their knowledge by orally presenting information. Because Mic Note is registered to student e-mails, a copy of the student audio files is sent to their e-mail accounts that can aid in the submitting and sharing of student work.

When communicating with students using one of the resources, it is recommended that teachers accept a less formal dialect or register from students. While it is acceptable to require formal language on assignments, to continue to build rapport, caring contexts, and authentic relationships, students may need a space for communicating informally with teachers and/or with students.

## DIVERSITY IN THE DELIVERY OF INSTRUCTION AS CULTURALLY RELEVANT PEDAGOGY

Pedagogical approaches, as outlined by the tenets of CRP and FoK, consider students' culture and interests in the instructional choices a teacher makes. To understand learner differences and learner similarities, it is still important to enact practices that are responsive for all. The eight components of responding to diversity in the delivery of instruction include: (a) preferred content, (b) strategies for learning tasks, (c) techniques for conveying thoughts, (d) physical and social settings, (e) arrangements for performance, (f) stimulation for demonstrating comprehension, (g) motivational learning, and (h) interactional style (Gay, 2002). While these components reference CRP in brick-and-mortar settings, they can easily be transferred to the middle level virtual classroom.

After getting to know students culturally, strategizing their learning tasks should consider the broadest possible range, to include *all* learners. The inclusion provides access to groups of learners that may otherwise not be included in the learning process. In a virtual classroom, this may include access to software or access to language, which means that the instructor needs to consider the ways that communication (in the previously described forms of reading, writing, speaking, listening, and viewing) occurs for all. These different forms of communication give students techniques to convey thoughts to either their peers or their teacher depending on the scenario.

### Physical and Social Settings and Arrangements for Performance

Virtual teachers should evaluate the physical setting of a virtual classroom. Determining the type of hardware, a student is using to access materials will help teachers understand how to offer flexibility. For example, if a student is using a Mac computer, a PC computer, or a tablet may present issues of access to various resources. As teachers continue to learn students' social interests, skills should also be identified and understood to decide for students in pairs, or triads for assignments and projects. These settings and arrangements may happen based on languages spoken, or other components related to the setting. As teachers' cultural competence increases, the instructional decisions for a CRP will continue to evolve (Gay, 2002).

## Stimulation, Motivation, and Interaction

Beyond the initial inventorying of what motivates students, teachers can begin to integrate culturally relevant resources based on other cultural factors (e.g., age). Teachers may also incorporate popular culture into their classrooms (Fotiyeva & Terrell Shockley, 2015; LaVoulle, 2016). Popular culture includes an integration of culturally relevant media images, or film into the classroom. Drawing on popular culture, teachers offer a diverse lens through which material is presented to meet the needs of the students (LaVoulle, 2016) and to recognize and affirm the diverse nature of the middle level student.

## DISCUSSIONS AS CULTURALLY RELEVANT PEDAGOGY

Establishing guidelines for discussions is an essential component of a middle level virtual classroom. Teachers suggest that a classroom that recognizes and affirms diversity ensures that the learning environment is safe, making students more comfortable in taking risks, participating in discussions, and possibly making errors, particularly as some students are learning a new language and new customs (Fisher, Frey, & Rothenberg, 2008). To engage middle level virtual learners and promote a sense of belonging through CRP, virtual teachers should consider how they might work with students to create and establish discussion guidelines because differing perspectives may create conflict or confusion during class or group conversations. Drawing on the principles of CRP, we suggest the following guidelines:

- allow a range of opinions
- respect other's opinions
- listen as one peer speaks at a time
- have humility and recognizing that others may have perspectives that we do not

- engage in synchronous practice conversations for difficult dialogues

Teachers may also consider providing each student with equal talking time. The speaker should avoid criticism of the listener, and the listener should avoid interjecting (Weissglass, 1997). Virtual teachers can strive to include students in establishing guidelines and participating in practice rounds of talk, especially with culturally, linguistically diverse students (Fisher et al., 2008).

**Getting started with discussions.** Given the different forms of communication available in a virtual classroom, teachers and students can engage in these forms in a structured format via a Discussion Board, a Wiki, an online journal, or in a format where students engage in conversations synchronously. To begin the discussion, teachers can randomly select students to respond to a question or issue. Class Dojo allows random selection of students for discussion participation, provides students with participation points, keeps track of their points, and includes a timer (see Figure 11.2). After uploading a class roster into Class Dojo, this can be modified at any time.

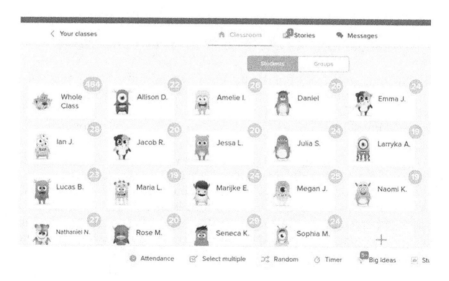

**Figure 11.2.**   Sample Class Dojo created by chapter authors.

After selecting a student to respond to a stated question, issue, or other course content, teachers can randomly select the next student using this resource or continue the discussions by having students select each other.

Overall, the goal of discussion in classrooms that employ CRP is to engage students in critical dialogue where they listen to each other, learn new perspectives, and accept differences.

## CONCLUSION

There are multiple ways to implement culturally responsive pedagogy in the virtual middle level classroom. As educators, it is essential that we consider and incorporate components of the culture that students bring to our classrooms (Ladson-Billings, 1995). The literature shows that teachers who employ CRP observe significant gains in achievement for diverse learners (Stoddard, Tieso, & Robbins, 2015). Without this approach, the diverse middle level virtual learner may continue to perform at a national average that is lower than their peers (National Center for Education Statistics, 2014, 2015).

Historically there may have been differences in achievement or performance among major ethnic groups; however this has more to do with inadequate instruction, and less to do with student's ability to learn (Abrams, Ferguson, & Laud, 2001; Howard & Rodriguez-Scheel, 2017). Zeichner (1992) listed components for teaching diverse learners including teachers having a sense of their cultural identity, making connections to the curriculum and to diverse learner's experiences and prior knowledge, maintaining students' sense of pride about their culture while teaching school culture, and believing that all their students are capable of succeeding. Transforming the virtual classroom to echo these sentiments is possible with the right mindset and even more possible with the right resources.

## REFERENCES

Adams, M., & Bell, L. (2016). *Teaching for diversity and social justice* (3rd ed.). New York, NY: Routledge, Taylor & Francis.

Abrams, J., Ferguson, J., & Laud, L. (2001). Assessing ESOL students. *Educational Leadership*, *59*(3), 62–65.

Chen, L., Zhang, R., & Liu, C. (2014). Listening strategy use and influential factors in web-based computer assisted language learning. *Journal of Computer Assisted Learning*, *30*(3), 207–219.

Erlandson, C., & McVittie, J. (2001). Student voices on integrative curriculum. *Middle School Journal*, *33*(2), 28–36.

Fisher, D., Frey, N., & Rothenberg, C. (2008). *Content-area conversations: How to plan discussion-based lessons for diverse language learners*. Alexandria, VA: Association for Supervision and Curriculum Development.

Fotiyeva, I., & Terrell Shockley, E. (2015, May). *Using traditional LMS for mathematics instruction: Lessons learned from instructor-made videos*. Paper presented at the International Conference on Computer Supported Education, Lisbon, Portugal. Retrieved from http://www.scitepress.org/PublicationsDetail.aspx?ID=j4otoeX%2fTjc%3d&t=1

Garrett, N. (2009). Computer-assisted language learning trends and issues revisited: Integrating innovation. *The Modern Language Journal, 93*(s1), 719–740.

Gay, G. (2000). *Culturally responsive teaching: Theory, research, and practice*. New York, NY: Teachers College Press.

Gay, G. (2002). Preparing for culturally responsive teaching. *Journal of Teacher Education, 53*(2), 106–116.

Gonzalez, R. J., Pagan, M., Wendell, L., & Love, C. (2011). *Supporting ELL/ culturally and linguistically diverse students for academic achievement*. Rexford, NY: International Center for Leadership in Education.

Howard, T. C., & Rodriguez-Scheel, A. (2017). Culturally relevant pedagogy 20 years later: Progress or pontificating? What have we learned, and where do we go? *Teachers College Record, 119*(1), 1–32.

Johns, J., & Lenski, S. (2001). *Improving reading: Strategies and resources* (3rd ed.). Dubuque, IA: Kendall/Hunt.

Kee, J. (2015). No excuses or no equity? Narrative and counternarrative themes within educational discourse in New Orleans. *Souls, 17*(3/4), 248–262.

Khalifa, M., & Briscoe, F. (2015). A counter-narrative autoethnography exploring school districts' role in reproducing racism: Willful blindness to racial inequities. *Teachers College Record, 117*(8), 1–34.

Ladson-Billings, G. (1995). Toward a theory of culturally relevant pedagogy. *American Educational Research Journal, 32*(3), 465–491.

LaVoulle, C. (2016). Effective instructional practices for diverse learners: Using popular culture resources to engage learners. *AMLE Magazine*. Retrieved from https://www.amle.org/BrowsebyTopic/WhatsNew/WNDet/TabId/270/ArtMID/888/ArticleID/746/Effective-Instructional-Practices-for-Diverse-Learners.aspx

Moll, L. C., Amanti, C., Neff, D., & González, N. (1992). Funds of knowledge for teaching: Using a qualitative approach to connect homes and classrooms. *Theory Into Practice, 31*(2), 132–141.

Moule, J. (2012). *Cultural competence: A primer for educators* (2nd ed.). Belmont, CA: Wadsworth.

National Center for Education Statistics. (2014). *Common core data 8*. Retrieved from https://nces.ed.gov/nationsreportcard/subject/publications/main2013/pdf/2014451.pdf

National Center for Education Statistics. (2015). *National score gaps*. Retrieved from https://www.nationsreportcard.gov/reading_math_2015/#reading/gaps?grade=8

Posey, G., Burgess, T., Eason, M., & Jones, Y. (2010, March). *The advantages and disadvantages of the virtual classroom and the role of the teacher*. Paper presented at the Southwest Decision Sciences Institute Conference, Dallas, TX. Retrieved from http://www.swdsi.org/swdsi2010/SW2010_Preceedings/papers/PA126.pdf

Robinson, H., Wolffe, R., Hunt, P., & Hoerr, N. (2002). Creating cross-cultural connections. *Urban Education, 37*(4), 533–547.

Stoddard, J., Tieso, C., & Robbins, J. (2015). Project CIVIS: Curriculum development and assessment of underserved and underachieving middle school populations. *Journal of Advanced Academics, 26*(3), 168–196.

Terrell Shockley, E. (2017). Field notes: Encouraging positive dispositions toward exceptional students. *ASCD Express, 12*(16). Retrieved from http://www.ascd.org/ascd-express/vol12/1216-toc.aspx

Toppel, K. (2015). Enhancing core reading programs with culturally responsive practices. *The Reading Teacher, 68*(7), 552–559.

U.S. Census Bureau. (2015). *Census Bureau reports at least 350 languages spoken in U.S. homes* [Press release]. Retrieved from http://www.census.gov/newsroom/press-releases/2015/cb15-185.html

Weissglass, J. (1997). Deepening our dialogue about equity. *Educational Leadership, 54*(7), 78–81.

Zeichner, K. M. (1992). *Educating teachers for cultural diversity*. National Center for Research on Teacher Learning Special Report. Retrieved from https://education.msu.edu/NCRTL/PDFs/NCRTL/SpecialReports/sr293.pdf

CHAPTER 12

# ORGANIZING AND FACILITATING ONLINE TEACHING, LEARNING, AND SCHOOLING VIA EFFECTIVE CLASSROOM ASSESSMENTS

**Nancy P. Gallavan**
*University of Central Arkansas*

**Shannon R. Maiden**
*Ruth Doyle Middle School*

During the 1960s, middle level education emerged focusing on the education of young adolescents, between the ages of 10 and 15 (Schaefer, Malu, & Yoon, 2016). Contemporary middle level education has advanced to encompass the ever changing and challenging contexts amid the transitional years of academic growth and personal development when young adolescents transform significantly: physically, intellectually, morally, psychologically, and socio-emotionally (National Middle School Association, 2010). To guide and support middle level education, as well as middle level teacher candidate preparation, the Association for Middle Level Education

*The Online Classroom:*
*Resources for Effective Middle Level Virtual Education,* pp. 205–224
Copyright © 2018 by Information Age Publishing
All rights of reproduction in any form reserved.

drafted *This We Believe: The Keys to Educating Young Adolescents* (National Middle School Association, 2010) as a framework for middle level schools. This seminal document helps middle level educators and teacher educators understand the concepts and practices necessary to optimize all middle level educational environments.

Middle level education has continued to evolve and expand over time and, like all K–12 educational environments, has become accessible as face-to-face, online, blended, or hybrid (a combination of face-to-face and online) educational environments. To address the development and various milieu of online education, the International Association for K–12 Online Learning (iNACOL) was established and subsequently published standards for online educators (iNACOL, 2011). However, even with the publication of standards from AMLE and iNACOL, along with documents published by many other national professional educational organizations, effective middle level online education poses new and difficult challenges both like and different from challenges encountered in face-to-face education (Beebe, Vonderwell, & Boboc, 2010; Robles & Braathen, 2002). Specifically, the increasing requirements for middle level teachers to document evidence of learner engagement and achievement; to analyze data associated with the teaching, learning, and schooling; and to demonstrate accountability to all stake-holders may seem elusive as middle level online teachers struggle with designing and delivering the required curriculum coupled with meaningful instruction. To these ends, this chapter offers online middle level teacher resources and tools for organizing and facilitating the teaching, learning, and schooling via classroom assessments. These resources and tools not only advance online learner growth and development, they also help teachers enhance their sense of responsibility or self-efficacy, building a sense of ownership or agency, and developing a sense of career professionalism.

## TEACHING, LEARNING, AND SCHOOLING TRIAD

Middle level learning in today's educational environments is defined by a signature pedagogy (Haselhuhn, Al-Mabuk, Gabriele, Groen, & Galloway, 2007; Schaefer, Malu, & Yoon, 2016) depicted by research-based classroom practices and professionalism developed specifically for middle level teachers to be effective with the range of today's middle level learners. Middle level teachers must be attentive to their learners' diverse characteristics, needs, and interests, as well as their learners' families and support systems. One aspect of this signature pedagogy advocates for immersion into the contemporary sociocultural context of the middle level teaching, learning, and schooling (Cochran-Smith, 1991) accompanied with reflective practices centered on teacher self-efficacy (Bandura, 1977, 1986).

Gallavan's triad of teacher self-efficacy (Gallavan & Merritt, in press) illustrates the presence and power of the three components contributing to teacher self-efficacy. The teaching, learning, and schooling are monitored and measured by analyzing documents and data related to (a) each learner's engagement and achievement, (b) the teacher's practices and modifications, and (c) the school's environment, materials, and resources. The goals are for teachers to increase the learning, enhance the teaching, and improve the schooling.

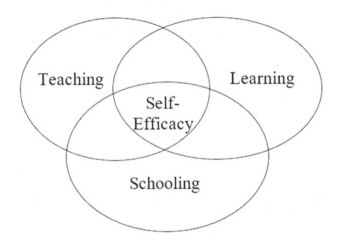

**Figure 12.1.** Gallavan's triad teacher self-efficacy.

However, all three aspects of the triad are dependent on the effectiveness of the teacher and teaching-the most critical factor affecting educational success and satisfaction (Darling-Hammond, 2006). As today's middle level schools grapple with the needs for middle level teachers to engage learners contextually and authentically in meaningful explorations to increase learners' achievement, middle level teachers must demonstrate accountability via assessments, analyses, and accommodations appropriate to middle level education.

## Teacher Self-Efficacy and Effectiveness

Bandura (1997) defined self-efficacy as "the belief in one's capacities to organize and execute the sources of action required to manage perspective situations" (p. 3). Coupled with awareness, application, and advocacy of human agency, the quest to enhance teacher self-efficacy compels a teacher to acknowledge and accept responsibility for organizing and executing the sources of action required to increase the engagement and achievement of *all* learners (Bandura, 1977, 1986). For the middle level teacher specifically, enhancing teacher self-efficacy entails taking responsibility for providing both the will and the way to do what is right and good because it is right and good. Thus, middle level teachers are attending constantly, consistently, and comprehensively to all aspects of the teaching learning, and schooling for each learner by monitoring, measuring, and modifying individual practices to optimize educational success and satisfaction within the dynamics descriptive of middle level learning and living. Only by documenting evidence of growth, analyzing data associated with processes and outcomes, and detailing accountability in each sphere of the triad (see Figure 11.1) can teachers appropriately guide and support early adolescents, providing the sustainability necessary for their significant transformation within the ever-changing and challenging sociocultural context of middle level virtual education.

## Middle Level Classroom Teachers and Learners

Many of today's middle level teachers (face-to-face, online, blended, and hybrid) are millennials and were educated in or influenced by the era of No Child Left Behind when teachers dedicated an abundance of classroom teaching and learning time to test preparation and state-mandated testing (National Center for Education Statistics, 2017). During the teachers' PK–12 years of schooling, technology was just beginning to become a viable part of the educational as well as home and social environments and was added—somewhat awkwardly at times--to the school day rather than integrated more naturally into the curriculum and instruction. During the early years of the 21st century, teachers used little or no technology for classroom assessments (Boss, 2011). Conversely, today's middle level learners are considered digital natives who have been immersed in technology throughout their lives and, most likely, have been educated in the era of technology where classroom teachers are dedicating an abundance of time to connectivity, using various devices, tools, or linking through virtual courses.

Approaching the organization and facilitation of teaching, learning, and schooling via effective classroom assessments equips and empowers online middle level teachers to align curriculum, instruction, and assessments (Wiggins & McTighe, 2005) and better manage the elicitation of authentic outcomes as learners express and exchange their new learning. Today's middle level learners are captivated by, conditioned to, and comfortable with learning with technology (both in and out of the classroom—educationally and socially). Therefore, the responsibility for online middle level teachers to select current, relevant, and appropriate technology to accommodate all needs and interests increases. Consequently, online middle level teachers provide learners with optimal platforms and multiple possibilities to address academic standards and fulfill expectations established by the state departments of education and national professional organizations, including iNACOL and the AMLE.

## THE CLASSROOM ASSESSMENT CLOCK

To assist online middle level teachers in the organization and facilitation of teaching, learning, and schooling through assessments, we offer the Classroom Assessment Clock (see Figure 12.2), named for the 12 steps of the cyclical sequence followed when reading a clock. The Classroom Assessment Clock is divided into four quadrants, each containing three steps: (a) Targets (planning, researching, and aligning), (b) Techniques (designing, conducting, and collecting), (c) Tools (documenting, analyzing, and communicating), and (d) Tips (reflecting, modifying, and enhancing). We describe and discuss the processes involved in employing the four quadrants and three corresponding steps for a unit of learning in the next sections.

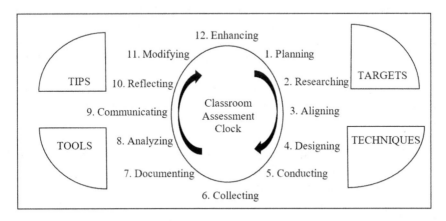

**Figure 12.2.**   The Classroom Assessment Clock developed by the authors.

## Targets

The "Targets" for a unit of learning designed and delivered in any educational format start with a careful review of the standards. For middle level units of learning, online middle level teachers must reference all relevant attributes and characteristics found in *This We Believe* (NMSA, 2010) and the iNACOL *Standards for Online Education* (2011) for courses with online formats and technological features, and content standards for the subject area. Additionally, online middle level teachers can benefit greatly by becoming acquainted with the *Classroom Assessment Standards for PK–12 Teachers* published by the Joint Committee for Standards of Educational Evaluation (Klinger, McDivitt, Howard, Munoz, Rogers, & Wylie, 2015). As the 21st century began, many classroom teachers had received little to no formal education related to classroom assessments (Sheppard, 2000). These standards supply the information that middle level teachers need to understand and apply classroom assessments effectively in all contexts throughout the school year.

Klinger et al. (2015) categorized the classroom assessment standards for pre-K–12 teachers into three broad domains: (a) foundations, (b) use, and (c) quality. "Foundations" include preparation, especially aligning curriculum, instruction, and assessments. "Use" involves facilitation, especially providing feedback to learners, reporting progress to parents and administrators, and analyzing data. "Quality" incorporates fairness, especially ensuring validity and reliability in the assessments. When teachers apply these standards across the teaching, learning, and schooling of young adolescents, in all educational formats and with all technological features, they can enhance self-efficacy. Awareness and incorporation of these assessment standards help online middle level teachers to align assessments with curriculum and instruction to maximize the limited time and opportunities teachers spend with learners.

Ultimately, online middle level teachers must design the purpose of the unit of learning placed in the appropriate scope and sequence of a course of learning, select the specific goals and objectives, and operate in terms of the assessment cycle. The assessment cycle starts with a preassessment conducted before the teaching and learning begin and is followed by formative assessments conducted during each class lesson. The assessment cycle highlighted by summative assessments such as papers, presentations, Power Points, projects, and so forth, showcasing overarching authentic outcomes for the unit of learning. Then the assessment ends with the postassessment—the same instrument used for the preassessment, conducted after the end of the unit of learning. Teachers should administer the same preassessment and postassessment instrument to compare the growth of each learner and the usefulness of each assessment item. Using the same instrument for the unit of learning preassessment and postassessment helps online middle level teachers recognize the major modifications needed for the curriculum, instruction, and assessments of this unit of learning during steps 11 and 12 of the Classroom Assessment Clock.

Formative assessments provide the primary opportunities for online middle level teachers to daily monitor and measure learners' knowledge, skills, and dispositions and helps teachers recognize the minor modifications that they need to make from day-to-day to advance the learning for each learner appropriately (William, 2006). Summative assessments offer opportunities for learners to apply new knowledge, skills, and dispositions to comprehensive productions that connect concepts and practices across multiple lessons and allow learners to express their individual interests. All outcomes associated with the preassessment/postassessment, formative assessments, and summative assessments must be established during the steps of planning, researching, and aligning.

**Step 1—Planning.** Planning involves many components including (a) understanding the structures and functions available with and specific to an online educational format; (b) the context of the unit of learning; (c) the academic readiness, cultural characteristics, and individual needs of the learners, particularly online learners; (d) the scope and sequence of the curriculum; (e) the length of the unit of learning; and (f) the length of each class session. Planning for online learners requires middle level teachers to think through both the long-term overview of the entire course and the specific unit of learning experience, as well as the short-term details of each class session to understand the direction of the teaching, learning, and schooling. Teachers must anticipate and prepare for every kind of interaction given the changes and challenges associated with online education, for example, individual responsibility for engagement online, technology issues, computer literacy, time management, and self-motivation (Kumar, 2015). Middle level learners are just beginning to acquire self-control; online education adds another dynamic that online middle level teachers must plan in detail. Technology applications (apps) such as Google Forms, Nearpod, and Planboard offer free and efficient tools to help virtual teachers through the planning process. They each include resources that help virtual teachers organize, align, and document classroom curriculum, instruction, and assessments.

**Step 2—Researching.** Researching requires online middle level teachers to (a) identify the standards, expectations, and outcomes in their academic subject areas and states; (b) network with colleagues; and (c) communicate with learners and families. Teacher can find information about standards, expectations, and outcomes on the web sites of several national professional organizations: National Council of Teachers of English, National Council for Teachers of Mathematics, National Council for the Social Studies, National Science Teachers Association, among other middle level curricular content areas. Live chats on the websites for the AMLE, Edutopia, and educational blogs for middle level teachers provide opportunities for educators to network with others in the field.

Researching also encourages online middle level teachers to find learner-centered and innovative strategies to incorporate into the course and unit of learning that are both appropriate and progressive. The American Association of School Librarians and the Northwest Evaluation Association have created web sites with some of the best apps for teaching and learning. Teachers are encouraged to evaluate educational apps for their classrooms noting the engagement, appropriateness, design, motivation, and accessibility as developed by Educational Technology and Mobile Learning (2017).

**Step 3—Aligning.** Although frequently overlooked, the step of aligning the curriculum, instruction, and assessment encompasses one of the most essential steps for instructional effectiveness (Martone & Sireci, 2009). The curriculum or selected content based on the class session objectives must align with the teaching methods and learning strategies so learners can demonstrate the appropriate outcomes during the process as monitored and measured on their formative assessments and after the process as monitored and measured on their post-assessments. When the in-class activities and/or out-of-class assignments constitute major outcomes, then the summative assessments also must align. Online middle level teachers should start by identifying the objectives and outcomes, followed by communicating opportunities for learners to select various options to explore, discover, and coconstruct new knowledge emphasizing individual connections. Then online middle level teachers should end by monitoring and measuring the learners' demonstrated outcomes, highlighting self-assessment, of the established objectives.

## EFFECTIVE ONLINE CLASSROOM ASSESSMENTS

Conducting, collecting, and analyzing classroom assessment data allow online middle level teachers to authentically inform and modify practices (Ferdig & Cavanaugh, 2011; Watson & Murin, 2014) to meet the needs of each learner. Online middle level teachers benefit by viewing assessments from three perspectives: (a) as the process, (b) for the process, and (c) of the process (Stiggins, 2005). When teachers view assessment *as* the process, the data relate to the learners and learning. These data constitute the outcomes that each teacher monitors and measures revealing the learners' engagement and achievement. When teachers view assessment *for* the process, the data relate to the teacher and teaching. These data constitute the outcomes that each teacher monitors and measures revealing the teacher's self-efficacy. When teachers view assessment *of* the process, the data relate to the school and schooling. These data constitute the outcomes that learners and each teacher both monitor and measure revealing the environment and various situational factors that the learners and the teacher may or may not be able to control or manage. All three sets of data contribute to the overall effectiveness of the teaching, learning, and schooling centered on enhancing the teacher's self-efficacy.

## Techniques

Techniques encompass the three ways that teachers conduct classroom assessments. Teachers can conduct assessments by watching or observing learners in action, listening to learners talking, or reading and reviewing learners' written and created products. Therefore, teachers are assessing informally, during presentations and discussions, and formally, during writing and creating a final paper or project, as part of their formative and summative assessments. Prior to the starting the unit, online middle level teachers must determine the forms and the types of assessments to be used when conducting the preassessments/postassessments, formative assessments, and summative assessments.

The forms of assessment include the ways items will be posed to the learners for them to demonstrate their learning. For example, when teachers are watching or observing learners, the form of assessment may ask the learner to show, draw, point to, and so forth, an outcome or object. Students demonstrate the outcome through an action and may or (may not) be accompanied with talking and/or writing. When teachers are listening to learners, the form of assessment may ask the learner to tell or say something to the class, peer, group of peers, teachers, and so forth, and may or may not be accompanied with an action and/or writing. When teachers are reading the learners' written products, the form of assessment may ask the learner to write as an in-class activity or out-of-class assignment that may (or may not) be accompanied with talking and/or an action.

In online education, teachers use technology for watching, which allows them to see the learner. Teachers may conduct their watching live via Google Hangouts, Skype, or by viewing a video using YouTube or VideoAnt. VideoAnt enhances learning by combining annotated statements into the documentation that the learner and teachers exchange with one another as a written conversation. Likewise, listening necessitates technology for online middle level teachers to hear the learner live or by listening to a submitted recording. Listening may be conducted through Google Hangouts, Skype, and, of course, individual telephone calls and texts.

Essential to the forms of classroom assessments is each teacher's preparation with questions and questioning techniques to use during class conversations. Online middle level teachers benefit greatly by preparing a learner selection system with every learner's name recorded on a checklist for easy reference. The checklist provides an ideal space for online middle level teachers to record formative assessment data for the entire group of learners during one class lesson. Teachers begin by identifying the assessment criteria across the top of the sheet and the learners' names down the side before the class lesson begins. As teachers conduct the lesson, they record notations. The Assessment Checklist Template and the Canva websites provide ways to customize classroom assessment checklists. For online formats, middle level teachers can conduct discussions and ask questions through synchronous connections such as Google Hangouts or Skype and asynchronous connections such as Voice Thread. Voice Thread allows learners to add their own narratives to their products to share with teachers and/or peers.

Types of assessment include the wording of items to promote higher order and critical thinking. Types of assessment need to include an array of recognition and recall; logical and reasoning; skills and applications; creativity and productivity; and outlooks and dispositions. These five types of assessment allow teachers to vary their questioning and further explore a topic or issue, particularly a topic of issue of interest to the learners. Ideament lets learners design diagrams that can integrate any or all levels of thinking to demonstrate individual understanding and application of concepts and skills for every middle level learner.

**Step 4—Designing.** When designing the assessment technique, online middle level teachers must consider the entire assessment cycle (when to assess), the technique (how to access), the form of assessment (how learners will express outcomes), and the type of assessment (what learners will provide as the outcome). Additionally, middle level teachers must supplement the given curriculum with resources for learners to access additional information to apply to all forms and types of assessments used throughout the assessment cycle. Middle level learners have a wide range of abilities, needs, and interests; the learning environment encapsulates an ideal time to stimulate their potential as they discover new information about the world around them.

Online middle level teachers will appreciate the educational information found on web sites such as BrainPop, Crash Course, Newsela, and Wolframalpha. BrainPOP provides learners with short animated videos coupled with activities and assessments. Crash Course includes an array of courses from which teachers and learners can glean additional knowledge. Newsela is comprised of information, writing prompts, annotations, and quizzes. Wolframalpha features various menus to delve into each of the topics in seemingly endless detail.

Forms of assessments include selected answers, constructed responses, demonstrated performances, and spoken conversations. In selected answers, the assessment provides all possible answers and the learner selects the most appropriate answer. Some common selected answer assessments are fill-in-the-blank, labeling a diagram, matching, multiple-choice, placing in order, and true/false. For selected answers, teachers can use the technological features on apps such as Gnowledge, Interact Quiz Builder, Kahoot!, Online Quiz Creator, and Socrative. Each of these apps enables teachers to develop the questions ideal for preassessments, formative assessments, and postassessments and quiz learners in a game-like fashion. Online middle level teachers can also ask their learners to write the questions. Varying the apps motivates learners to attend class, prepare for the game, and participate more fully.

In constructed responses, the learner must write the response in words. The written response may range in length from one word to a lengthy essay or report. For constructed responses, teachers can use the technological features of Evernote, Google Docs, Google Forms, Questbase, and Wiki-Spaces for learners to write long and short fictional and nonfiction entries. Then teachers and peers can share and assess entries.

In demonstrated performances, the learner acts, demonstrates, performs, points to, and so forth, without using spoken and/or written words. Learners can conduct their demonstrated performances alone or as members of a group; teachers must be clear on the ways each member of the group will be assessed individually. For demonstrated performances, teachers can use the technological features on Flipboard, Glogster, Google Drawings, Google Forms, Google Presentations, Google Slides, and Live-binders for learners to delve into topics (individually, as partners, or in small groups) to organize information and inquiries to share with the class. Demonstrated performances transfer the responsibility for learning as well as teaching peers to the learners themselves.

In spoken conversations, the learner speaks with teachers, the class, a peer, or a group of peers, and so forth, without demonstrating or using written words. Again, spoken conversations may be limited to a single word or a lengthy description. For spoken conversations, teachers can use the technological features on AudioNote, Poll Everywhere, Screencast-o-matic, and Tell About This for learners to record their oral messages again individually, with partners, or in small groups with or without notes. Additionally, online middle level teachers can easily combine the four forms of classrooms assessments and use the technological features on Google Forms.

**Step 5—Conducting.** Online middle level teachers should be conducting classroom assessments constantly both formally and informally. As middle level teachers monitor engagement and measure achievement, teachers are assessing the learners by watching, listening, and reading written products. Likewise, all learners should also be constantly assessing themselves; teachers need to ask learners to proofread their individual responses and products. In addition, they gauge themselves (formally and informally) against the responses and products of their peers. Some educational resources for conducting polls include AnswerGarden, ExitTicket, Lino, and Plinkers. Teachers and learner need to co-construct some classroom assessments collaboratively— deciding jointly the process and the outcomes.

Learners should be shown ways to proofread carefully and self-assess honestly as part of their guided and independent practice during in-class activities and out-of-class assignments. "Students need to self-assess to know when they are learning, how much effort they must expend for success, when they have been successful, when they are wrong, and which learning strategies work well for them" (McMillan & Hearn, 2008, p. 44) in order "to discover their own learning potential" (Nonyel, 2015, para. 3). Increased opportunities to connect the major concepts and related practices strengthen learners' understanding and application across the curriculum and contextualization in the real world. Providing learners with written instructions that include expectations and assessment tools allows learners to guide themselves while allowing parents and other family members to assist the learners. Learners can share their products with peers, teachers, and families using DropBox, Google Photos, Moodle, and WeVideo.

**Step 6—Collecting.** All teachers, especially teachers educating in virtual contexts who are not physically interacting with their learners, should be attentive to collecting and recording assessment data constantly. Maintaining electronic records using charts, rubrics, spread sheets, and so on, as online middle level teachers observe, listen, and read learners' written products both informally and formally helps teachers to quickly identify learners' strengths and weaknesses and to readily modify teaching practices to better meet the needs and interests of learners. Teachers can maintain data collected from daily classroom assessments as anecdotal records, and on Google Sheets, Microsoft Excel, and other online grade display systems frequently required and provided by schools and school districts.

Google Sheets and Microsoft Excel allow teachers to design specific categories appropriate to classroom assessments: raw scores, percentages, and so forth, and enter corresponding data. Features on these systems let teachers interact with the data to analyze outcomes associated with an assessment, assessment item, and/or learner. Likewise, teachers can analyze progress over time. Analyzing data provides teachers with the knowledge needed to modify their practices and professionalism to increase learner engagement and achievement and enhance their self-efficacy and effectiveness.

## Tools

Assessment techniques describe the ways that teachers conduct assessments, whereas, assessment tools describe the ways that teachers record assessment data. Tools include class rosters, checklists, rubrics, apps, and grade books. Each of the assessment tools allows online middle level teachers to record progress corresponding with the assessment criteria and each learner's name as teachers watch, listen, and read written products. Various electronic tools available for recording preassessment/postassessment data include Diagnoser, Flubaroo, Naiku, and Grade Ninja. These tools include features that calculate scores and generate patterns.

Checklists are the most popular tools for recording formative assessment data; rubrics are the most popular tools for recording formative assessment data collected by reading written products and all summative assessment data. Checklists and rubrics can be generated using iRubric, QuickRubric, QuizStar, Rubric-Maker, and RubiStar. These tools provide an array of templates enabling teachers to design developmentally appropriate rubrics. Teachers should include spaces for learners to self-assess too. Moreover, teachers can save their rubrics and return to it later to edit for other lessons and units. Using similar rubrics helps learners feel comfortable with the assessment process and the teacher in order to demonstrate competence with the content.

**Step 7—Documenting.** After online middle level teachers have created the appropriate assessment tools and are beginning to conduct the assessments, they must document the data immediately. Too often, teachers will watch or listen to the learners and not record the assessment data right away; frequently teachers tend to believe that they will remember the learners' words or actions until later in the day and they can modify their teaching appropriately at that time (Brookhart, 2004). However, ongoing information and a multitude of events to monitor, manage, and measure inundate most middle level teachers; consequently, their memories become overloaded. Teachers may not remember the intricate details related to each learner's progress and outcomes; therefore, teachers need to document data immediately as they assess. After data are recorded, for example on checklists or rubrics while assessing in-class activities and out-of-class assignments, the teacher must record the data in electronic documents that can be easily accessed for each teacher's analysis and communication with learners and learners' families.

With online education, everyone needs to be well acquainted with the procedures in advance of completing activities and assignments. Distribution of the checklist or rubric accompanies communication with learners and their families prior to the teaching, learning, and schooling. The checklist or rubric helps to reinforce the goals and purpose of the unit of learning, the objectives and expectations of each lesson, fairness and transparency of scoring, availability of and access to assistance, choice and voice for customizing outcomes, and frequency and detail of anticipated feedback. When a teacher establishes a format to follow throughout a course, the learners and their families can concentrate on the known academic process and product rather than the unknown personalities and presumptions.

**Step 8—Analyzing.** At every step of the Classroom Assessment Clock, online middle level teachers must analyze all aspects of the teaching, learning, and schooling by asking 12 key questions:

- What content standards were assessed?
- What content standards were not assessed and why not?
- What were the levels and indicators of learner proficiency?
- What percent of learners demonstrated each level and indicator of proficiency?
- What are the levels of proficiency by subgroups (e.g., but not limited to, race, gender, free and reduced lunch, abilities, English language learners)?
- What are the implications of learner achievement for the teacher at each step of the Classroom Assessment Clock?
- What modifications should the teacher make to increase learner engagement and achievement? (The teacher should consider the curricular content, instructional strategies, assessment procedures, in-class activities, and out-of-class assignments.)
- After modifications, what percent of learners demonstrated each level and indictor of proficiency?
- Did modifications or other interventions improve learner performance?
- What modifications need to occur in the next unit of learning?
- What modifications need to occur in the general approaches and attitudes of the teaching, learning, and schooling?
- What overarching steps does the teacher need to take to ensure continuous attention to documenting evidence of learner engagement and achievement; analyzing data associated with the teaching, learning, and schooling; and demonstrating accountability to all stake-holders?

When analyzing preassessment and postassessment data, online middle level teachers can use tools such as Desmos, Excel, Google Developers, and Graph Maker. Graphs provide visual displays that help teachers see the data quickly and easily. Teachers can identify the patterns among both the items and the learners. From these data, teachers can conduct an item analysis corresponding to the curriculum instruction, activities, assignments and assessments as well as the individual learners. Creating similar graphs to record preassessment and postassessment data using the same instrument allows teachers to analyze data readily, allowing the virtual teacher to note change over time.

**Step 9—Communicating assessment data.** Many learners and their families want and appreciate communication with teachers regarding the learner's progress. Communicating involves providing immediate, accurate, and encouraging feedback, so online middle level teachers must be purposeful in their comments. Suggestions for effective feedback include (a) using the learner's name so the teacher can individualize the communication (and ensuring that the correct learner is receiving the correct communication) followed by complementary statements reinforcing accomplishments; (b) sharing one or two statements communicating corrections or redirections to items and areas needing more attention; and (c) asking for explanations to items or areas that seem unclear and/or incomplete. Teachers should avoid using generic words such as "great" or "terrific" without specificities (Brookhart, 2012; Bruno & Santos, 2010).

Unfortunately, many learners (and their families) tend to focus more on numeric scores or grades, rather than the descriptive narratives used for feedback (Brookhart, 2012). Therefore, online middle level teachers must ensure that the descriptive narratives communicate the numeric scores or grades clearly emphasizing the importance and value in understanding areas of strength, and areas of demonstrated development, and inviting continuous conferencing with learners and their families to support growth. Classkick allows teachers to provide learners with immediate private individual feedback on iPad screens and answer questions posed electronically. (Review the suggestions from Techniques Step 4). Learners can reflect using a tool called Recap to provide feedback accompanied by videos.

## Tips

The fourth quadrant of the Classroom Assessment Clock consists of three tips that are essential for middle level teachers to provide the will and the way to do what is right and good because it is right and good. Through purposeful and mindful reflection on and modification to practices, particularly classroom assessment practices, middle level teachers realize the presence and power of effectiveness across the triad of teaching, learning, and schooling.

**Step 10—Reflecting.** After analyzing data, teachers should reflect on their practices to increase their awareness of accomplishments and to assess their own self-efficacy (Brookfield, 2017; Tschannen-Moran & Hoy, 2001; Tschannen-Moran & McMaster, 2009). We recommend that teachers reflect on four questions: (a) What did I ask/tell my learners to do (show, say, and/or write) to demonstrate their learning? (b) Why did I ask my learners to demonstrate their learning that way? (c) What were the criteria that guided the learning and demonstration of learning? and (d) How well were learners prepared with knowledge, skills, and dispositions to demonstrate their highest achievement of the learning? These four questions prompt teachers to revisit the entire unit of learning starting with the outcome, then looking at the assessment. Teachers must be sure that the assessment aligns with and builds upon the instruction and curriculum based on clearly articulated objectives.

Online education demands more attention to the step of reflecting. Teachers organize many of the documents and resources used during online education in advance of the facilitation. Unlike face-to-face education, teachers cannot alter or augment the selected documents and resources during facilitation of online education. Communicating alterations and augmentations can easily create cumbersome situations that online educators want to avoid. Digital tools helpful for teachers to record their own reflections include Edublogs; Teach, Learn, Lead; and WordPress. Teachers can pose inquiries, share information, and make powerful insights by expressing themselves and exchanging ideas with other educators. Teachers can use these same tools for classroom social networking in addition to Edmodo, Seesaw, and Twiducate. Edmodo facilitates communication with families; Seesaw and Twiducate allows teachers to communicate with their learners.

**Step 11—Modifying.** In this step, teachers must be open to modifying five areas by asking themselves important questions as a form of self-assessment. The first areas begin by examining curriculum, instruction, and assessment. Questions related to curriculum include: (a) Was the selected content appropriate for the lesson?, (b) Was the content appropriate for learners' needs, cultures, interests?, (c) Was it appropriate in length, breadth, and depth?, and (e) Were the materials or resources appropriate? Questions related to instruction include: (a) Were the methods appropriate for the curriculum and learners?, (b) Was it appropriate in length?, (c) Did it include appropriate accommodations and modifications for individual learners?, (d) Were the materials and resources appropriate?, and (e) Was the instruction learner-centered and not primarily teacher-directed? Questions related to assessment include: (a) Was a preassessment and postassessment conducted?, (b) Were formative assessments conducted and data collected throughout the lesson?, and (c) Was the assessment data analyzed?

Additionally, teachers must assess in-class activities and out-of-class connections and assignments. Questions related to in-class activities include: (a) Were the learners provided written instructions with expectations and self-assessments?, (b) Were individual and group activities organized appropriately and equitably?, and (c) Were learners provided appropriate and adequate time, materials, and resources? Questions related to out-of-class connections and assignments include: (a) Were learners provided written instructions with expectations and self-assessments?, (b) Were learners provided with appropriate and adequate time, materials, and resources?, and (c) Were learners' out-of-school situations considered in relationship to the assignment? When these five areas are seamlessly smooth, the teacher, learners, and the learners' families will notice the clarity as learners increase their engagement and achievement reported on assessments by the learners and teachers.

**Step 12—Enhancing.** For online middle level teachers to achieve the sense of success and satisfaction evident in the teaching, learning, and schooling, the teacher needs to center on enhancing self-efficacy, the teacher's beliefs in one's abilities to achieve a goal. Simply stated, self-efficacy is saying, *I think I can; I know I can; I can, I will, and I know a way*. Once the teacher has experienced the full sequence of the assessment cycle illustrated here by our Classroom Assessment Clock, especially to guide and support online middle level education, the middle level teacher's sense of self-efficacy tends to increase and the teaching, learning, and schooling improve (Ross & Bruce, 2007).

## MAKE THE MOST OF CLASSROOM ASSESSMENTS

Middle level teachers readily acknowledge the importance of increasing learner engagement and achievement (typically reported as test scores), especially as results are integral to teachers' career evaluations, professional development, and future opportunities (Finnegan, 2013). However, increasing learner engagement and achievement occurs effectively only when assessment procedures (a) align with the curriculum and instruction, (b) are appropriate to the ever-changing and challenging middle level sociocultural context, (c) are administrable electronically through various documents, discussions, and devices, and (d) are adaptable to the needs and interests of *all* learners individually and as members of various groups.

Awareness of Gallavan's triad of teacher self-efficacy (Gallavan & Merritt, in press) makes visible the importance for online middle level teachers to develop the will and the way to organize and facilitate teaching, learning, and schooling with attention to the presence and power of classroom assessments. Only by documenting evidence of learner engagement and achievement, analyzing data associated with each sphere of the triad, and demonstrating accountability to all stakeholders, can middle level teachers fully advance and achieve classroom success and satisfaction.

Middle level online educational environments pose risks that contribute underestimating teacher self-efficacy. Without face-to-face interactions with learners and void of step-by-step guidelines to organize and facilitate the steps of classroom assessment, teachers are more susceptible to using fewer less accurate assessment practices (Arend, 2007). Following the Classroom Assessment Clock equips and empowers online middle level teachers with targets, techniques, tools, and tips to document evidence, analyze data, and demonstrate accountability that "yield affordances" (Kearns, 2012, para. 28) that enhance teacher self-efficacy and effectiveness.

## REFERENCES

Arend, B. (2007). Course assessment practices and student learning strategies in online courses. *Journal of Asynchronous Learning Networks, 11*(4), 3–13.

Bandura, A. (1977). Self-efficacy: Toward a unifying theory of behavioral change. *Psychological Review, 84*(2), 191–215.

Bandura, A. (1986). *Social foundations of thought and action: A social cognitive theory.* Englewood Cliffs, NJ: Prentice-Hall.

Bandura, A. (1997). *Self-efficacy: The exercise of control.* New York, NY: W. H. Freeman.

Boss, S. (2011, September 11). Technology integration: A short history. *Edutopia.* Retrieved from https://www.edutopia.org/technology-integration-history

Brookfield, S. D. (2017). *Becoming a critically reflective teacher* (2nd ed.). San Francisco, CA: Jossey-Bass.

Brookhart, S. M. (2004). Classroom assessment: Tensions and intersections in theory and practice. *Teachers College Record, 106*(3), 429–458.

Brookhart, S. M. (2012). *How to give effective feedback to your students* (2nd ed.). Alexandria, VA: Association of Supervision, and Curriculum Development.

Bruno, I., & Santos, L. (2010). Written comments as a form of feedback. *Studies in Educational Evaluation, 36*(3), 111–120.

Beebe, R., Vonderwell, S., & Boboc, M. (2010). Emerging patterns in transferring assessment practices from f2f to online environments. *Electronic Journal of e-learning, 8*(1), 1–12.

Cochran-Smith, M. (1991). Reinventing the student teaching. *Journal of Teacher Education, 42*(2), 104–118.

Darling-Hammond, L. (2006). Constructing 21st century teacher education. *Journal of Teacher Education, 57*(3), 300–314.

Educational Technology and Mobile Learning. (2017, February 4). A very good visual on how to evaluate educational apps to use in your class. [Online blog post] Retrieved from http://www.educatorstechnology.com/2017/02/a-very-good-visual-on-how-to-evaluate.html

Ferdig, R. E., & Cavanaugh, C. (2011). *Lessons learned from virtual schools: Experiences and recommendations from the field.* Vienna, VA: International Association for K–12 Online Learning.

Finnegan, S. (2013). Linking teacher self-efficacy to teacher evaluations. *Journal of Cross-Disciplinary Perspectives in Education, 6*(1), 18–25.

Gallavan, N. P., & Merritt, J. P. (in press). Reinforcing MAT course goals during internship experiences via Gallavan's seven essential elements. In L. G. Putney & N. P. Gallavan (Eds.), *ATE Yearbook XXVI; Building upon inspirations and aspirations with hope, courage, and strength: Teacher educators' commitment to today's teachers and tomorrow's leaders.* Landham, MD: Rowman & Littlefield.

Haselhuhn, C. W., Al-Mabuk, R., Gabriele, A., Groen, M., & Galloway, S. (2007). Promoting positive achievement in the middle school: A look at teachers' motivational knowledge, beliefs, and teaching practices. *Research in Middle Level Education Online, 30*(9), 1–20. Retrieved from https://www.tandfonline.com/doi/abs/10.1080/19404476.2007.11462042

International Association for K–12 Online Learning. (2011). *National standards for quality online teaching* (Version 2). Vienna, VA: Author. Retrieved from https://www.inacol.org/wp-content/uploads/2015/02/national-standards-for-quality-online-teaching-v2.pdf

Kearns, L. R. (2012). Student assessment in online learning: Challenges and effective practices. *Journal of Online Learning and Teaching, 8*(3). Retrieved from http://jolt.merlot.org/vol8no3/kearns_0912.htm

Klinger, D., McDivitt, P., Howard, B., Munoz, M., Rogers, T., & Wylie, C. (2015). *The classroom assessment standards for preK-12 teachers.* Joint Committee for Standards of Educational Evaluation. Retrieved from http://www.jcsee.org/the-classroom-assessment-standards-new-standards

Kumar, S. (2015, July 10). 5 common problems faced by students in elearning and how to overcome them [Online blog]. Retrieved from https://elearningindustry.com/5-common-problems-faced-by-students-in-elearning-overcome

Martone, A., & Sireci, S. G. (2009). Evaluating alignment between curriculum, assessment, and instruction. *Review of Educational Research, 79*(4), 1332–1361.

McMillan, J., & Hearn, J. (2008). Student self-assessment: The key to strong student motivation and higher achievement. *Educational Horizons, 87*(1), 40–49.

National Center for Education Statistics. (2017). *Digest of educational statistics: Teacher trends 2017.* Washington, DC: U.S. Department of Education, Institute of Education Sciences. Retrieved from https://nces.ed.gov/programs/digest/d17/tables/dt17_209.20.asp

National Middle School Association. (2010). *This we believe: Keys to educating young adolescents.* Westerville, OH: Author.

Nonyel, N. P. (2015, June 19). Self-assessment is essential to lifelong learning. *Educational Theory and Practice.* Retrieved from http://edtheory.blogspot.com/2015/06/self-assessment-is-essential-to.html

Robles, M., & Braathen, S. (2002). Online assessment techniques. *Delta Pi Epsilon Journal, 44*(1), 39–49. Retrieved from http://www.acousticslab.org/dots_sample/module2/RoblesAndBraathen2002.pdf

Ross, J. A., & Bruce, C. D. (2007). Teacher self-assessment: A mechanism for facilitating professional growth. *Teaching and Teacher Education, 23*(2), 146–159.

Schaefer, M. G., Malu, K. F., & Yoon, B. (2016). An historical overview of the middle school movement. *Research in Middle Level Education Online, 39*(5), 1–27. Retrieved from https://www.tandfonline.com/doi/full/10.1080/19404476.2016.1165036

Sheppard, L. A. (2000). The role of assessment in a learning culture. *Educational Researcher, 29*(7), 4–14.

Stiggins, R. (2005). From formative assessment to assessment FOR learning: A path to success in standards-based schools. *Phi Delta Kappan, 87*(4), 324–328. Retrieved from http://68.77.48.18/RandD/Phi%20Delta%20Kappan/Assessment%20FOR%20Learning%20-%20Stiggins.pdf

Tschannen-Moran, M., & Hoy, A. W. (2001). Teacher efficacy: Capturing an elusive construct. *Teacher and Teacher Education, 17*(7), 783–805.

Tschannen-Moran, M., & McMaster, P. (2009). Sources of self-efficacy: Four professional development formats and their relationship to self-efficacy and implementation of a new teaching strategy. *Teacher and Teacher Education, 110*(2), 228–245.

Watson, J., & Murin, A. (2014). A history of K-12 online and blended education in the United States. In R. E. Ferdig & K. Kennedy (Eds.), *Handbook on research on K–12 online and blended learning* (pp. 1–24). Pittsburgh, PA: Entertainment Technology Center Press, Carnegie Mellon University.

Wiggins, G., & McTighe, J. (2005). *Understanding by design* (2nd ed.). Alexandria, VA: Association for Supervision and Curriculum Development.

William, D. (2006). Formative assessment: Getting the focus right. *Educational Assessment, 11*(3/4), 283–289.

# SECTION V

## DIVERSE POPULATIONS

CHAPTER 13

# MIDDLE SCHOOL VIRTUAL CLASSROOM DEVELOPMENT AND INSTRUCTION FOR STUDENTS WITH DISABILITIES

**Sucari Epps**
*California Lutheran University*

Given the increased interest in virtual learning, one might ask if virtual contexts are appropriate for all grade levels and types of learners, specifically, students with disabilities (Keeler & Horney, 2007). As this demographic of student continues to enroll in virtual courses, there is a need to examine how they are included, supported, and instructed in a virtual school placement (Carnahan & Fulton, 2013). Regardless of the plan type assigned (504 or Individualized Education Plan), students with disabilities (SWDs) are turning to virtual learning environments because they can work at their own pace (Sorensen, 2012), and because instruction can be customized to meet their specific needs (Blomeyer & Hemphill, 2005). However, there is little information to inform educator practices regarding how SWDs are instructed and accommodated successfully in online courses. Virtual school curriculum designers, administrators, educators, and educational stake-

*The Online Classroom:*
*Resources for Effective Middle Level Virtual Education,* pp. 227–245
Copyright © 2018 by Information Age Publishing
All rights of reproduction in any form reserved.

holders who influence virtual educational policy must explore approaches and delivery methods that are most beneficial and appropriate to ensure the broad scope of these learners' academic needs are met in the virtual school environment (Carnahan & Fulton, 2013; Keeler & Horney, 2007).

There is a unique opportunity for research regarding learning tools and applications that could help distribute the access of virtual-based learning judiciously among interested learner population types. Equalizing and making education equitable is the overall goal of the Office of Special Education Programs (U.S. Department of Education, 2018); virtual education is therefore part of this mission. This national government agency began to explore the possibilities of virtual instruction for SWDs in 2002 after the introduction of the No Child Left Behind legislation (Meyer & Rose, 2000). Part of that national effort to equalize education was the recognition that a one-size-fits-all curriculum created barriers to progress for students with special needs (Individuals with Disabilities Education Improvement Act, 2004). Technology has provided a new avenue, or an alternative pathway, to success for this demographic of students. Currently, "states, districts, publishers, advocates, disability organizations, parents, and most importantly students with a range of disabilities" (Meyer & Rose, 2000, p. 68) have recognized the potential benefits of virtual learning mediums. For example, incorporating large font, text to speech or speech to text, a highlighting tool, and digital versions of print materials into an online course design exemplify the basic universal tools that curriculum designers could begin to use to give students with special needs permission to take ownership of their disabilities and progress academically.

Although researchers have made a solid and significant case for new media and modern technologies, learners with diverse needs are not considered a core target market for virtual curriculum designers (Hitchcock, Meyer, Rose, & Jackson, 2002). Rather, diverse learners are considered outliers, so building a virtual curriculum with an inherent flexibility that includes a range of options for access, use, and engagement from the very beginning has not yet generated sufficient momentum. It will take a significant shift in thinking to convince online course designers, developers, and virtual educators to implement scaffolds and tools that fully support SWDs and users with varying backgrounds or multiple disabilities. Language, socioeconomic, and cultural diversity are additional layers to consider (Chu, 2014).

Virtual schools should aim to provide multimodal instructional options to help all learners recognize or ascertain which ideas they understand and to support educators' effort to engage their pupils (Hall, Cohen, Vue, & Ganley, 2015). This universal design for learning (UDL) requires virtual schools to adapt their curricula to meet the varied needs of students who encounter considerable barriers such as physical, perceptual, or cognitive to academic performance. Moreover, by eliminating or significantly minimizing barriers to learning, SWDs may also see an increase in performance on state required assessments designed to exhibit mastery of grade-level objectives.

Certain aspects of virtual education remain a mystery to local school districts, whereas other districts are well informed and choose to explore the use of virtual contexts. It is vital to the virtual learning movement to raise the awareness and level of understanding for all educational stakeholders regarding the real possibility of achieving academic success for middle school students, especially middle school learners with disabilities, when the infrastructure for their supports and services are strong. The aim of this chapter is to provide resources for meeting the needs of virtual middle school learners with disabilities. The virtual middle school design has been broken into four main areas: (a) virtual context, (b) virtual curriculum, (c) instructional strategies, (d) and personalized learning. By concentrating on these specific areas, this chapter offers virtual teachers, administrators, and curriculum designers with resources to further their efforts to create and sustain effective virtual school programs for middle school virtual students with disabilities.

## THE VIRTUAL CONTEXT:
## SPACES FOR COLLABORATION AND COMMUNICATION

Students with disabilities who participate in virtual school contexts should have a team of people who are working together to support their individualized education plans' (IEP) academic goals. It is beneficial when parents/guardians understand the nature of the learning space in which their children are gaining knowledge, receiving special education services, and acquiring life skills. It is vital to students' success to encourage active parent/guardian and student participation in ongoing meetings, conferences, trainings, and other school related virtual events (Sorensen, 2012). Virtual middle schools will need to be prepared to provide a space that is conducive to all stakeholders. Therefore, multiple communication pathways are key in meeting the needs of middle school students with disabilities (Lozik, Cooney, Vinciguerra, Gradel, & Black, 2009). What follows are virtual contexts that contain communication resources that promote not only parent/guardian involvement, but also collaboration among students, staff, and other key stakeholders.

## Virtual Meeting Rooms

Parent/guardian involvement is vital to the academic success of all middle school learners (Flores de Apoda, Gentling, Steinbus, & Rosenberg, 2015). For SWDs, the need for this involvement increases (Weishaar, 2010). In brick-and-mortar classrooms, educators have physical spaces in which to hold parent/guardian meetings to discuss student academic and social concerns. Given that virtual classrooms are not defined by physical space, how can educators and administrators meet this need in virtual contexts? One suggestion is using virtual meeting rooms.

**Blackboard Collaborate.** Blackboard Collaborate is an example of a virtual meeting room that allows for collaboration. Each virtual room has a unique call-in number and personal identification number (PIN), making it private. Even without an Internet connection, all stakeholders can join the room by dialing in via a phone. This virtual environment also includes a group and private chat capability (with emojis) that offers teachers and administrators a context in which to hold both private conferences or connect with several parents/guardians at a time. Such meetings provide virtual teachers, students, and families the opportunity to discuss matters of academic, social, and emotional significance to the student's progress within the virtual environment. Providing a space for these meetings benefits SWDs in that they are given a confidential and secure means to advocate and negotiate for their needs to be met online (Carter & Rice, 2016).

Blackboard Collaborate can also be used to encourage student-to-student collaboration. This virtual meeting space provides an interactive whiteboard where students and teachers can write, solve problems, and post text and images. Visual aids work well in the virtual platform, which can be important for students with specific disabilities as such aids help make the curriculum more relatable, interpretable, and translatable (Bourgoyne & Alt, 2017; Meadan, Ostrosky, Triplett, Michna, & Fettig, 2011; Munday, 2017).

The Blackboard Collaborate platform also offers students and teachers the opportunity to share a variety of applications such as computer screens, audio and video files, and other types of documents. These features are incredibly important and essential to the online teaching and learning environment for SWDs because they support the clear majority of learning modalities

**GoToMeeting.** Supports and services, consultations, and other strategies used to present curriculum to SWDs, must be wide-ranging and diversified enough to appeal across disability needs, especially for students who present with more than one special education eligibility. Virtual middle school programs should survey a range of meeting room options to find the most suitable match. Another meeting space gaining momentum among virtual school programs is GoToMeeting. This virtual conference space offers similar features to Blackboard Collaborate such as the whiteboard, drawing tools, and screen sharing. GoToMeeting can be accessed from a Mac, PC, Chromebook, or a mobile device. Meetings can be set up for a one-time use or used as a recurring open meeting space. The GoToMeeting virtual room allows for webcams and multi-audio access (microphone, speaker, or call in by phone). Sessions can also be recorded and viewed later. GoToMeeting is limited to 100 participants and can be cost prohibitive depending on the needs of the organization and school. Therefore, it is important for school programs to shop around and survey their audience of users; schools that have gone virtual must know the range of devices students are using to access their meeting space and curriculum.

## Instant Messaging

Another useful resource for communication is instant messaging. Students who do not feel comfortable with or the ability to use the microphone or webcam may opt for instant messaging (IM). Blackboard Messenger is an instant messaging and voice chat tool that allows parents/guardians, students, and instructors to communicate online privately or in groups when working from laptops or desktops. Blackboard Instant Messenger offers many features like those offered by other instant messaging chat tools such as Windows Live Messenger, Skype, Google Hangouts, Yahoo, AIM and Jabber. However, Blackboard Instant Messenger is unique because it can populate each student's contact list each semester with the names of every student and staff member in their virtual school; it is an in-house tool that a virtual middle school program can use to expand it avenues and pathways for communication. Students and staff can also customize a contact list. Additionally, students can instantly see who is online and available from their virtual classroom.

IM is an incredibly important feature for virtual middle students with disabilities because of its convenience and instant access. It allows for synchronous communication between SWDs and teachers and staff without having to search for contact phone numbers or email addresses. The software application is easily downloaded to a desktop or laptop computer. Students can be set up to be automatically launched into IM when turning on computer devices after first registering login information. Chatting offers students with social anxieties, auditory deficits or complete hearing loss, or an emotional disturbance an alternative mode of communication to using a microphone or webcam. Selections from these communications can be copied into desktop post it notes, Word files or Google documents, or saved as screen shots for ongoing or future reference. If students prefer a combination of communication modes, however, then video conferencing may be more suitable to their needs.

## Video Conferencing

Skype is a free virtual tool that focuses on video conferencing, but also allows users to share their screens. Skype also allows for group interactions for up to ten people at no cost to users. If ongoing access for more than 10 people is required, Skype does offer business plans. When reviewing the general instructional and communication needs of a virtual course and the delivery of specialized academic instruction or special education related services (e.g., speech, individual counseling, or occupational therapy), having ongoing access to a whiteboard or other document sharing applications should be a priority.

Having access to a screen-sharing tool during video conferencing is a non-negotiable for virtual middle school students with disabilities. Providing visual explanations and examples enhances the learning experience. Taking students on virtual tours improves their Internet research skills by demonstrating how to narrow searches using key words while also showing them how to utilize suggested websites to enrich their learning.

A whiteboard is one of the essential components of general education instruction. The whiteboard allows teachers to model how to apply and solve math formulas or present diagrams for science or English language arts, and whiteboards provide a platform for drawing historical timelines. These images can be saved as screen shots and filed shared with all participants for later reference. Students with disabilities can use these shared files or whiteboard images as notes in a group activity or on a test. The virtual meeting space's whiteboard has many similar functions to the interactive whiteboards appearing in the traditional classroom (drawing tools, writing tools with adjustable sizes and color pens) that may help new virtual educators feel more comfortable transferring from the brick-and-mortar setting.

Collaboration and communication are fundamental to the success of middle school students, especially those who have special needs (Chu, 2014). All adults who serve as members of a student's IEP team need to be operating with the same set of strategies, knowledge, and understanding of a student's needs. Parent conferences and other informal meetings with staff can be held regarding high school plans and goals, attendance, social needs, or behavioral plans using whiteboard and document sharing applications to discuss and disseminate information.

## Phones and Text Messaging

Another form of communication is the phone. Middle level educators encourage phone calls to SWDs and their families as the primary individualized mode used by staff because they are synchronous and directed to the targeted constituents (Madden, Jones, & Childers, 2017). In striving to establish clear communication with virtual learners and their families/guardians, virtual teachers can engage in regular phone calls and messaging for primary offline communication modes while engaging in their daily online routine. Virtual educators can also employ free texting applications that send text messages to students' phones and messages from their personal or work computer or other digital device via e-mail. Doing so enables teachers to communicate with all students in a manner that matches one of the most popular 21st century modes of communication—texting. Students with disabilities also need to be well trained and versed in the use of electronic communication interactions, such as texting, to adapt and participate in their educational and often social communities (Pennington, Saadatzi, Welch, & Scott, 2014). Text messaging has been the most popular form of communication since 2007 surpassing phone and traditional mail (Burke, 2015). Given this level of engagement in text messaging by young adolescent learners, helping middle school SWDs master this type of communication encourages inclusion and serves as a gateway for acceptance and connection with their same aged, nondisabled peers.

## CURRICULUM RESOURCES FOR TEACHING SWDs IN THE MIDDLE SCHOOL VIRTUAL CLASSROOM

Some virtual middle school educators contend that prescribed online curriculum can be a bit advanced and require more guided instruction and teacher interaction than might be feasibly accessible for students with special needs. Curricula aimed at a target market of true independent learners often results in the need for more interaction between educators and students. Some lessons might be perceived as rushed based on a predetermined timeline requiring students to spend more time offline to complete embedded projects or extended writing assignments. Course customization has opened a whole new world for supporting instruction. Virtual educators who merge prepackaged curricula with teacher-generated activities, inserting lessons and messages to readjust the lesson timeline, and tailoring the courses to support the needs of all virtual students find greater success in meeting the needs of diverse learners (Greer, Rowland, & Smith, 2014).

Regardless of specific curriculum design, SWDs should have certain, readily available features and tools. Screen magnifier applications, screen reading applications, a highlighting tool, text to speech, closed caption for videos, transcripts for videos, electronic note-taking, visual images with explanatory text, a built-in dictionary, a glossary of terms, and thesaurus are the bare minimum (Hitchcock et al., 2002). What follows are some curriculum design resources that include these features and tools and that can aide in the teaching of SWDs in the virtual classroom.

## Edgenuity

Edgenuity is a digital content design with a platform and curricular structure that is aligned most congruently with a UDL model. Edgenuity offers closed captioning and transcripts for the instructional videos. Using a word pad, students can take electronic notes that are stored in each lesson and can be available for assessments if teachers choose to customize settings in this way. Personalized settings and access allows student users to take ownership over their own learning and the process of learning the skills and material. Often, SWDs believe that their lack of success in the curriculum signals a need for more support, when all they really need is an educational team (e.g., administrators, educators, parents/guardians, related services professionals, and academic counselors) to discover their learning needs and remove the barriers (Fernandez & Streich-Rodgers, 2010; Hitchcock, Rao, Chinn, & Yuen, 2016). The long-term goal of implementing an IEP is to find avenues that help facilitate learning in the most suitable fashion possible. Edgenuity pairs well with educational teams working online with SWDs because course customization furnishes superior methods for personalizing learning.

Edgenuity course customization does not allow content to be altered, but there are many creative details, such as adjusting time, dates, order of assignments, and access to assignments, embedded in the course settings that furnish the curriculum with individualized access. In small ways, Edgenuity is on the forefront of producing a formula for academic success not just for SWDs, but all learners. For instance, the universal tools that are already available are on the brink of UDL mastery, including text to speech, closed caption, video transcript, highlighting tool, student-generated electronic notes storage, calendar, saving and exiting. However, by adding speech to text, more visual impairment options, and written and audio language translations, the value of the product for the market could become priceless for virtual educators who teach SWDs.

## Edmentum

Edmentum is a diagnostic assessment data center that provides instant access to student performance levels. With more SWDs enrolling in the virtual learning environment, being able to customize and individualize learning is a necessity (Meyer & Rose, 2000). Edmentum provides teachers the opportunity to meet students where they are at their personal learning level and prescribe lessons that will build a bridge to help them access their grade level curriculum. The Edmentum curriculum spans grades K–8 where students' most fundamental educational skills are developed. Edmentum offers a skill performance report to view learning path progress and an edit learning path placement that allows educators to edit student learning path skill placement as needed to further personalize skill building. Also, middle school SWDs may benefit from having choices regarding the skills they develop and in the order they feel ready to learn. The students' team members will have to work closely with the student and families/guardians during meetings to pair academics needs with the appropriate lesson prescriptions.

Although Edmentum lacks the span of universal tool applications of Edgenuity, it provides the supplemental tools and strategies that support students' acquisition of information. These two digital content designers have separately developed great modes for providing instruction, yet paired together for a middle school delivery model, both tools paired together creates a fuller, richer, and more holistic curricular experience that is personable and equitable. Having these components organically embedded in a virtual school program fosters a community of support. In such a litigious and unprecedented area of education (special education paired with virtual learning), it is much more advisable that online school programs provide the highest levels of support and curricular accommodations to the maximum extent possible. Not only is this both the moral and ethical approach (Northouse, 2015) to education, it is also the most equitable and inclusive form of education to provide as it effectively internally encompasses tiers of support manipulation that does not limit user employability.

## ADVANCEMENT VIA INDIVIDUAL DETERMINATION AS AN INSTRUCTIONAL RESOURCE

In the 2014–15 school year, a virtual middle school in California began training and implementing advancement via individual determination (AVID) strategies in language arts and social studies courses for the purpose of piloting these strategies for effectiveness before moving school-wide (Carr, 2017). Students who participated in the AVID elective course received support in the form of daily virtual live sessions that aimed at learning and practicing college vocabulary, Cornell Notes, creating smart goals, employing graphic organizers, demonstrating mastery via multiple means of assessment, creating journals, and engaging in group work and independent work.

One popular AVID teaching and learning strategy used in this pilot was Philosophical Chairs (Carr, 2017), a form of a debate (see Figure 13.1). Participants make a choice between agreeing, disagreeing, or remaining neutral on a topic after critical discussion. A virtual version of Philosophical Chairs is conducted using the whiteboard and allowing student participants to use the writing tools to place their name next to the image of a chair.

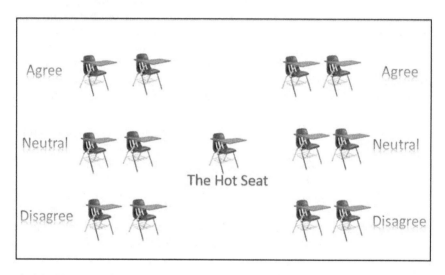

**Figure 13.1.**   Author created example of Philosophical Chairs slide for the Collaborate Whiteboard.

For example, a Philosophical Chairs activity can be implemented for a class debate on a newspaper article in history or a poem in English language arts. A math course can discuss the justification for the next step in a geometric proof. After all ideas, research, questions and analysis from prior preparation, students will yield a final stance on the topic under debate. It is important that students come to the virtual session prepared with general notes and thoughts about the topic. Therefore, the preparation should be assigned prior to this activity.

Next, the teacher should create an image (similar to Figure 13.1) on the whiteboard. The chairs on the whiteboard should represent a stance or perspective depending on the issue that may change as students make comments and additional questions are presented. Upon their login to the online classroom, each student should be presented with a reminder of the focus and topic under debate and select their initial stance. After each question and discussion session, student participants should be given an opportunity to write their name on a different chair given their stance, perspective, or response may have changed as a result of their participation in the debate. The teacher can determine how many times students can change their stance depending on the amount of discussion.

Students will sit in or write their name on the hot seat when they are sharing information, refuting ideas, agreeing with, or explaining comments. This process allows participants to share the microphone and practice virtual etiquette. All other participants must listen and wait for their turn to share. Virtual educators can take notice of who changes their name on the whiteboard or the number of changes. This activity discussion can be customized to meet the requirements of several standards across disciplines.

Virtual middle school SWDs could benefit from the opportunity to have the topic information presented in multiple ways from multiple perspectives via group and peer interaction. Guided social interaction allows for a slow and moderately controllable atmosphere fostering positive communication, sharing ideas, and expanding SWDs' experiences with grade level information. In other words, guided social interaction encourages more opportunities for inclusion in the general education setting.

Another strategy that AVID offers is a virtual binder that serves as a virtual container for students' work. Housing student files in one central place online acts as an organizational support tool for the SWDs in the virtual middle school classroom. School related items such as calendars and the student handbook, which explains school policies, can be uploaded and included. Assignments and assignment feedback can be stored in the virtual binder. The virtual binder is an easily accessible document management method that relieves the stress of having to search for items. This way students, staff, and other support providers can share a common format for arranging student work, copies of notifications, or other school related records.

Lastly, AVID offers gallery walks that allow students to move themselves through breakout rooms. These rooms can present higher-order questions, ideas, images, or stories that call students to think critically and participate in small group discussions. Many of the other supporting strategies found in this resource appear in the form of documents: concept maps, Cornell notes, graphic organizers, learning logs, posters, projects, and quick writes. These can be shared and manipulated via a shared document, presented while sharing a computer screen, or as a whiteboard image to complete as a class or in small groups in virtual meeting breakout rooms. Multi-modality instruction is essential to meeting the needs of students with special needs. Seeing examples of work from other students, moving from virtual room to virtual room, and having an opportunity to collaborate and share with their peers' mirrors a kinesthetic hands-on experience in the virtual environment. Additionally, this real-time shared experience and access allows for continued support, modeling and guidance towards IEP goals or grade level objectives in the general education setting.

Although AVID does not specifically target SWDs, the tools and strategies offered within support pre-teaching, repetition, and using scripts or graphic organizers which are some of the best practices that can be used for all learners in the virtual classroom. Because SWDs flourish in environments that offer room for differentiation and customization, allowing choices in how to learn or demonstrate learning while providing tiered levels of support, are important practices to have present in the virtual classroom.

When working with students who have special needs, the virtual teacher should consider the following attributes when deciding on a strategy or tool: auditory, memory, visual, attention, oral, emotional, or physical. Having options that appeal to the gamut of both learning styles and specific needs, should be a key consideration when designing a virtual school classroom and the instructional delivery presented.

## VIRTUAL COLLABORATION AND SOCIALIZATION RESOURCES

Virtual school students and parents/guardians typically expect programs that can be tailored to meet the diverse and ever-changing needs of their student. Middle school students need tiered levels of responsibilities, expectations, and supports (California Department of Education, 2016; Pullen, Tuckwiller, Konold, Maynard, & Coyne, 2010; Stuart, & Rinaldi, 2009). In 2014, the California Department of Education began to promote an expanded and more comprehensive framework for schools to follow to support the use of Common Core curriculum, and keep instruction student centered and tailored to meet individual needs via differentiation (California Department of Education, 2016). Tiered level of supports aligns school stakeholders with data-driven practices that are intended to be used to match learner multifariousness. One way to accomplish this is through grouping. Grouping SWDs with a same grade-leveled peer as a support helps to remove the stigma that the label of special education arbitrarily places on early adolescent learners (West, Novak, & Mueller, 2016). It is helpful and motivating to SWDs when virtual educators can find and employ effective practices that encourage them to participate and engage with the general education curriculum and their peers.

Preparation for high school is a key benefit of grade grouping at the middle level. For example, virtual sixth graders can be assigned to work with one teacher their first year of middle school (like the elementary school structure). All subjects can be taught by the same virtual teacher. When students move into seventh grade, they can be introduced to the responsibility of working with an additional online teacher. Mathematics and science can now be taught by one middle school virtual educator, while social studies, English language arts, and physical education can be instructed by another. Once students reach eighth grade, four educators become part of their school schedule, emulating the structure they will experience in high school. By creating tiered levels of interaction, middle school virtual SWDs receive the opportunity to ease into working with multiple staff members, thus preparing them for the next phase of their education.

Online learning has great potential to become an isolated phenomenon. However, virtual educators understand the significance of providing middle school learners opportunities to collaborate and socialize with peers. Virtual middle school programs have to become creative and tap into the imagination of their educators and support staff to develop favorable and comfortable events for appropriate fraternization. For example, one virtual middle school program that serves southern California launched weekly study halls, monthly assemblies, and workshops (Greer et al., 2014; Hitchcock et al., 2002). The middle school virtual educators encouraged their middle school students to join a virtual school club and participate in virtual fields trips when the in-person field trips were not available. Given that middle school virtual education does not require many offline meetings other than state testing, it will be imperative to the attractiveness of a virtual school program to have social opportunities for students to participate in.

## Virtual Study Hall

To engage learners in an academically focused conversation, one resource that virtual teachers can implement is an online study hall. Students and teachers can meet in a synchronous fashion to discuss course lessons and assignments, and solicit assistance from peers. A virtual study hall affords students a virtual space on a daily, monthly, or semester basis to work independently or receive support from the teacher or a peer. There may be times when a middle school student with disabilities feels alone, isolated, or separated from others. By having a virtual space that permits academically related chat interactions or additional synchronous discussions about assignments, projects, or tests, middle school SWDs are further supported towards success and feel like they are part of a community. All social interactions cannot revolve around academics. This will eventually discourage middle school students because they will start to sense the absence of fun and entertainment. This is where school-wide or classroom based virtual assemblies and workshops can fill in the convivial gap.

## Virtual Assemblies and Workshops

Another resource that virtual middle school staff can implement to promote socialization is monthly virtual assemblies and workshops. Teachers can invite students to an assembly through the Google Calendar invitation setting, and convene in a virtual platform such as Blackboard Collaborate. Given the global capabilities of online learning, faculty can invite community members and speakers from around the world to share and present on an assortment of topics of interest to middle school students. Key speakers and presenters can be provided moderator privileges, allowing them to upload slides, documents, and other resources to share out with students and faculty during the assembly session.

Middle school virtual workshops can also be offered to students and parents as a platform to review various subjects and skills such as: notetaking, navigating courses, or completing autograded assignments. Continuous reteaching and constant exposure to solid study practices are needed to keep SWDs in an ongoing educational routine that sometimes appears absent when schooling takes place via the Internet (Lynch, 2016; O'Keefee & Medina, 2016). Stakeholders no longer have to worry about missing out on important informational sessions because middle school program workshops can be recorded, shared, and reviewed as many times as needed. With so many distractions and time commitments in the lives of families who have students with special needs, the convenience of knowing that a workshop will be offered each month to keep the lines of communication and collaboration between home and school open and active is reassuring.

## Virtual Field Trips

Middle school students can be encouraged to participate in virtual field trips as not all students have the financial means or transportation access to attend field trips that take place in person. Although having in person field trips is highly encouraged, many virtual schools operate with a small staff that wear multiple hats to keep the virtual program in operation. It would be unfair to deprive SWDs (or any students) of the chance for exposure to exotic and horizon-expanding adventures and experiences. Rather than focus on a lack of personal resources, virtual middle school educators can furnish SWDs an opportunity to see the geographic landscape and travel to remote islands or watch tribal dances or ceremonies (Taylor, 2017). They can also view a play or theatrical performance via the Internet in their virtual classroom or meeting space. Moreover, SWDs can take virtual tours of museums and art galleries of interest. These are just a few examples of the kind of activities that can transpire online. These types of opportunities may not be affordable or available in another school placement setting virtual education parent from the brick-and-mortar. Middle school SWDs would be able to share in these experiences with their nondisabled peers giving them additional grounds for inclusive connections and peer bonding activities rooted in academic and social growth.

## Virtual School Clubs

By participating in virtual school clubs, students can meet to share their personal passions. Making friends is difficult for any student, but the pressure and circumstances can be even more intimidating to a SWD, who may be afraid of not belonging, not being good enough, or appearing different. Virtual school clubs allow students to be as visible or anonymous as they wish and feel comfortable. Additionally, regardless of disability status participating in club activities and events helps middle school students gain team building skills, enhance time management skills, and engage in confidence building because doing so requires clear communication and consistent collaboration. Virtual school clubs can be used as an extracurricular commitment related to a career path that gives any middle school student real world experience that can later transfer into the workforce. Virtual community groups or social clubs help to relieve some of the stress and anxiety that many students in middle school face when trying to find a place to belong.

## PERSONALIZED LEARNING

Personalizing learning is key in meeting the needs of students with special needs (APLUS+, 2017; Basham, Hall, Carter, & Stahl, 2016; Davis, 2015). Personalized learning represents a collaborative effort among school staff to customize learning and school-related activity participation via students' personal interests, strengths, or needs (Basham et al., 2016). Several tools that virtual educators can utilize in meeting individual student needs can be embedded in their course settings. For example, SWDs could have access to text to speech and speech to text tools, as well as direct access to instructional videos that include transcripts and closed captioning. Additionally, through the course settings, virtual educators could offer SWDs opportunities for additional assessment accommodations and attempts. In terms of timed assessments, SWDs could be given the option to save and exit the exam to take a break, work on a problem offline, revisit notes, or consult instructional videos, or video transcripts. Customized course settings and access capitalizes on flexibility which is how personalized learning is achieved. Students with disabilities benefit from a personalized learning environment because it is furnished with supports and strategies designed to match their individual learning style, preference, and competency rather than struggling to catch on to what is presented to the masses.

## CONCLUSION

Virtual education offers a unique and extraordinary instructional space that has the potential to dramatically shift and change how, when, and where students learn. Online learning offers students choices that were not even available 5 years ago, which indicates the rapid changes in learning and learning contexts that technology brings. With access to this new form of learning, SWDs are afforded opportunities that once were not available to them in the brick-and mortar-classroom. Via a well-designed virtual school model, middle school SWDs may find that online learning platforms are more apt in meeting their individual needs. As such, middle school virtual stakeholders must design curriculum and plan instructional strategies to include a focus on the virtual middle school student with disabilities. Additional supports and tools within these contexts are necessary in creating a personalized learning environment that aims to meet the needs of this demographic group.

Technology is no longer limited or bound by time and space. Instead, the marriage of the Internet and free or low cost virtual education technologies has revolutionized the way SWDs can and will learn. Academic achievement for SWDs depends on the educational placement where their individualized education plan must be implemented. Regardless of the plan type assigned, SWDs are turning to virtual learning environments. Virtual school curriculum designers, administrators, and other educational stakeholders who influence educational policy have a legal and ethical obligation, as defined by the Individuals with Disabilities Improvement Act (2004), to find the approaches, academic content, and delivery methods that are the most beneficial and appropriate for SWDs to ensure the broad scope of these learners' academic needs are met in the virtual school environment (Carnaham & Fulton, 2013; Keeler & Horney, 2007). This chapter provides virtual educators with resources and strategies to help meet the unique needs of these students through thoughtful, designed curricula and instructional approaches. Aiming to support all learning styles and student types, virtual middle schools can begin to make learning more fluid and positive for middle school students with disabilities.

## REFERENCES

APLUS+. (2017). *FAQs about personalized learning.* Retrieved from https://theaplus. org/?s=About+personalized+learning

Basham, J. J., Hall, T. E., Carter, R. A., Jr., & Stahl, W. M. (2016). An operationalized understanding of personalized learning. *Journal of Special Education Technology, 31*(3), 126–136.

Blomeyer, R., & Hemphill, H. (2005, August). *Online learning in K–12 schools: "What works."* Paper presented at the 18th Annual Conference on Distance Teaching and Learning, Madison, WI.

Bourgoyne, A., & Alt, M. (2017). The effect of visual variability on the learning of academic concepts. *Journal of Speech, Language & Hearing Research, 60*(6), 1568–1576.

Burke, K. (2015, October 19). What's the most popular form of communication in 2018? It's still texting [Web log post]. Retrieved from https://www.textrequest. com/blog/people-under-50-prefer-texting-to-all-other-communication/

California Department of Education. (2016). *Definition of multi-tiered system of supports.* Retrieved from http://www.cde.ca.gov/ci/cr/ri/mtsscomprti2.asp

Carnahan, C., & Fulton, L. (2013). Virtually forgotten: Special education students in cyber schools. *TechTrends, 57*(4), 46–52.

Carr, A. (2017). *Philosophical chairs.* Retrieved from http://slideplayer.com/ slide/6214505/

Carter, R. A., Jr., & Rice, M. F. (2016). Administrator work in leveraging technologies for students with disabilities in online coursework. *Journal of Special Education Technology, 31*(3), 137–146.

Chu, S. (2014). Perspectives of teachers and parents of Chinese American students with disabilities about their home–school communication. *Preventing School Failure, 58*(4), 237–248.

Davis, M. R. (2015). Online course taking evolving into viable option for special ed. *Education Week, 34*(26), 10–11.

Fernandez, D., & Streich-Rodgers, K. (2010). *A glossary of strategies and activities.* Retrieved from http://www.edison.k12.nj.us/cms/lib2/NJ01001623/Centricity/ Domain/58/InstructionalStrategiesActivities.pdf

Flores de Apoda, R., Gentling, D. G., Steinbus, J. K., & Rosenberg, E. A. (2015). Parental involvement as a mediator of academic performance among special education middle school students. *School Community Journal, 25*(2), 35–54.

Greer, D., Rowland, A. L, & Smith, S. J. (2014). Critical considerations for teaching students with disabilities in online environments. *Teaching Exceptional Children, 46*(5), 79–91.

Hall, T. E., Cohen, N., Vue, G., & Ganley, P. (2015). Addressing learning disabilities with UDL and technology: Strategic reader. *Learning Disability Quarterly, 38*(2), 72–83.

Hitchcock, C., Meyer, A., Rose, D., & Jackson, R. (2002). Providing new access to the general curriculum. *Council for Exceptional Children, 35*(2), 8–17.

Hitchcock, C. H., Rao, K., Chinn, C. C., & Yuen, J. W. L. (2016). TeenACE for science using multimedia tools and scaffolds to support writing. *Rural Special Education Quarterly, 35*(2), 10–23.

Individuals with Disabilities Education Improvement Act (IDEIA) 2004. Pub. L. No. 108–446, § 1–306, 118 Stats. 2647–2808.

Keeler, C. G., & Horney, M. (2007). Online course designs: Are special needs being met? *The American Journal of Distance Education, 21*(2), 61–75.

Lozik, P. L., Cooney, B., Vinciguerra, S., Gradel, K., & Black, J. (2009). Promoting inclusion in secondary schools through appreciative inquiry. *American Secondary Education, 38*(1), 77–91.

Lynch, J. M. (2016). Effective instruction for students with disabilities: Perceptions of rural middle school principals. *Rural Special Education Quarterly, 35*(4), 26–36.

Madden, L. M., Jones, G., & Childers, G. (2017). Teacher education: Modes of communication within asynchronous and synchronous communication platforms. *Journal of Classroom Interaction, 52*(2), 16–30.

Meadan, H., Ostrosky, M. M., Triplett, B., Michna, A., & Fettig, A. (2011). Using visual supports with young children with autism spectrum disorder. *Teaching Exceptional Children, 43*(6), 28–35.

Meyer, A., & Rose, D. H. (2000). The future is in the margins: The role of technology and disability in educational reform. In D. H. Rose, A. Meyer, & C. Hitchcock (Eds.), *The universally designed classroom: Accessible curriculum and digital technologies* (pp. 13–35). Cambridge, MA: Harvard Education Press.

Munday, J. (2017). Successful study strategies for students with special needs. *The Old Schoolhouse, Summer*(4), 124–125.

Northouse, P. G. (2015). *Leadership: Theory and practice.* Thousand Oaks, CA: SAGE.

O'Keefee, S. B., & Medina, C. M. (2016). Nine strategies for helping middle school students weather the perfect storm of disability, diversity, and adolescence. *American Secondary Education, 44*(3), 72–87.

Pennington, R. R., Saadatzi, M. N., Welch, K. C., & Scott, R. (2014). Using robot-assisted instruction to teach students with intellectual disabilities to use personal narrative in text messages. *Journal of Special Education Technology, 29*(4), 49–58.

Pullen, P. P., Tuckwiller, E. D., Konold, T. R., Maynard, K. L., & Coyne, M. D. (2010). A tiered intervention model for early vocabulary instruction: The effects of tiered instruction for young students at risk for reading disability. *Learning Disabilities Research & Practice, 25*(3), 110–123.

Sorensen, C. (2012). Learning online at the K–12 level: A parent/guardian perspective. *International Journal of Instructional Media, 39*(4), 297–307.

Stuart, S. K., & Rinaldi, C. (2009). A collaborative planning framework for teachers implementing tiered instruction. *Teaching Exceptional Children, 42*(2), 52–57.

Taylor, D. (2017). *Fullscreen 360*. Retrieved from http://www.fullscreen360.com/

U.S. Department of Education. (2018). Office of Special Education Programs. Retrieved from https://www2.ed.gov/about/offices/list/osers/osep/index.html

Weishaar, P. M. (2010). Twelve ways to incorporate strengths-based planning into the IEP process. *The Clearing House, 83*(6), 207–210.

West, E. E., Novak, D. D., & Mueller, C. M. (2016). Inclusive instructional practices used and their perceived importance by instructors. *Journal of Postsecondary Education & Disability, 29*(4), 363–374.

CHAPTER 14

# CREATING EFFECTIVE INCLUSION PRACTICES FOR STUDENTS WITH EXCEPTIONALITIES IN THE VIRTUAL STEM CLASSROOM

**Jennifer Gallup and Cory A. Bennett**
*Idaho State University*

Each year, teachers return to their classrooms eager to teach and help students reach their potential. Within the past decade, there has been a change in the way students attend school; many students are now attending classes in a fully online or virtual classroom setting. As with traditional face-to-face classroom settings, when considering standards that need to be met on an annual basis, expectations and goals remain the same for students in virtual classrooms. However, virtual classrooms are not cookie cutter versions of face-to-face contexts, especially for students with exceptionalities.

As of 2015, it was estimated that about 44,000 middle level students are enrolled in an online course (Miron & Gulosino, 2015), and enrollment for underrepresented populations such as individuals with exceptionalities has increased exponentially (Barrett, 2011). Students with exceptionalities

*The Online Classroom:*
*Resources for Effective Middle Level Virtual Education,* pp. 247–266
Copyright © 2018 by Information Age Publishing
All rights of reproduction in any form reserved.
247

include those individuals with a physical, cognitive, mental health, or learning disability. These students have particular needs that must be considered when developing and presenting learning experiences in a virtual setting for several reasons. First, students who have exceptionalities are often reluctant to engage in complex school-related tasks such as working in dynamic groups, engaging in complex problem solving, inductive and deductive reasoning, which leads students with disabilities to fall further behind their peers as they transition to secondary schools (Mastropieri et al., 2006). This is especially true for technical content areas—such as science, technology, engineering, and mathematics (STEM) as they can be perceived as more difficult due to the increased complexity in vocabulary and theoretical concepts (Mastropieri et al., 2006). The marginalization and chronic underrepresentation of students with exceptionalities in STEM courses becomes more pronounced in high school and college (Shattuck et al., 2014). Additionally, many adolescents with exceptionalities feel that failure is likely, and often unavoidable, and, as a result, feel that no matter how hard they try, success is not obtainable (Shattuck et al., 2014).

Middle level students with exceptionalities encounter daily obstacles such as not being able to read a textbook, difficulty decoding complex vocabulary, trouble retaining sufficient background knowledge to engage in the learning or self-check progress, or being allowed too little time to work on a specific academic task (Masteroperi et al., 2006). Additional non-academic challenges experienced by many young adolescents include dealing with transitions, to a new school, to a new grade level, or from class to class-bullying, limited access and opportunities to explore classes of interest, or being provided with adequate technology supports that would ensure equitable access to the curriculum remain scant (Beck, Egalite, & Maranto, 2014).

In the traditional face-to-face classroom, many of these students' days are filled with barriers that can make learning complex material, specifically in STEM content areas, more difficult (Beck et al., 2014). However, virtual classrooms hold the potential to eliminate barriers to learning for young adolescents, specifically those with exceptionalities, when paired with the construct of universal design for learning (Center for Applied Special Technology [CAST], 2011). Universal design for learning (UDL) is a framework that supports the purposeful development of flexible learning to ensure equitable access for all students and their individual learning differences. While UDL is appropriate for any middle level classrooms, virtual classrooms are uniquely positioned to harness the power of technology and directly address the unique needs of individual learners when lessons are intentionally designed and planned from inception using the UDL framework (Meyer & Rose, 2005). A UDL lesson has the potential to provide greater autonomy over individual student and classroom work, whereby students accrete innovation, critical and computational thinking, through flexibility in expressing their understandings (CAST, 2011).

Flexibility in the middle level virtual classroom provides students the opportunity to focus longer on one specific course. Additionally, the virtual nature of the classroom provides online learners a broader range of course offerings. Virtual schooling can also serve young adolescents who have a physical or learning disability that may otherwise hinder them from engaging in a traditional learning experience. Students now have the flexibility to attend classes at any time of the day, or the flexibility to make up classes on evenings or weekends. Virtual learning environments provide students the opportunity to learn at their own convenience and pace. In this way, virtual learning empowers students to take accountability for their own learning.

Many students with exceptionalities struggle with multiple academic behaviors and habits of mind (Dalton, Morroco, Tivnan, & Mead, 1997). These habits include activating prior knowledge, articulating a question, systematically approaching problems, making inferences or using inductive and deductive reasoning, and transferring knowledge across contexts. These are all skills needed to be successful in STEM content areas that rely on conceptual understanding and using logical and structured ways of thinking within the content (Grover & Pea, 2013). Ultimately, individuals with exceptionalities require increased structure and guidance that can easily be incorporated through a UDL in virtual classrooms, along with dedicated time, to manage the cognitive demands associated with successful learning of STEM content.

To ensure that all students have equitable access to high quality learning experiences, teachers need to understand learner differences that focus on student strengths, and thus design differentiated learning opportunities. It is for this reasons that a UDL is ideal for developing virtual learning experiences in STEM content areas, specifically for individuals with exceptionalities, as beginning with student strengths will allow teachers to build in goals that will support the student's developmental needs.

This chapter presents resources on designing and implementing UDL lessons to maximize learning for middle level students with exceptionalities to actively engage in virtual STEM classrooms. We begin by dissecting some fundamental features and constructs of UDL, and examine how more traditional STEM lesson plans designed for face-to-face instruction can be modified using UDL to support students with exceptionalities within virtual classrooms. For the purpose of this chapter, we have chosen to focus on mathematics. However, all concepts can be applied to any content-area virtual lesson.

## TEACHING AND LEARNING STEM CONTENT
## FOR STUDENTS WITH EXCEPTIONALITIES
## IN VIRTUAL CONTEXTS

The most difficult subjects for young adolescents with exceptionalities are often STEM courses due to complex and specialized vocabulary, the abstract nature of the concepts, the required critical and complex thinking with respect to these abstract concepts (Wei, Yu, Shattuck, McCracken, & Blackorby, 2013). Additionally, the process of engaging in the content wherein the student should assume the role of the STEM content expert (i.e., a scientist, engineer, or mathematician) instead of just memorizing facts and procedures can also present a challenge. Conceptual understanding, critical analysis, and computational thinking are too often absent in individualized education programs with more rote or procedural skills being the focus of academic growth for STEM courses. However, technical habits of mind are key to becoming a proficient student across STEM-related professions (Bennett & Ruchti, 2014; The National Academies Press, 2013).

To compound the issue, the presence of virtual education adds a layer of complexity that can present challenges for teachers and students alike. For example, young adolescents with exceptionalities often experience difficulty when reading to learn. Specifically, students with exceptionalities struggle with decoding and obtaining content acquisition without sufficient background knowledge (Hall, Cohen, Vue, & Ganley, 2015). Students might also struggle in understanding abstract concepts within prescribed contexts or timeframes, as is often the case in face-to-face middle level mathematics and science classrooms. This raises the question of how to best create virtual learning experiences in technical STEM content areas for middle-level students with exceptionalities.

To demonstrate integration of UDL in virtual STEM classrooms, we focus on how best to support students with diverse learning needs and exceptionalities when the nature of support appears to be different than otherwise provided in traditional face-to-face STEM classrooms. Ultimately, this comes down to examining two key questions: (a) What is the nature of learning technical content areas and presenting understanding through a traditional lesson compared to a UDL lesson for a virtual classroom? and (b) How do the supports provided to students with exceptionalities in these class contexts differ?

### The Nature of Learning in STEM Content Areas

The teaching and learning of STEM content is a complex and dynamic process. Over the last few decades, teachers' understandings on what and how to teach STEM courses has changed from a heavy emphasis on memorizing facts and applying rote procedures to more open-ended and self-guided learning through problem solving (Hadani & Rood, 2018). This change is key, as learning about scientific or mathematical relationships by engaging in the practices exhibited by scientists, mathematicians, and engineers is fundamental to learning STEM content, In other words, students must behave like a scientist or an engineer. The sophistication of specific content knowledge presented, depth of understanding expected, complexity or degree of abstraction encountered, and the technical vocabulary used, increases greatly in middle level STEM classes.

Essentially, STEM courses in the middle level represent key moments in students' academic careers. They are essential building blocks needed for more complex applications in technical professions that require advanced content knowledge. Meaning, that without a firm conceptual grasp of STEM concepts at this time, students will be poorly positioned for opportunities that rely on critical and analytical thinking in future course work or careers. Additionally, critical and analytical thinking are life-long cognitive skills that substantially coalesce during adolescence, but these are often missed opportunities for individuals with exceptionalities as such individuals are chronically underrepresented in core content classes (Gallup, Duff, Serianni, & Gallup, 2016).

It is important to understand what it means to *do* mathematics, *be* a scientist, or *design* as an engineer so that appropriate virtual experiences can be created for online learners. Essentially, virtual STEM teachers should engage online learners in actively using tools to explore, study, and make sense of a situation and then provide students opportunity to express ideas and understandings in a quantitative, systematic, and logical manner. Such behaviors and ways of doing STEM are the backbone of differentiation through the UDL lens and are the core-foundational pieces often missing in the ways students with exceptionalities have previously engaged in STEM classes. Virtual teachers should carefully consider these views and challenges when planning STEM curriculum within the virtual classroom to maximize participation and learning for students with exceptionalities.

## Effective Inclusion in the Middle Level Virtual STEM Classroom

Effective inclusion for middle level students starts with a proactive approach to teaching that considers the social, emotional, behavioral, and academic needs of all students. de Boer (2009) indicated the concept and practice of inclusion focuses on the "membership and participation" of students with exceptionalities, as well as the overall climate and culture of learning within the classroom. While such tenets for middle level learners have been recognized and espoused by a variety of educational experts and advocates for decades (e.g., National Middle School Association, 2010), recognizing how to support students with exceptionalities in virtual STEM classrooms has not been thoroughly developed. With an increase in the number of students with exceptionalities enrolling in online K–12 schools served under the Individuals with Disabilities Education Improvement Act (2004), there is a need to maximize participation and content acquisition in general education STEM content areas. Teachers who can harness the power of technology in their instructional practices increase their capabilities to leverage the principles of UDL for the benefit of their students (Edyburn, 2010). Therefore, UDL becomes a necessary part of designing and delivering efficacious virtual curriculum.

## MULTIPLE MEANS OF PHYSICAL ACTION, EXPRESSION, AND ENGAGEMENT IN THE VIRTUAL STEM CLASSROOM

Physical action describes where, when, and how a student navigates their learning environment (e.g., turning pages, handwriting in spaces provided, clicking through an online module) that leads into the expression of knowledge. When considering a virtual environment, physical interaction can drastically change, which will affect expression and engagement (CAST, 2011). For example, physical interactions might include such things as using voice-over, speech-to-text, text-to-speech, graphic organizers, virtual keyboards, interactive games, virtual manipulatives, online graphing programs, virtual checkpoints or voice activated switches to check for student comprehension of course material. Properly designed curricula provide a seamless interface with common technologies that individuals with exceptionalities can navigate and express what they have learned. Some of the tools that can be used for this purpose include Canva, Lucid Press, Google + tools, Google Classroom, Livescribe Pens to build a pencast or living wall, or other video-based presentations.

Expression is defined as the presentation of new information beyond the current realm of knowledge and traditional forms of expression (CAST, 2011). In a traditional face-to-face classroom, expression typically consists of paper and pen production of work wherein students are provided with only conventional instructional methods and inflexible options for demonstration of meeting standards and acquisition of new knowledge (e.g., written response and multiple choice). By addressing all aspects of the curriculum and appropriate instructional methods, as UDL does, the exceptional student is physically, intellectually, emotionally, and behaviorally supported within the classroom (Hitchcock, Meyer, Rose, & Jackson, 2002). Curriculum design using UDL creates "social, psychological, and intellectual processes that result in initial success, greater sense of belongingness, and a belief that students can learn more than they thought possible" (Fullan, 2013, p. 19). These critical tenets of middle level education have the potential to positively shift students' academic growth (Fullan, 2013). Therefore, multiple means of expression allow a student to move beyond traditional forms of knowledge acquisition by creating opportunities for expression and demonstration of learning that aligns learning outcomes with the student's learning preferences and strengths.

Unless specific media and materials are critical to a set learning goal defined by the standard, it is important to provide alternative media for expression allowing all students, especially those with exceptionalities, options to create and demonstrate understanding in ways appropriate to them. For example, one science standard might require students to "conduct an investigation to provide evidence that living things are made of cells; either one cell or many different numbers and types of cells" (The National Academies Press, 2013, Standard MS-LS1-1, p. 61). In a traditional lesson plan, the teacher might require a written report of the investigation. However, through a UDL approach, many options of expression are available for students to demonstrate understanding and mastery beyond writing. For example, students could create and deliver a live demonstration using a web-based tool such as Google Hangouts, make a video and embed it within a PowerPoint, create a free interactive website using Google Sites, or record a speech using options such as a Voki. Students might also decide to create a virtual illustration using Procreate (see Figure 14.1), a music video, digital storyboard, comic strip, animation, or other complex multi-media presentation based on their familiarity and comfort with specific web-based tools. Regardless, resources similar to the ones listed above increase opportunities for students with exceptionalities to develop a wider range of expression in a media-rich world.

## SAMPLE VIRTUAL STEM LESSON: MATH

So, what does a UDL-designed STEM lesson for a virtual classroom look like? What follows is a comparison of two sixth-grade math lessons that specifically support students with exceptionalities utilizing UDL principles. On the left side of Tables 14.1 and 14.2 is a lesson reflective of a typical face-to-face classroom, and on the right side is a modification of this lesson for a virtual classroom. This particular lesson is designed to explore the relationship between the net of a prism and the application of calculating the surface area for the same prism. For clarity, a mathematical net is essentially a two-dimensional representation of the faces from a three-dimensional object. Think of cutting a cardboard box in such a way that it can lay flat, as one piece of cardboard, with the sides of the box still connected.

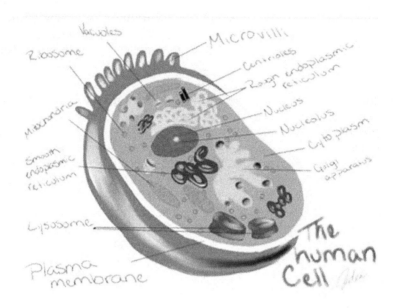

**Figure 14.1.**   Diagram of a cell using Procreate.

The differences between the two lessons is not a change in content, standards, or learning outcomes, but rather a change in how the learning experiences are purposefully created to support a virtual setting as well as deliberately taking into consideration variations in how students learn and how teachers expect students to demonstrate and apply critical thinking skills in STEM classes.

While the lesson on the left side could be implemented in a traditional face-to-face classroom by an experienced teacher, there are some aspects of this lesson that become instructional design flaws when considered for students with exceptionalities enrolled in a virtual classroom. For the purpose of this topic, we have organized the discussion of the mathematics lesson into four categories: (a) the grade level, standard, and learning objectives; (b) the learning progression of the lesson which includes: an opening, anticipatory set, a developing stage, a closing, and the materials needed for this exploration; (c) the formative assessments used; and (d) the adaptations anticipated for diverse learners in the typical lesson. Each of these categories also includes a discussion on why UDL would strengthen the learning experience for students with exceptionalities in virtual classrooms.

While this example is in mathematics, other STEM content area lessons can be adapted in a similar fashion. As such, teachers should pay attention to the intended nature of the learning and academic behaviors, as these are very similar to behaviors and interactions expected in science or engineering classes (Bennett & Ruchti, 2014).

## Developing Learning Objectives

Carefully crafting learning objectives that align with content standards is an important first step in designing a lesson. An objective guides the learner to the final destination by asking three important questions: (a) What are students' current level of understanding, (b) What are the specific content connections or expected learning outcomes, and (c) What is the best route for reaching the learning outcomes for the students' needs, readiness, and learning preferences?

An objective grounded in UDL can be compared to a global positioning system (GPS) in one's car; the GPS helps the traveler identify the best route to reach the final destination based on a series of options and navigational choices. This process is similar to developing objectives in a UDL designed lesson in two ways. First, all travelers—or students—start at a unique spot, yet, the goal is to get everyone to the same destination in an efficient way. Second, a GPS must provide multiple routes to account for individual preferences and varied needs and interests. A well-crafted objective includes the standard, task at hand, and allows the learner flexibility to reach the goal. Table 14.1 lists the learning objectives for our sample math lesson on examining the relationship between surface area of a prism and the corresponding net of this prism and how that lesson can be modified within a UDL framework

Notice the objective statement in the modified UDL allows the student flexibility in navigating their learning environment, developing their understanding of the information, and presenting their understanding of the information, yet maintains consistent outcomes related to the content. This suggests that teachers should provide alternate media options to support individualized expression, thereby emphasizing a student-centered approach to learning. When students become familiar with options available for content expression, they are more likely to use different tools to explore a given topic and develop a product to represent their understanding in a way that is conducive to their learning preference and readiness.

For example, a student may find that utilizing a PowerPoint with voice-over narration maximizes their ability to express their understanding of a given topic in a way that meets the instructor's requirements. While another student may find it more beneficial to create a multimedia product using hyperlinks, a web-based product, or perhaps a video to demonstrate their

**Table 14.1.**

**Sample Standards and Objectives in a Typical Lesson and How These Can Be Modified Within a UDL Framework**

| Typical Lesson | Modified UDL Lesson |
| --- | --- |

**Grade:** 6th Grade

**Standard:** CCSS.Math. Content.6. G.A.4

Represent three-dimensional figures using nets made up of rectangles and triangles, and use the nets to find the surface area of these figures. Apply these techniques in the context of solving real-world and mathematical problems.

| Typical Lesson | Modified UDL Lesson |
| --- | --- |
| **Objectives:** Students will explain in an essay why: (a) the 2-dimensional faces of a rectangular prism can be used to calculate the surface area of this prism and (b) why nets are an efficient technique to arrange and organize these faces. | **UDL Objectives:** Students will learn about and present information on the relationship between the area of a prism's faces and surface area to demonstrate why (a) the 2-dimensional faces of a rectangular prism can be used to calculate the surface area of this prism, and (b) how nets are an efficient technique to arrange and organize these faces. |
| | *(Similar to the mathematics standard above, a web-based tools can be utilized to create a multimedia product to demonstrate mastery of the standard in this sample lesson. As teachers begin to build their repertoire of web-based tools and students become familiar with exploring other options to express content, collectively the teacher and students will work together to develop options for action, expression, and engagement. Some options to begin will be discussed throughout this chapter such as Google slides.)* |

understanding of the topic. Each student can address the given standard based on rubric requirements, again, utilizing tools that best meet the student's learning preference and readiness that ultimately improves their learning outcomes and retention of material (CAST, 2011).

## Learning Progression and Materials

The development of a coherent progression of concepts is equally important to the quality and nature of learning. It is in this design phase the details and nuances of UDL become most apparent (see Table 14.2). In particular, the inclusion of digital tools is purposefully embedded, the nature and structure of the progression supports all students, and the manner in which "discussions" are managed to leverage multiple means of action and engagement (MMAE) and multiple means of expression (MME) become apparent.

**Table 14.2.**
**Comparison of a Typical and Modified UDL Math Lesson**

| Typical Lesson | Modified UDL Lesson |
|---|---|
| **Opening** (20 min): Review homework from the previous day (calculating area of rectangles and triangles and identifying the number of, and shape of, the 2-dimensional faces in a rectangular and triangular prism).<br><br>Next, show students a rectangular prism and ask them to consider how to calculate the area of the object. Introduce the vocabulary word Surface Area. What do they already know about area? How would their ideas relate to the prism? Tell students that today they will be learning how to calculate surface area using a net, or a flattened version of the rectangular prism. | **Opening:** Explore the following app: https://illuminations.nctm.org/Activity.aspx?id=3544<br><br>Create and share a way to convince someone how the sides of the shape can be used to calculate surface area during your asynchronous class. If students are unsure about how to begin, provide them with a list of options such as *Geogabra*, *Procreate* (can be shared as a video), or develop a 3-D model and video to share with the class/teacher. |
| **Developing (25 min):** Pass out the Surface Area worksheet showing the rectangular prism and the net of the same prism. Have students work in groups of two or three to explore how the net relates to the surface area. Once students are able to share the correct answer, have them move on to the practice exercises on the worksheet for other rectangular prisms. Move around the classroom to support students. | **Developing:** Use the following app, students create their own prism and the accompanying net (can be setup as virtual stations, individual or group): https://illuminations.nctm.org/Activity.aspx?id=3521<br><br>Prompt 1: Find additional sources and information on nets. Explore how the faces of a prism relate to the surface area of the prism. (can be individual or group)<br><br>Prompt 2: Locate additional information on where prisms are found in the real-world and how surface area relates to these contexts. (Options: group or individual—list in shared drive such as Google Documents)<br><br>Prompt 3: Using both apps provided and the sources found on your own, develop a multimedia presentation that represents your understanding of (a) the two-dimensional faces of a rectangular prism and how they can be used to calculate the surface area of this prism, and (b) how nets are an efficient technique to arrange and organize these faces that meet the above standard. |

*(Table continues on next page)*

**Table 14.2.**
**(Continued)**

| Typical Lesson | Modified UDL Lesson |
|---|---|
| **Closing (15 min):** Have a class discussion on the relationship between 2 dimensional faces of a 3-dimensional prism and the overall surface area of the 3-dimensional prism. Ask students to consider how they would go about finding the surface area of pentagonal prism and explain why they can be very helpful in calculating surface area. | **Closing:** Multimedia presentations will be displayed in a class forum such as Padlet, Google Drive, Moodle, or one with a shared page housing links to related media such as Canva, Lucidpress, Google Expedition, Keynote, or other related platforms. |
| Pass out exit ticket on surface area and collect before bell rings | Within the digital format for collaborative sharing of information (i.e., discussion boards) provide feedback and comments to other students using a teacher developed feedback form, (e.g., Google Forms). |
| Assign next homework exercises from textbook | |
| **Materials:** Worksheets from textbook/ curriculum | **Materials:** Access to the Internet, computer, digital forum for collaboration, online textbook, online apps or games. |

The structure of planning in the typical lesson greatly restricts the learning and levels of engagement for all students, especially those with exceptionalities within virtual classrooms. The potential for differentiation, flexibility, and student expression or communication of understandings is greatly diminished through the use of a traditional approach to planning in the virtual context. For example, the process of including an opening, developing, and conclusion within specific timeframes implies a teacher-centric model where the pace, format, and representations of what is to be learned is controlled. This is not to say that planning for virtual classroom experiences will not contain this construct, but to create greater engagement for all students, especially those with exceptionalities, a different approach is necessary.

In the UDL modified lesson, the opening section offers students with exceptionalities flexibility. First, even though the argument they present must demonstrate their understanding of the goal, to whom they present it is flexible: to the class, to a parent, to the learning coach, or the teacher. In addition, the modified lesson contains no specific timeframe assigned to the opening activity. Often, restricted timeframes create undue stress for students with exceptionalities and can inhibit their ability to maximize opportunities to acquire a productive learning state of mind (Csíkszentmihályi, 2008). By removing potentially restrictive timeframes and offering choice in presentation audience, virtual teachers can eliminate distractions and align learning goals to intended outcomes while removing obstacles to learning that many students with exceptionalities encounter.

As students work through the opening section, they will analyze the relationship of the surface area of a prism and a net through navigation of the technology application. This inquiry process systematically builds towards understanding. By situating the opening task as such, students with exceptionalities have an alternate environment for engaging in the learning process while meeting the same standard.

During the development section of the traditional lesson, purposeful mathematical tasks and explorations designed through a UDL allows for the "low floor and high ceiling" of rich explorations, meaning there is "room to grow" in the learning because of the inherent design. The learning is substantially developed in the process, not just in the completion of the calculations involved.

In the developing section of the face-to-face lesson, grouping is used to support learning; but group work does not support all students (CAST, 2011). Collaborative groups can be effective for exceptional learners in virtual classrooms as the tools used to facilitate collaborative learning frequently create a working visual model of the ideas shared. Tools such as Trello (see Figure 14.2) can help group members assign tasks, organize materials, and manage information asynchronously.

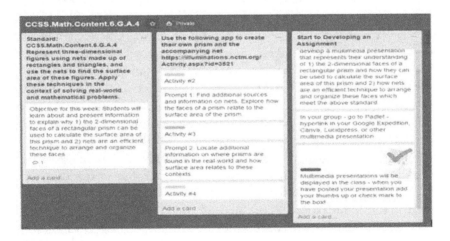

**Figure 14.2.** Sample asynchronous mapping of content related ideas and discussion threads in Trello.

Another construct often seen in the traditional face-to-face classroom is student group work stations. In a virtual environment, rotating in stations can be challenging; therefore, active engagement, content navigation, and expression may take on another form during collaboration. Within the virtual classroom, students with exceptionalities can navigate through the content and participate in different stations. Through workflow spaces such as Trello, the teacher can use these stations as checkpoints, monitoring students' progress.

Using Trello in a science lesson, the teacher could create several stations. For example, one station could require students to use slides. These slides would contain a prompt for students to develop a collaborative presentation on the topic of study. Station two could contain a Google Sheet having students develop descriptions of resources on the topic of study, and discuss how the topic is relevant to the real-world. Station three might contain a compilation project—either written or a multimedia product. Students could then present findings on the given science standard and experiment utilizing a modality that works for the group. All the steps to complete the project would be organized in Trello maximizing workflow, communication, and assigned tasks.

The materials section in this math lesson offers students multiple ways to navigate the information in both a physical and virtual form. A video on the internet, such as one from Khan Academy, and voice-over PowerPoints help students understand the content because students have multiple opportunities to revisit and consider the nuances presented. For students with exceptionalities this matters because timely and responsive feedback from teachers creates opportunities to reconsider the content, or it can provide longer time to make the necessary connections to real world applications that are often common accommodations for these students.

In traditional classrooms, after students complete collaborative work, they are often pulled back together as a class and asked to participate in activities such as a think-pair-share or debrief sessions. Students are also asked to present their work to the class and are often encouraged to ask questions and engage in reflective dialogue. Teachers can use similar strategies in a synchronous virtual classroom setting. Online chat rooms such as Google Hangouts or Zoom are forums for sharing information and can also be used as breakout sessions that provide opportunities for students to engage in collaborative conversations and other work opportunities. In a virtual asynchronous classroom, questions can be posted on forums such as Padlet. Padlet looks like an open page where students can double click on the "pad" and add a typed, verbal, or video response for others to see. Regardless of format, teachers should consider identifying specific times to have information or final products posted for discussion to ensure timely feedback and student engagement.

## Using Formative Assessments

Because instruction should be centered on student needs, it is important that teachers, no matter the learning context, gather data daily and use this data to modify their teaching in an effort to improve student outcomes. Using data gathered through formative assessments, teachers can provide feedback to students as a means of assisting students in monitoring their own academic effort, practice, and progress (see Table 14.3). For students with exceptionalities, frequent and on-going feedback helps them understand the details within the learning outcomes, as well as helps students stay on task; this is especially true in technical STEM content (Mastropieri et al., 2006).

**Table 14.3.**
**Comparison of Typical and UDL Modified Lesson Assessments**

| Typical Lesson | Modified UDL Lesson |
|---|---|
| Listen for conversations about matching 2-dimensional shapes to corresponding faces on 3-Dimensional prism | Video conversation using *Animoto*. Padlet discussion. Screen share. Video presentation of information related to exploration of related apps and websites. |
| Look for accurate calculations for the area of each 2-dimensional polygon | Accurate calculations for the area of two-dimensional objects are presented along with descriptions or other representations of objects that are two-dimensional polygons in real world settings. |
| Closing discussion and exit slip on the relationship between the net of a 3-Dimensional prism and its surface area to check for understanding | Find an article, website, or app related to the relationship between the net of a 3-D prism and its surface area—describe understanding. Present evidence of understanding using tools of choice. |

Teacher feedback can take many forms in a virtual STEM classroom, all of which embrace the UDL principles. Feedback can be provided through multiple means of communication, such as written or highlighted text and through voice over annotations. Many forums or discussion threads in virtual classrooms also provide rich opportunities for formative feedback. For example, a closed Facebook group may be more amenable for some students with exceptionalities and middle level learners, as online social forums are often a part of their daily activities. Within a closed social media group, students can embed hyperlinks, engage in live chats, and even share photos adding a personal touch to the often impersonal online space.

Feedback does not always have to come from the teacher. It is important that reflective student-led conversations also occur as a means of feedback. Students should be encouraged to discuss drafts of their work with each other through digital formats. Through virtual collaborative sharing of information, teachers can encourage students to provide feedback to fellow classmates to further guide their learning. By setting up student-generated feedback, teachers have increased opportunity to help students engage in reflective and formative "conversations" that help both the giver and the receiver to learn within a student-centric lesson.

In both synchronous and asynchronous formats, teachers should provide formative feedback during the iterative process students undergo when demonstrating their understanding of course content. One way to accomplish this is for teachers to provide feedback on class notes submitted during different learning sessions. These notes can vary in style. For example, some notes can be comprised of text or voice recordings, while others could include diagrams drawn by hand and photographed into text, or diagrams drawn using software, such as Procreate, Geogebra, or Educreations, all of which are dynamic mediums for creating and manipulating content. Software such as these are helpful for supporting UDL in STEM curricular for middle level learners. Regardless of the medium used, formative feedback is a powerful way to support all students in learning key connections (Cobb, Boufi, McClain, & Whitenack, 1997) and cannot be abandoned because of the virtual nature of the classroom.

The quality and timeliness of formative feedback has an impact on students' overall learning (National Mathematics Advisory Panel, 2008). It is important to remember that the assessment portion of the lesson should be flexible; no two students need to be assessed in the same way, or at the same time. Some students may need to be assessed orally, some written, and others using a combination of both; as long as the student can demonstrate understanding of the standards, the format can remain flexible.

## Making Modifications and Adaptations for Students With Exceptionalities

Teachers use modifications and adaptations within lessons to help students with exceptionalities achieve their learning goals. An adaptation, also known as an accommodation, is implemented within the curriculum to help the student meet the same expectations as their peers. A modification changes what a student is taught or what the student is expected to learn in the curriculum such as, a shorter assignment, different readings, or an alternate assessment. Modifications and adaptations can be accomplished through individualized instruction that is focused on student's strengths, readiness, learning preferences, and unique needs. Lesson modifications and adaptations are important for individuals with exceptionalities as such adjustments level the playing field; meaning that if they were not in place, students with exceptionalities would not have equitable access to information. Therefore, appropriate modifications and adaptations can be the key to success in the classroom. While the goal of curricular adaptations is not to reduce rigor by lowering standards, typical modifications and accommodations are often a reactive approach to a curriculum (Dieker & Hines, 2014).

Modifications and accommodations are no longer necessary within a UDL lesson plan, as the lesson is developed using UDL principles that are based on the belief that all students can learn, including students with exceptionalities, when provided equitable access. Students with differing needs and abilities are considered within the scope of the lesson). That is, specific supports for students with individual education plans are purposefully included from the beginning of the lesson planning process. As is the case when civil engineers design ramps into curbs at street intersections, the ramps are useful to a variety of users and not just those who require the accommodation.

A UDL lesson plan requires proactive planning to account for *all* students, rather than trying to retrofit a lesson plan to meet the needs of individual students through added accommodations. In this section of the lesson design, both the students and teacher take ownership of learning and the teacher becomes a facilitator of learning. Through these purposefully designed experiences, students sustain engagement and personally connect to the content.

Choice is another key component within a modified UDL lesson that supports exceptional learners. Middle level learners often seek opportunities to be more autonomous. Providing situations for student choice is one way to create opportunity for such autonomy. By offering choices, young adolescents develop as capable and proficient learners in STEM content areas and are often more engaged, motivated, and take on greater responsibility for their own learning (Bennett, 2012). UDL works on the premise that all students can learn and if an adaptation, accommodation, or modification is good for one student, it should be available to all.

## MOVING FORWARD

In this chapter, recommendations for UDL implementation in virtual lesson planning have been highlighted through a specific mathematics lesson, though they apply to all STEM content areas. It is important to note that we did not target a specific population of students with exceptionalities, rather we describe UDL as a means to meet the widest range of young adolescents while recognizing that some students may require individualization related to specific areas. This individualization might include explicit strategy-instruction or assistive technology such as an augmented communication device for a nonverbal student. However, when teachers use the UDL framework to proactively plan for student learning diversity within the virtual classroom, the need for individualization decreases. Teachers should begin by asking three critical questions: (a) am I representing information in multiple ways, (b) am I allowing students to demonstrate their knowledge and understanding in multiple ways, and (c) am I providing students with multiple ways of engaging in the learning process? By asking and answering these three questions, teachers are harnessing the power of UDL and addressing the curriculum in a way that meets the needs of exceptional middle level learners in a virtual classroom. These three questions serve as a baseline to help teachers get started with integrating UDL and developing curriculum to meet the needs of all students, especially those with exceptionalities.

In middle level education, the achievement gap in technical STEM content areas between students with exceptionalities and their typically developing peers increases substantially (Wei et al., 2013). Yet, students who were thought to be "unreachable" because of their exceptionalities, can learn when provided appropriate materials and instruction, based on UDL, in virtual classrooms (Greer, Rowland, & Smith, 2014). The assumption that students cannot learn has been predicated on something being "wrong" with a student. However, Meyer and Rose (2005) noted that what is "wrong" is the curriculum that has been inadequate to meet the individual needs of students.

Current educational practices for students with exceptionalities are often dictated by pacing charts and tests tied to standards and benchmarks. This approach, while not inappropriate as a component of a learning plan, fails to account for learner diversity within inclusive classrooms (Meyer & Rose, 2005). Purposefully designing for learner variability using the UDL framework is a powerful proactive approach for students with exceptionalities, particularly in technical content areas like STEM. Within a virtual classroom, there is the potential to reach a greater number of students with differing strengths and foster learning environments that are conducive to all types of learners. Greater autonomy, motivation, and ownership over learning is possible for all students in virtual STEM classrooms with the deliberate and intentional design through UDL. Therefore, virtual STEM teachers are encouraged to become familiar with instructional practices and effective frameworks for instruction like UDL, so it becomes a natural part of the lesson planning process. Additionally, STEM teachers should proactively seek out Internet-based tools and apps related to their content to support content acquisition, exploration, and expression in these virtual contexts.

## REFERENCES

Barrett, B. G. (2011) Strategic tool for students with disabilities: Creating and implementing virtual learning environments without barriers. *Journal of College Teaching and Learning, 8*(9), 35–40.

Beck, D., Eglite, A., & Maranto, R. (2014). Why they choose and how it goes: Comparing special education and general education cyber student perceptions. *Computers and Education, 76,* 70–79.

Bennett, C. A. (2012). Using tiered explorations to promote reasoning. *Mathematics Teaching in the Middle School, 18*(3), 166–173.

Bennett, C. A., & Ruchti, W. (2014). Bridging STEM with mathematical practices. *Journal of STEM Teacher Education, 49*(1), 17–28.

Center for Applied Special Technology. (2011). *Universal design for learning guidelines version 2.0.* Wakefield, MA: Author. Retrieved from http://www.udlcenter. org/sites/udlcenter.org/files/updateguidelines2_0.pdf

Cobb, P., Boufi, A., McClain, K., & Whitenack, J. (1997). Reflective discourse and collective reflection. *Journal for Research in Mathematics Education, 28*(3), 58–277.

Csíkszentmihályi, M. (2008). *Flow: The psychology of optimal experience.* New York, NY: Harper Perennial.

Dalton, B., Morocco, C. C., Tivnan, T., & Mead, P. L. (1997). Supported inquiry science: Teaching for conceptual change in urban and suburban science classrooms. *Journal of Learning Disabilities, 30*(6), 670–684.

de Boer, S.R., (2009). *Successful inclusion for students with autism: Creating a complete ASD inclusion program.* San Francisco, CA: Jossey-Bass.

Dieker, L. A., & Hines, R. A. (2014) *Strategies for teaching content effectively in the inclusive secondary classroom.* Upper Saddle River, NJ: Pearson.

Edyburn, D. L. (2010). Would you recognize universal design for learning if you saw it? Ten propositions for new directions for the second decade of UDL. *Learning Disability Quarterly, 33*(1), 33–47.

Fullan, M. (2013). *Stratosphere: Integrating technology, pedagogy, and change knowledge.* Toronto, Canada: Pearson.

Gallup, J., Duff, C. K., Serianni, B., & Gallup, A. (2016). An exploration of friendships and socialization for adolescents with autism engaged in massive multiplayer online role-playing games (MMORPG). *Education and Training for Autism and Other Developmental Disorders, 51*(3), 223–237.

Greer, D., Rowland, A. L., & Smith, S. J. (2014). Critical considerations for teaching students with disabilities in online environments. *Teaching Exceptional Children, 46*(5), 79–91.

Grover, S., & Pea, R. (2013). Computational thinking in K–12: A review of the state of the field. *Educational Researcher, 42*(1), 38–43.

Hadani, S. H., & Rood, E. (2018). *The roots of STEM success: Changing early learning experiences to building lifelong thinking skills.* San Francisco, CA: Center for Childhood Creativity. Retrieved from http://centerforchildhoodcreativity. org/wp-content/uploads/sites/2/2018/02/CCC_The_Roots_of_STEM_Early_ Learning.pdf

Hall, T. E., Cohen, N., Vue, G., & Ganley, P. (2015). Addressing learning disabilities with UDL and technology: Strategic reader. *Learning Disability Quarterly, 38*(2), 72–83.

Hitchcock, C., Meyer, A., Rose, D., & Jackson, R. (2002). Providing new access to the general curriculum. *Teaching Exceptional Children, 35*(2), 8–17.

Individuals with Disabilities Education Improvement Act (IDEIA) 2004. Pub. L. No. 108–446, § 1–306, 118 Stats. 2647–2808.

Mastropieri, M. A., Scruggs, T. E., Norland, J. J., Berkeley, S., McDuffie, K., Tornquist, E. H., & Connors, N. (2006). Differentiated curriculum enhancement in inclusive middle school science: Effects on classroom and high-stakes tests. *The Journal of Special Education, 40*(3), 130–137.

Meyer, A., & Rose, D. H. (2005). The future is in the margins: The role of technology and disability in educational reform. In D. H. Rose, A. Meyer, & C. Hitchcock (Eds.), *The universally designed classroom: Accessible curriculum and digital technologies* (pp. 13–35). Cambridge, MA: Harvard Education Press.

Miron, G., & Gulosino, C. (2015). Full-time virtual schools: Enrollment, student characteristics, and performance. In A. Molnar (Ed.), *Virtual schools in the U.S. 2015: Politics, performance, policy, and research evidence* (pp. 59–85). Boulder, CO: National Education Policy Center.

The National Academies Press. (2013). *Next Generation Science Standards: For states, by states.* Washington, DC: Author. Retrieved from https://www.nap.edu/ read/18290/chapter/1

National Mathematics Advisory Panel. (2008). *Foundations for success: The final report of the National Mathematics Advisory Panel.* Washington, DC: U.S. Department of Education. Retrieved from https://www2.ed.gov/about/bdscomm/list/math-panel/report/final-report.pdf

National Middle School Association. (2010). *This we believe: Keys to educating young adolescents.* Westerville, OH: Author.

Shattuck, P. T., Steinberg, J., Yu, J., Wei, X., Cooper, B. P., Newman, L., & Roux, A. M. (2014). Disability identification and self-efficacy among college students on the autism spectrum. *Autism Research and Treatment, 20*(14), 1–7.

Wei, X., Yu, J. W., Shattuck, P., McCracken, M., & Blackorby, J. (2013). Science, technology, engineering, and mathematics (STEM) participation among college students with an autism spectrum disorder. *Journal of Autism and Developmental Disorders, 43*(7), 1539–1546.

# APPENDIX

## LIST OF ONLINE RESOURCES AND APPLICATIONS

| OnlineResource | Description | Website/URL |
| --- | --- | --- |
| Actively Learn | Online literacy platform for English, history, and science instruction. | activelylearn.com |
| Adobe Connect | Online meeting space for collaboration in virtual classrooms. | adobe.com |
| Adobe Spark | Allows users to create a variety of graphics, web pages, papers, and presentations. | spark.adobe.com |
| Air Pano | Offers aerial photographs featuring 360° panoramas and videos. | airpano.com |
| Animoto | Allows users to create video slide shows. | animoto.com |
| Annotate | Document-sharing tool that allows students to work collaboratively. | annotate.net |
| Answer Garden | Offers capability of providing real-time feedback and collaborative online brainstorming. | answergarden.ch |
| Apple Facetime | Apple's video and calling service. | itunes.apple.com/mw/app/facetime |

*The Online Classroom:*
*Resources for Effective Middle Level Virtual Education,* pp. 267–281
Copyright © 2018 by Information Age Publishing
All rights of reproduction in any form reserved.

| | | |
|---|---|---|
| Articulate | Online library of two million images and slide templates for teachers to utilize in creating online coursework and learning modules. | articulate.com |
| Audacity | Audio editor and recorder. | audacityteam.org |
| Audio Note | Allows you to combine note-taking with voice recording. | luminantsoftware.com |
| Better Explained | Powerful resource of step-by-step articles, interpretations, and graphic explanations over hundreds of difficult math topics that can support a student's path to success. | betterexplained.com |
| Big Huge Labs | Transform photos into posters, calendars, book covers, collages and more. | bighugelabs.com |
| Bingo Baker | Allows users to generate hundreds of random bingo cards. | bingobaker.com |
| Blackboard Collaborate | Service that allows teachers to reach learners via digital media (conferencing, messaging, etc.). | blackboard.com |
| Blackboard (Instant) Messenger | Instant collaboration system between students and teacher and among students in a course. | blackboardim.com |
| Blogger | Platform used to easily create a blog (pre-made templates). | blogger.com |
| Bloomboard | Allows teachers to earmark and share teaching resources. | bloomboard.com |
| Book Widgets | Allows educators to create interactive exercises to share with students using iPads or other devices. | bookwidgets.com |
| Brain Pop | Collection of resources and videos covering various topics within particular subjects. | brainpop.com |
| Brainscape | Platform used to find, make, and share flashcards. | brainscape.com |
| Camtasia | Downloadable software for video editing and screen recording. | discover.techsmith.com/camtasia-brand-desktop/ |
| Canva | Graphic-creator with drag and drop feature that allows the user to create and download graphic designs and documents. | canva.com |
| Canvas | Cloud-based learning management system suitable for K–12 and higher education. | canvaslms.com |

| | | |
|---|---|---|
| ChatterPix Kids | Create talking pictures. | commonsense.org |
| Cisco Telepresence | Immersive collaboration experience via installed video monitors. | cisco.com |
| Class Dojo | Connects teachers with students and parents to build classroom communities. | classdojo.com |
| Class Kick | Teachers can provide real-time feedback or allow students to give each other anonymous feedback. | classkick.com |
| Clyp It | Sharing audio clips online. | clyp.it |
| Constant Contact | E-mail marketing service with templates and integrated marketing services. | constantcontact.com |
| Commonsense | Online source to assist teachers and students in successfully navigating the growing world of technology. | commonsense.org |
| Crash Course | YouTube channel with animated style miniseries videos tutorials. | thecrashcourse.com |
| Desmos | Integrates art with math functions, data, and graphs. | desmos.com |
| Diagnoser | Web-based assessment program that houses diagnostic instructional tools for middle and high school teachers and students. | diagnoser.com |
| Discussion Board | Feature of Blackboard that allows participants to carry on discussions online. | blackboard.com |
| Doppel Me | Avatar maker where users can use their character in forums, instant messenger, blogs, and more. | doppelme.com |
| Dropbox | Secure file sharing and storage. | dropbox.com |
| Easelly | Website with thousands of templates for infographics, timelines, and reports. | easel.ly |
| Edgenuity | Online platform offering tools such as text to speech, closed caption, video transcript, highlighting tool, student-generated electronic notes storage, and more. | edgenuity.com |
| Edmentum | Diagnostic assessment data center providing instant access to student performance levels. | edmentum.com |
| Edmodo | Communication tool for teachers, students, and parents. | edmodo.com |

| | | |
|---|---|---|
| Edmondo Seesaw | Similar to Edmodo, this site hosts student-driven digital portfolios to be shared with parents and teachers. | web.seesaw.me |
| EdPuzzle | Teachers can make video lessons and track students' understanding of course material. | edpuzzle.com |
| Edublogs | Platform for educational teacher and student blogging. | edublogs.org |
| Educreations | Interactive screen-casting tool that allows teachers to animate and narrate content. | educreations.com |
| Edu Planet 21 | Software for curriculum design and collaboration. | eduplanet21.com |
| Edutopia | Online-learning community group that contains hundreds of pages of resources, blogs, discussions, and videos to support teaching online and in hybrid contexts. | edutopia.org |
| Evernote | Note-taking app that allows users to write and share notes from anywhere across devices. | evernote.com |
| Exit Ticket | Engagement tool where teachers can quickly test if students have understood the lesson. | theteachertoolkit.com/index. php/tool/exit-ticket |
| Explain Everything | Cloud collaboration platform that acts as a digital whiteboard for explanation and idea creation. | explaineverything.com |
| Facebook | Online social networking platform. | Facebook.com |
| Facing History and Ourselves | Online platform featuring resources and professional learning webinars on democracy and civic engagement. | facinghistory.org |
| Field Trip Zoom | Synchronous online field trip opportunity. Students and teachers can engage in pre-arranged virtual field trips and live guided tours from over 500 options. | fieldtripzoom.com |
| Flipboard | News platform that can be personalized based on different interests. | flipboard.com |
| Flubaroo | App for instant grading and student performance analysis. | flubaroo.com |
| Free Books | App with unlimited library storage for eBooks (in app purchases). | itunes.apple.com/us/app/ my-books-unlimited-library/ id364612911?mt=8 |

| | | |
|---|---|---|
| Free Technology for Teachers | A website dedicated to helping teachers with everything technology-related, including podcasts, PDFs, learning guide,s and app recommendations. | freetech4teachers.com |
| Fuel Education | Blended-learning curriculum and online system. | fueleducation.com |
| G Suite | G Suite is a brand of tools and products developed by Google. | gsuite.google.com |
| Geogebra | Provides a variety of free online calculators and classroom activities. | geogebra.org |
| Glogster | Tool for users to create virtual posters they can with others electronically. | edu.glogster.com |
| Gnowledge | An education platform where students and teachers can create and take tests and course assignments. | gnowledge.com |
| Go Animate | Cloud-based, animated video creation platform. | goanimate.com |
| Google + tools | Google Input. Tools provides users a custom dictionary for new or uncommon words and names. | google.com/inputtools/ |
| Google Calendar | Online calendar which teachers and students can use to keep track of important deadlines and course dates. | google.com/calendar |
| Google Classroom | Online learning platform that allows the teacher to create classes, distribute course assignments, communicate with students, and stay organized. | classroom.google.com |
| Google Developers | Program that provides teachers with information and professional development from Google experts and product developers. | developers.google.com |
| Google Docs | Online platform that allows users to collaborate and share documents from their own personal devices. | google.com/docs |
| Google Drawings | Users can create diagrams and charts from a variety of shapes. | docs.google.com/drawings |

| Google Earth | Online site that allows the user to search and view locations from all around the world. | google.com/earth |
| Google Forms | Online collaboration site that allows the user to create and share surveys and analyze results. | google.com/forms |
| Google Hangouts | Social collaboration platform that provides space for students and teachers to chat, talk, and share with one another. | hangouts.google.com |
| Google Photos | Online photo storage system. | photos.google.com |
| Google Presentation | Online collaboration platform the creation, sharing, and storage of slides and Power Point presentations. | docs.google.com/presentation |
| Google Sheets | Online collaboration platform that allows the user to create, share and store spreadsheets. | google.com/sheets |
| Google Sites | Web-page creation tool that allows users to create a site where multiple people can collaborate and share files. | sites.google.com |
| Google Slides | Online collaboration tool that allows users to create, share and store slides. | google.com/slides |
| Google Translate | Online service that translates words, phrases, and web pages between English and more than 100 other languages. | translate.google.com |
| GoToMeeting | Online platform for real-time collaboration and discussion. | gotomeeting.com |
| Grade Ninja | App that allows teachers to scan, grade, and analyze student data in a fast, streamlined approach to record keeping. | gradeninja.com/ninja.php |
| Grammarly | Online site for editing one's documents. | grammarly.com |
| Graph Makers | Online graph maker that allows the user to create, design and share a variety of original charts within minutes. | chart-maker.com |
| Guide to Everything | Online blog dedicated to providing educators resources on technology and online education. | schrockguide.net |

| History Project | Users store and share images, videos, timelines, and more as a means of documenting life moments online. | historyproject.org |
|---|---|---|
| Ideament | Create original diagrams and outlines. | ideament.en.softonic.com |
| infogram | Infographic and chart maker. | infogram.com |
| Interact Quiz Builder | Online quiz maker. | tryinteract.com |
| International Association for K-12 Online Learning | International non-profit organization dedicated to providing high standards and information on K–12 online education and blended learning. | inacol.org |
| International Society for Technology in Education | Standards for the use of technology in teaching and learning. | iste.org |
| iRubric | Free online rubric generator. | rcampus.com |
| Intervention Central | Resource on behavior and social development and interventions. | interventioncentral.org |
| Cisco Jabber | Offers free instant messaging, voice and video calls, voice messaging, desktop sharing, conferencing, and presence. | cisco.com |
| Kahoot! | Game-based learning platform. | kahoot.com |
| Khan Academy | Nonprofit educational organization that offers custom-created videos that are screen captures of processes, explanations, and concepts in mathematics and science. | khanacademy.org |
| Kidblog | Offers tools to publish student writing. | kidblog.com |
| Kidlogger | Tool for parental control of apps. | kidlogger.net |
| Library of Congress | Online portal to the largest library in the world; houses a wide array of resources and information. | loc.gov |

| Literacy Design Collaborative | Online planning tool and resources allowing teachers to access and share best practice materials, processes, and insights. Offers free online courses, a library of teacher created instructional resources, and a space to build curriculum and share instructional resources. | ldc.org |
| --- | --- | --- |
| Lino | Online web sticky note service. | en.linoit.com |
| Livebinders | Online digital binder. | livebinders.com |
| Livescribe Pens | Smartpens that allow students to transcribe information with ease. | livescribe.com |
| Lucid Press | Web-based drag and drop publishing app. | lucidpress.com |
| Mail Chimp | E-mail platform. | mailchimp.com |
| Make Beliefs Comix | Online comic generator. | makebeliefscomix.com |
| Mic Note | Voice recorded and notepad. | micnote.audio |
| Michigan Virtual Learning Research Institute | Provides access to helpful resources including webinars, podcasts, research reports, and school district blended learning readiness guidelines. | mvlri.org |
| Microsoft Excel | Data analysis tools and spreadsheet templates. | microsoft.com/excel |
| Microsoft PowerPoint | Create presentation slides, handouts, and templates. | microsft.com/powerpoint |
| Mobymax | Online program providing differentiated instruction and personalized learning with a focus on most core subjects. | mobymax.com |
| Moodle | Create and manage your courses. Teachers can upload files, track student progress, open discussion forums, create workshops for peer collaboration and even assess students all through this app. | moodle.org |
| My Nature Animal Tracks | Application packed full of nature guides providing users information on identifying and tracking animals in their surrounding environment. | mynatureapps.com |

| | | |
|---|---|---|
| Naiku | App allowing teachers to share common and formative assessments, track student performance, and engage in virtual professional learning communities. | naiku.net |
| National Archives | Website providing access to a plethora of primary source documents from the past 200 years. | archives.gov |
| National School Reform Faculty Harmony Education Center | Hosts over 200 protocols to develop teaming processes, analyze success, and improve efforts. Although not explicitly written for virtual PLCs, these protocols offer questions, prompts, and process descriptions that translate well to the virtual environment. | nsrfharmony.org |
| National Museum of American History | Resources in the teaching of history from the Smithsonian's National Museum of American History. | si.edu/museums/american-history-museum |
| Nearpod | Ready-to-teach interactive lessons for all grade levels and subject areas. | nearpod.com |
| Newsela | Combines real-time assessments with differentiated content from daily news sources. | newslea.com |
| Notability | Note-taking app with a variety of tools for the user. | gingerlabs.com |
| Office Mix | Provides teachers and students with space to create and share interactive online videos. | mix.office.com |
| Online Learning Consortium (OLC) | Professional online learning society devoted to advancing quality e-Education by providing educators access to thousands of instructional resources. | onlinelearningconsortium.org |
| OLC Future of Blended Learning Blog | Online posts related to blended learning. Users can also join the blog community, and offer their own posts. | onlinelearningconsortium.org/insights-field-future-blended-learning |
| Online Quiz Creator | Online quiz generator. | onlinequizcreator.com |
| Online-stopwatch | Online timer. | online-stopwatch.com |
| Open Culture | Website hosting free educational materials including online textbooks, audio books, eBooks and more. | openculture.com |

| Openstax | Non-profit ed-tech initiative that provides openly licensed textbooks. | openstax.org |
| Over Drive Media Console | Online application that provides students access to eBooks, audiobooks and streaming videos from their local library. | app.overdrive.com |
| Padlet | Online forum that allows students to share work and collaborate on the creation of a webpage, online bulletin board, or virtual document through video, image, and textual form. | padlet.com |
| Pan Open | Open source educational content platform built to be functional and user-friendly on any device. Users are able to interact, take notes, highlight text, and watch videos. Instructors are able to set calendar dates, assign grades, and track student progress. | panopen.com |
| Participate | Platform that allows teachers to learn and collaborate together through online professional learning. | participate.com |
| PBS | Online database of digital content for student learning. | pbs.org |
| Photo Collage | Website for creating a photo collage without the need to upload images. | photocollage.com |
| Photo Peach | Online slideshow creator and platform. | photopeach.com |
| Pico Vico | User-friendly application for video making. | picovico.com |
| Piktochart | Application for creating infographics, charts, and slideshows. | piktochart.com |
| Pinterest | Website providing space to curate and share educational resources and instructional ideas. | pinterest.com |
| Pixton | Create an original comic strip. | pixton.com |
| Plagiarism | Online comprehensive set of resources to assist students in writing with integrity. | plagiarism.org |
| Planbaord | Application designed to assist teachers in organizing lessons, unit plans, and teaching schedule. | chalk.com/planboard |

| Play Posit | Interactive tool that allows teachers to create interactive videos for student engagement. | playposit.com |
| Plickers | Classroom polling tool that allows the teacher to immediately collect student assessment data. | plickers.com |
| Poll Everywhere | Online polling tool for quick classroom assessment. | polleverywhere.com |
| Positive Learning Blog | Blog containing articles focused on a variety of education topics and featuring seven ways to get funding for technology in the classroom. | positivelearning.com/blog |
| Powtoon | Create an informative or entertaining cartoon by combining images, text, and an action sequence. | powtoon.com |
| Procreate | iPad friendly painting application that allows students to generate sketches, diagrams, paintings, and illustrations. | procreate.art |
| Prodigy Game | Interactive math program that supports learners at many different math instructional levels. | prodigygame.com |
| Project Exploreer | Online resource that houses over four hundred videos centered on cultures from 14 different countries. | projectexplorer.org |
| Project Noah | Provides students the capacity to contribute their own nature experience using their smart device. The project's goal is to build a go-to platform for documenting all of the world's organisms. | projectnoah.org |
| Questbase | Online assessment generator. | questbase.com |
| Quick Rubric | Online rubric generator. | quickrubric.com |
| Quill | Site that has 150 activities built around Common Core standards that include proofreading, sentence correction, and collaborative writing. | quill.org |
| Quiz Star | Online quiz generator. | quizstar.4teachers.org |
| Quizlet | Database of millions of study set notecards and notecard generator. | quizlet.com |

| Quizizz | Quiz generator that allows teachers to share interactive assessments and engage students in interactive assessment in a fun and effective way. | quizizz.com |
| --- | --- | --- |
| ReCap | Online tool that that provides teachers opportunity to encourage student reflection and critical thinking through a video moderated, question-led dialogue. | letsrecap.com |
| Remember The Milk | Task management application for creating a digital to-do list. | rememberthemilk.com |
| Remind | Online site that allows teachers to schedule and send out important reminders to students and families. | remind.com |
| Report Card for America's Infrastructure | Provides students access to expert maps, videos, infographics, and interactive content about state and national bridges, water, budgets, and environmental issues | infrastructurereportcard.org |
| Rubistar | Online rubric generator. | rubistar.4teachers.org |
| Rubric Maker | Online rubric generator. | rubric-maker.com |
| Schoology | Online learning management system for today's virtual classrooms. | schoology.com |
| Screencast-o-matic | Screen-capturing tool that allows the user to record screenshots with audio commentary. | screencast-o-matic.com |
| Screenr | Provides fast, visual feedback. | screenr.co |
| Sevenzo | Online platform for professional learning and collaboration. | sevenzo.org |
| Skype | Online conferencing call and video platform. | skype.com/en/ |
| Slack | Cloud-based collaboration tool for conferencing and file sharing. | slack.com |
| Smart Voice Recorder | Voice-recording application. | recorder.smartmobdev.com |
| Smithsonian Educator | Website that provides resources such as lesson plans, activities and teaching tools focused on art, history, science and technology. | smithsonianeducation.org/educators |
| Socrative | Online learning platform that promotes student and teacher collaboration, online assessment and grading tools. | socrative.com |

| | | |
|---|---|---|
| Stop Motion Studio | Application that allows the user to create stop motion animated videos. | itunes.apple.com/us/app/stop-motion-studio/id441651297?mt=8 |
| Storybird | Website that provides access to free books and resources for creating original texts. | storybird.com |
| Teach, Learn, Lead | Application that provides a forum for teacher collaboration and professional learning. | teachlearnlead.org |
| Teaching Partners | Allows teachers to create or join collaborative groups of educators with the same interests to facilitate problem-solving and professional growth.  It provides a space for PLCs to work as well as helps virtual educators locate supportive networks. | teachingpartners.com |
| Teaching History | Provides a variety of teaching materials, history content, and information on best practices for the classroom. | teachinghistory.org |
| Teachers With Apps | Resource for teachers, students and families to learn more about quality virtual tools and resources. | teacherswithapps.com |
| The Center for Teaching Quality | Catalyzes teacher leaders across the U.S. to share expertise.  Training in facilitating virtual teams, focused advocacy efforts, professional learning and networking are offered. | teachingquality.org |
| Tell About This | Application that promotes storytelling through visual and auditory prompts. | tellaboutapp.com |
| Thing Link | Interactive infographic generator. | thinglink.com |
| Thrively | Virtual resource to assist teachers in providing students a personalized learning experience with online lessons tailored to meet the individual student's needs. | thrively.com |
| Time and Learning | Nonprofit organization dedicated to expanding learning time to enhance student success and educational achievement. | timeandlearning.org |

| Toodledo | Site that enables learning coaches and virtual learners to create a daily to-do list and then prioritize the tasks. | toodledo.com |
| Trello | Web-based project and learning management system to enhance student collaboration, learning, and managing student progress. | trello.com |
| Tricider | Social voting tool for today's classrooms. | tricider.com |
| Twiddla | Online collaborative whiteboard. | twiddla.com |
| Twiducate | K–12 social networking platform that provides space to share links, resources, questions and more. | livelingua.com/twiducate/ |
| Twitter (Chats) | Educators can follow a variety of educational hashtags on this social media platform as a means of continuous professional development and collaboration. | twitter.com |
| Typing | Assists users in improving their typing skills and speed. | typing.com |
| Typing Club | Assists users in learning and enhancing their typing abilities. | typingclub.com |
| Vark-Learn | Online questionnaire designed to assist teachers in identifying and understanding student learning styles. | vark-learn.com |
| Video Ant | Web-based video annotation tool. | ant.umn.edu |
| View Pure | Tool for filtering advertisements out of online videos for educational viewing. | viewpure.com |
| Vocaroo | Online voice recorder. | vocaroo.com |
| Voice Memos | Online application for recording voice memos directly to one's computer or iPad. | voice-memos.appspot.com |
| Voice Thread | Cloud-based tool that allows that allows students to collaborate through asynchronous discussions with the use of voice, text, image, and video. | voicethread.com |
| Voki | Online avatar generator. | voki.com |
| We Video | Online video editing program that allows the user to capture, create, and view their unique movie creations. | wevideo.com |

| Web Quest | Online source of information and premade web quests on a variety of educational topics. | webquest.org |
|---|---|---|
| Wiki Spaces Classroom | Virtual environment that offers tools for teaches to organize and monitor their classrooms and a platform for students to collaborate and socialize. | wikispaces.com/content/classroom |
| Windows Live Messenger | Communication platform. | windows-live-messenger.en.softonic.com |
| Wolframalpha | Comprehensive online search engine that organizes varied learning material via visual representations. | wolframalpha.com |
| Word Press | Online blogging platform. | wordpress.com |
| Wordle | Digital word cloud generator. | wordle.net |
| Yammer | Social networking tool provided by Microsoft Office to ease communication and networking within a defined online community. | yammer.com |
| You Tube | Popular online video hosting platform. | youtube.com |
| Zoom | Online video conferencing platform. | zoom.us |
| Zunal | Web-based software to assist teachers in constructing a Web Quest and Web Quest rubrics. | zunal.com |

# ABOUT THE CONTRIBUTORS

## THE EDITORS

**Brooke Eisenbach** is assistant professor of middle and secondary education at Lesley University. She is a member of AERA's Middle Level Education Research SIG. She is a former middle level English teacher, young adolescent literature teacher, and virtual school teacher with over 10 years of experience. E-mail: brooke.eisenbach@gmail.com

**Paula Greathouse** is assistant professor of secondary English education in the Department of Curriculum and Instruction at Tennessee Tech University. She is a member of AERA's Middle Level Education Research SIG. She is a former public school teacher with more than 15 years of experience teaching adolescents, three of which she spent teaching online English credit retrieval courses. E-mail: pgreathouse@tntech.edu

## THE CONTRIBUTORS

**Jason Beach** is associate professor in curriculum and instruction within the College of Education at Tennessee Tech University. He currently teaches a variety of courses that relate to technology application, research methodologies, and adult education as it pertains to teacher training. He is focused on technology integration and its ability to enhance the delivery of content in the classroom. E-mail: JBeach@tntech.edu

**Cory A. Bennett** is associate professor in the Department of Teaching and Educational Studies at Idaho State University. He is an expert in mathematics instruction and in understanding how to attend to learning this content in both in the virtual and physical classrooms. He has focused his research on developing inclusive opportunities that support inclusion through the lens of UDL within the traditional setting and online settings. E-mail: benncor3@isu.edu

**Eve Bernstein** is associate professor in the Division of Education at Queens College. She has extensive teaching experience in secondary and primary schools. Her research examines how middle school students perceive and how teachers structure competitive activities. In 2014, the Society of Health and Physical Educators name her the Margaret Paulding lecturer scholar. E-mail: eve.bernstein@qc.cuny

**Arquimen Chicas** is a graduate of the master's certification program at the University of Maryland, College Park. He is originally from El Salvador and is a former middle school English for speakers of other languages (ESOL) student who is now a middle level ESOL and Spanish teacher. He has over five years of experience teaching young adolescents. E-mail: Arquimen_G_Chicas-navarro@mcpsmd.org

**Matthew Duvall** is a doctoral candidate in Drexel University's educational leadership and learning technologies program. He previously worked as an application developer and high school teacher. He has written articles and book chapters on game-based learning and educational technology. E-mail: md697@drexel.edu

**Natalie Duvall** is a graduate of the inaugural mind, brain, and teaching cohort of the Johns Hopkins University doctoral program, where she now serves as an instructor and doctoral adviser. She is a former high school English teacher with over 10years of experience, with most of that time spent at a private residential school serving adolescent students in social and economic need. Email: Nduvall1@jhu.edu

**Sucari Epps** received her PhD in educational leadership from California Lutheran University. She has been a middle school special education teacher for over 15 years. Eight of those years have been spent coordinating special education services for a secondary virtual public charter school. Her research focuses on accommodating students with disabilities and needs in the virtual school, classroom, and curriculum, specifically learning outcomes and learning tools. E-mail: sepps@callutheran.edu

**Shelly Furuness** is associate professor of education in Butler University's College of Education. With the Center for Academic Technology, she co-developed the faculty-training course supporting the creation and delivery of online university courses. She has been recognized for her work on transforming learning through summer enrichment and virtual practicum experiences. E-mail: sfurunes@butler.edu

**Nancy P. Gallavan** is professor of teacher education at the University of Central Arkansas. She specializes in classroom assessments, cultural competence, and social studies education. With 160+ publications, Nancy has authored/co-authored/edited/co-edited 20 books including two volumes of *Developing Performance-based Assessments: Grades K–5 and Grades 6–12.* She is active in the American Educational Research Association, Association of Teacher Educators (past president), Kappa Delta Pi, National Association for Multicultural Education, and National Council for the Social Studies. E-mail: ngallavan@uca.edu

**Jennifer Gallup** is assistant professor in the Department of Teaching and Educational Studies at Idaho State University. She has dedicated her career to supporting the needs of individuals with disabilities, specifically those with autism, in science, technology, engineering, and mathematics (STEM). Her area of expertise is in universal design for learning, visual supports, and alternate assessments for students with significant intellectual disabilities. E-mail: galljenn@isu.edu

**Kyleigh B. Harrell** serves as a virtual mathematics teacher at Odyssey Online Learning in Columbia, South Carolina. She has experience teaching in both the traditional face-to-face learning environment and the online learning environment. She is currently pursuing her doctoral degree at Liberty University with a focus on the community of inquiry framework and perceived learning with K–12 blended and online learning environments. E-mail: Kyleigh.harrell@odysseyonline.com

**Mary Kirk** is a graduate student in the Department of Curriculum and Instruction at Tennessee Tech University. Her research focuses on the teaching of math in the virtual classroom. E-mail: mmgordon42@students.tntech.edu

**Shannon R. Maiden** is a sixth-grade teacher at Ruth Doyle Middle School in Conway, Arkansas. She earned her Master of Arts in Teaching (MAT) degree in 2012 from the University of Central Arkansas receiving the Outstanding Graduate Student Award in 2012 and the Watts Scholar Award from the Southeastern Association of Teacher Educators in 2012. E-mail: maidens@conwayschools.net

**Andrea Mosenson** is assistant professor and program coordinator for family and consumer sciences education at Queens College. She has over 30 years of teaching experience at the secondary and collegiate levels. Her research focuses on strategies for integrating 21st century skills into the secondary classroom with an emphasis on active learning and technology. E-mail: Andrea.Mosenson@qc.cuny.edu

**Cachanda Orellana** is a doctoral student in the College of Education at the University of Maryland College Park and a secondary English teacher in Washington, DC. She has designed professional development experiences for teachers around infusing e-learning in public school classrooms, examining students' research into culturally relevant pedagogy, and becoming reflective practitioners. Her research interests include the impact of digital text on reading comprehension and best practices in virtual charter schools. Email: corellan@umd.edu

**Kerry Rice** is a 2012–13 and 2015 Fulbright Scholar and professor in the Department of Educational Technology at Boise State University. Her research focuses on best practices in K-12 online education. She is a former middle school teacher and author of *Making the Move to K–12 Online Teaching: Research-Based Strategies and Practices* (Pearson, 2012). She serves as coordinator of the Idaho K–12 Online Teaching Endorsement Program at Boise State. Email: krice@boisestate.edu

**Mary Rice** is assistant professor in the Department of Language, Literacy, & Sociocultural Studies at the University of New Mexico, and a former junior high school teacher. Her research interests include curriculum development for the literacy development of diverse students and the identity construction of teachers developing this curriculum. She is the author of *Exploring Pedagogies for Diverse Learners* (2015) published by Emerald Press. E-mail: maryrice@unm.edu

**Amanda J. Rockinson-Szapkiw** is associate professor in the Instructional Design and Technology Program at the University of Memphis. She has over 10 years of experience teaching in and designing courses for the virtual environment. Her innovative technologies have received national and international recognition, including a feature in a Microsoft case study and a Campus Technology Innovators award. E-mail: Amanda.Rockinson-Szapkiw@memphis.edu

**Ebony Terrell Shockley** is assistant clinical professor in the Department of Teaching and Learning, Policy and Leadership at the University of Maryland, College Park. She is also the diversity officer and the director of the Office of Teacher and Leader Education. She is a former middle school ESOL/Science teacher and Reading Specialist. E-mail: eterrell@umd.edu

**Shannon Skelcher** is a doctoral student in the Department of Educational Technology at Boise State University where she also works as a graduate assistant. Her research interests include K–12 online education, classroom technology integration, and flipped learning. E-mail: skelcher@gmail.com

**Barbara Smith** is director of Partnerships and Professional Development for the Literacy Design Collaborative (LDC), a nationally recognized non-profit organization dedicated to helping educational systems improve teacher practice and student learning using a blended, competency-based approach. E-mail: basmith2007@gmail.com

**Mark Stevens** teaches seventh-grade social studies. He has 22 years of experience in a large school district in the Mid-Atlantic region. He is also doctoral student in the Department of Learning Technology Design Research at George Mason University, where his specialization is K–12 blended learning. He has conducted and published numerous studies on blended learning curriculum and implementation as a teacher researcher. E-mail: mastevens54@gmail.com

**Jeremy Wendt** is professor and chair of the Department of Curriculum and Instruction at Tennessee Tech University. He has worked with all things related to ed tech since 2003. He has taught undergraduate and graduate ed tech courses while serving the university and the community. Being very active in grant-writing and local K–12 schools, he is engaged with the most current ideas, tools, and processes in ed tech. E-mail: jwendt@tntech.edu

**Jillian L. Wendt** is assistant professor of science education at the University of the District of Columbia in Washington, DC. She has experience teaching in both the traditional face-to-face learning environment and the distance learning environment at the K–12, undergraduate, graduate, and doctoral levels. She routinely engages in research and publication on technology in education, science literacy, collaborative learning, teacher professional development, preservice teacher education, international education, and K–12 science education. E-mail: jillian.wendt@udc.edu

**Suzanne Wolfinger** earned her doctoral degree in educational leadership and management at Drexel University. She has been a virtual school instructor for the past nine years, serving middle school students across Pennsylvania. E-mail: swolfinger71@gmail.com

CPSIA information can be obtained
at www.ICGtesting.com
Printed in the USA
BVHW041936310519
549850BV00002B/13/P